D0864867

FROM BATAAN TO SAFETY

FROM BATAAN TO SAFETY

The Rescue of 104 American Soldiers in the Philippines

Malcolm Decker

McFarland & Company, Inc., Publishers

Jefferson, North Carolina, and London

LIBRARY OF CONGRESS CATALOGUING-IN-PUBLICATION DATA

Decker, Malcolm, 1946–
    From Bataan to safety : the rescue of 104 American
soldiers in the Philippines / Malcolm Decker.
        p.   cm.
    Includes bibliographical references and index.

    ISBN 978-0-7864-3396-4
    softcover : 50# alkaline paper ∞

    1. Fassoth, Bill, 1890–1957.   2. Fassoth, Martin, 1890–1982.
3. Bataan Death March, Philippines, 1942.   4. World War, 1939–
1945 — Prisoners and prisons, Japanese.   5. World War, 1939–
1945 — Conscript labor — Philippines.   6. Prisoner-of-war
escapes — Philippines — History — 20th century.   7. Prisoners of
war — Philippines — Biography.   8. Prisoners of war — United
States — Biography.   I. Title.
D767.4.D39   2008
940.54'7252095991— dc22   2008016998

British Library cataloguing data are available

©2008 Malcolm Decker. All rights reserved

*No part of this book may be reproduced or transmitted in any form
or by any means, electronic or mechanical, including photocopying
or recording, or by any information storage and retrieval system,
without permission in writing from the publisher.*

On the cover: *from top left* Bill, Catalina and Martin Fassoth;
Presidential Medal of Freedom (courtesy Ron Fischer); Death March
(National Archives)

Manufactured in the United States of America

McFarland & Company, Inc., Publishers
    Box 611, Jefferson, North Carolina 28640
    www.mcfarlandpub.com

To Vernon and Aurora Fassoth
for keeping the Fassoth legacy alive

Acknowledgments

Thanks go out to so many that it is impossible to list them in any order implying importance or amount of support. Thanks to Vernon Fassoth, who supplied several documents, interviews and pictures and spent over ten hours with me on the phone going over the material in the book, giving me additional background material. In addition. Monica Fassoth, his daughter, helped with family genealogy and pictures.

Wayne Sanford and Doug Clanin in Indianapolis held three reunions in the mid-eighties of the surviving men who organized guerrilla units on Luzon. It is from their interviews that much of the material in this book was garnered. Earl Oatman, a member of Fassoth's camps, wrote and self-published *Bataan: Only the Beginning,* and encouraged me to use material from his book to better tell the story of Bill, Martin, and Catalina's endeavors to aid the escaped American soldiers from Bataan. In addition, he and his good friend Hank Winslow met with me and Bob Mailheau in Riverside, California, for an interview in 1996. Thanks also to Edwin Ramsey for encouragement and allowing me to use excerpts from his book, *Lieutenant Ramsey's War.*

Jim Conner, son of Henry Clay Conner, has been most gracious in supplying me with his father's manuscripts and pictures.

Thanks go to Paul Brockman at the Indiana Historical Society for his help in locating research materials at the Society's beautiful Indianapolis facility.

Thanks to Don (Nano) Lucero for his interviews about Fassoth's camps and his time evading the Japanese. To Chris Schaefer, the author of *Bataan Diary: An American Family in World War II, 1941–1945,* who has forwarded me material for this book, including interviews with Vernon Fassoth. And to John Burton and his son Andrew Burton for helping with the map of Luzon. John Burton is the author of *Fortnight of Infamy: The Collapse of Allied Airpower West of Pearl Harbor.*

Many thanks also go out to the veterans of the war against the Japanese in the Philippines who have written of their experiences, and in particular to those who spent time recovering from the ravages of war and malnutrition in the jungle camps of the Fassoths. These books have substantiated the humanitarian work done by Bill, Catalina, and Martin Fassoth and helped give their story amplified integrity.

Contents

Preface

The surrender of Bataan on April 9, 1942, was a sad chapter in American history. Twelve thousand American soldiers and 60,000 Filipino compatriots slowed the conquering Imperial forces of the Japanese for four long months while enduring starvation rations and insufficient ammunition. They were asked to arrest the Japanese onslaught on the Philippine Islands without any help from outside sources.

Nearly 400 American soldiers either escaped from the Death March or did not surrender and slogged their way out of the Bataan peninsula into southern Luzon. They were aided by many Filipino families who put their own families and lives at risk to feed and shelter these men during their escape.

None put forth more effort than the Fassoths. Bill and Martin, twin brothers who were American cane growers, and Catalina, Bill's wife, expended immeasurable resources in ministering to over 104 American soldiers from April 17, 1942, to April 4, 1943.

Many Filipinos paid with their lives, but many were reimbursed by the U.S. government at war's end. Because Bill Fassoth would not turn his camps over to military control, insisting they remain rest and recuperation centers, he was denied the meager compensation for money he personally spent in providing food, shelter, and medicine for his "boys."

The army in one paragraph of their denial said: "You were not authorized to incur the expenses for which you seek reimbursement; it was a voluntary act on your part which does not create any obligation, legal or implied on the part of the United States to reimburse you."

Though Bill, Catalina, and Martin Fassoth were recognized by President Harry Truman with the Presidential Medal of Freedom in 1947, to date the Fassoth family has not received one penny in compensation for the untold

1

efforts they performed in saving over 25 percent of the men who escaped Japanese control.

The following story chronicles where the soldiers were when the war began, how they escaped from the Japanese and found their way to Fassoth's camps, the care the men received while in the camps and what became of them after the camps were raided and Bill and Martin Fassoth surrendered to the Japanese.

I have relied on material from more than twenty books, as well as archives, personal letters, unpublished notes and interviews from many of the men. I have changed verb tenses in some of the material and paraphrased some of the longer stories for continuity. For every story, source material is credited in my endnotes. Many who read this book will want to find the books I've quoted for more information about these remarkable men.

It is with great humility that I tell this story of epic humanity. It is a small effort for what this noble family has done, including saving the life of my father, Doyle Decker.

Chapter 1
War: December 8, 1941

In his preface to Bataan: Our Last Ditch, *John W. Whitman described the battle for Bataan as being the last battle of World War I and the first battle of World War II. It used weapons only marginally improved from World War I, and therefore tactics not unfamiliar to First World War veterans. It was also the first U.S. battle of World War II, and because it ended in disaster and few men escaped to carry the tale to U.S. citizens, it slipped into obscurity as better news of bigger battles drew the attention of correspondents, and later historians.*

The Second World War started differently for the men on Luzon, in the Philippine Islands, depending on their unit and area of service. The first word of the attack on Pearl Harbor came over the radio and then in the Monday-morning headlines of the *Manila Tribune.*

Second only to the Hawaiian Islands, the Philippines were considered an exotic duty station with tropical weather and a relatively high standard of living. Even a private in the army could afford some of the glamour the islands offered foreign visitors.

Bill and Catalina Fassoth were in Manila when the attack on Pearl Harbor was announced in the Philippines. Their fifteen-year-old son Johnny had been stricken in November and taken to Doctor's Hospital in Manila. In spite of the attention of several doctors, Johnny died on December 22, 1941, of an unknown internal ailment.

When the war started Bill and Catalina's family was spread over Luzon. Bill's twin brother Martin was working for the U.S. Navy Yard in Cavite. Bill Jr., the oldest son, was in the U.S. Navy and his brother Vernon had a position with the U.S. Army Transport services as a clerk. When Johnny died,

Bill obtained special permission from the Army Transport to have the body moved to the family plot of the Roman Catholic cemetery at Lubao, Pampanga, on December 24.

Lieutenant Edwin Price Ramsey was assigned to the Twenty-sixth Cavalry in June 1941. The Twenty-sixth was located at Fort Stotsenburg in the foothills of the Zambales Mountains, seventy-five miles northwest of Manila. It was the major military post protecting Central Luzon, a large plain that stretched between two mountain ranges from Lingayen Gulf in the north to Manila Bay.

Ramsey described life at the fort as like that of the old colonial army. They had servants who roomed in the back of the house and cooked their food and cleaned their uniforms, and each officer had an orderly to take care of their horses. The commanding general strictly enforced the imperial image. The officers were required to wear dress-white mess jackets to evening meals and social events. The tropical heat and humidity forced the officers to shower and change uniforms twice a day.

It was not until Ramsey reached Stotsenburg, that he realized the immediacy of the war. Every conversation turned to the Japanese and the radio constantly reported the seizures of Indochinese bases by the Imperial Army.

Captain Russell Volckmann, having graduated from West Point in June 1934, had put his name on the volunteer roster for duty in the Philippines. In the spring of 1940, he had his orders and he arrived in Manila on a steamy day that July, assigned to H Company of the Thirty-first Infantry, the only American infantry unit in the islands.

When Japanese aircraft bombed Fort Stotsenburg and nearby Clark Field on December 8, Private Pierce H. Wade had already heard at 4:30 that morning of the attack on Pearl Harbor. The war, which the men had known for several weeks was imminent, had begun.

Wade's unit, the Seventeenth Ordinance Company, evacuated three kilometers southeast of Stotsenburg and set up a maintenance area in a dense bamboo thicket. Wade's assignment that morning was to serve as chief of section, artillery, small arms, and instrument repair for the two tank battalions dispersed at Clark Field.

At noon Wade and his fellow soldiers observed the return of the planes that had been out on reconnaissance duty that morning. After landing their aircraft, the pilots went into their quarters for lunch, and it was then that the bombing of Clark Field started. From out of the northwest there appeared a large squadron of what Wade thought to be U.S. Navy bombers, flying at high altitude. As the formation came closer it veered to the left, flying directly over Clark Field. Then the men heard the shrill, whistling sound of bombs — a sound with which they were soon to become familiar.

Wade described the next few seconds as a lifetime. He stood paralyzed as men poured out from the barracks and watched in astonishment as Japanese aircraft let loose their bombs. Flying fragments were everywhere, and black smoke billowed in immense clouds from the gas dumps and planes on the ground. Many of the hangars were partially destroyed and one side of the Post Exchange Restaurant, which the men called "The Chinks,"[1] was razed.

Realizing the danger of their position, the men dived into a ditch. Ditches had recently been dug around the field for construction of a water main, and there is no doubt that these new trenches protected many of the men.

As Wade crawled from a ditch during a lull, he heard Jim Boyd call, "Put on your masks, boys, it's gas!"[2] Soon they learned that the gas fumes had resulted from the smoke of the gas dumps burning on the field. A fire truck from the fort rushed into the black cloud of smoke, but in about two minutes it rushed back out. It was impossible for fire fighters to get near the flames because of the vaporizing fuel.

Wade's small group had moved down the road about fifty yards when they again heard approaching planes. Unable to see overhead through the black clouds of smoke, they decided that the Japanese were returning. In this second attack the planes came from the east, brushing treetops and strafing everything around Clark Field. They flew so low that the American soldiers shot at them with pistols and rifles. Wade was carrying a Thompson submachine gun and used it to shoot at the planes, his first meeting with the enemy. Five enemy fighters were shot down. When the first one fell, Wade jumped from the ditch and yelled, "Yippee! We got one of the bastards."[3] Just as he was reveling in that triumph, another Japanese pilot shot out the wall of the barracks four feet behind where the men were crouched.

Wade continued firing his tommy gun at each plane cruising within his range, while Jim Boyd sat calmly plinking away at them with a .45 pistol. Wade thought at the time and is still convinced of the suitability of this Texan's nickname, "Cactus."[4] His display of courage — and his survival — were evidence that the name was deserved.

The men later were reunited with their commanding officer, Captain Richard C. Kadel, who cried, "Thank God, boys, you weren't killed! We were afraid you had gotten your tickets punched over there."[5]

Earl Oatman and Hank Winslow arrived in the Philippines on November 21, 1941, as part of the Thirty-fourth Pursuit Squadron and were stationed at Nichols Field just north of Manila. Though they lived in tents, for 3 pesos

($1.50) a month they had Filipino boys sweep the floors, make their bunks, shine their shoes and do latrine and KP duty. This was helpful since the Thirty-fourth worked long hours loading supplies and equipment onto trucks after the material had been unloaded from ships at the dock.[6]

On November 28, the Thirty-fourth moved out from Nichols Field by truck convoy, using blackout lights, on their way to Del Carmen Field, 15 kilometers south of Clark Field in Central Luzon.

It didn't take Earl or Hank long to get to know the Filipinos in the area. They learned some Tagalog phrases, including "*Maganda dalaga*" ("beautiful lady"), appreciated by the pretty young girls. These Filipinos enjoyed Hank and Earl's harmonizing, especially when they sang "San Antonio Rose." But the good life on the Pacific island did not last.

Early on the morning of December 8, Earl Oatman was waiting to go to Clark Field when a radio message was received saying that Pearl Harbor was being bombed by Japanese planes. With significant apprehension, several men in Oatman's group, including two medics and the first sergeant, left for Clark Field, 15 kilometers away. After sick call they ate lunch in the mess hall before starting back. Clark Field was a veritable bee hive[7] of activity. Armed men were posted in tactical locations and scurried about. B-17 bombers and P-40 pursuit planes sat on the runway apron with motors running and pilots and ground crews standing by.[8] All were awaiting orders to take off, but none were received. The radio station in Manila had announced that Clark Field was being bombed. This was considered a joke at the time as the men at Clark Field could see they were not under attack.

Oatman's group started back to Del Carmen Field. On the way, they stopped at a bar in a small town a short distance from Clark Field, as several of the group wanted to have a beer. Oatman was drinking a Coke when loud explosions were heard. The men rushed outside and saw that Clark Field was being bombed. Flames leaped from burning buildings and planes on the ground while black smoke billowed into the air above the field. Flights of silvery bombers in formation were dropping explosives, and, with no opposition, Zero fighters were strafing targets on the ground.

As they stood and watched, Oatman realized that war with Japan had started. Someone went to the second floor of the bar to get their first sergeant and one of the medics, both being serviced by prostitutes. Oatman has often thought what an unusual circumstance to be caught in at the start of a war, in bed with a prostitute. Acting under order of the first sergeant, their driver drove fast and irresponsibly back to Del Carmen Field. Upon their arrival, Oatman saw three or four of their P-35s had nosed over, leaving propellers bent and partially buried in the ground. Some of their pilots had been overly anxious to get their planes into the air to engage the Japanese in combat over Clark Field.[9]

Doyle Decker, Battery H, 200th Coast Artillery, was in Sternberg Hospital in Manila on December 8, awaiting transportation by ship to San Francisco's Letterman Hospital on December 12. Down to 135 pounds from his usual 150 pounds on his six-foot frame, the doctors couldn't find the reason for his low-grade fever, but surmised he must depart the tropics or die.

Decker wished the Japanese would wait to start a war with the United States until he could get home. But his hopes were dashed on the morning of the eighth as word came in on the Manila radio station that the Japanese had commenced a surprise attack on Pearl Harbor.

Though running a fever, Decker was ambulatory, and at 4:00 P.M. the first ambulance arrived with wounded at Sternberg Hospital. Someone yelled at Decker to help them unload the men and take care of the gory blankets. He dodged the first blood-soaked blanket thrown at him and then worked the rest of the afternoon aiding the wounded and dying. Some moaned in pain and others yelled that they didn't want to die or called for their mothers, wives, or girlfriends. One soldier looked at Decker, pleading, "Don't let them take off my leg."

Decker looked at the soldier's stump, wrapped and bleeding, and nearly fainted with shock from the sight of bones protruding from the wound.

An Army chaplain moved through the chaos from one bloody cot to another, talking softly to the men and giving last rites to those mortally wounded. The soldier's bodies had been ripped into grotesque shapes. The mixed smell of sweat, urine, and warm blood was pervasive. The scene was surreal: a continuous stream of bodies delivered by the white ambulances riddled with bullet holes from being strafed by Japanese fighter aircraft as they sped to the hospital.

The Japanese attack of white ambulances marked with a red cross disgusted the doctors and nurses.

Decker was drenched in sweat and about to faint when a young army doctor grabbed him by the shoulder and walked him away from the scene. Smoking a cigarette and taking a break, they discussed the carnage. Decker asked the doctor how he handled the chaos. The young doctor replied that they just did best they could and hoped they didn't go crazy in the process.

The doctor needed the break as much as Decker. After a few minutes he slapped Decker on the back. "We better get in there. They need both of us. Think you can handle it?" Nodding his head in the affirmative, Decker returned to his gruesome task. At the rate the bodies were coming into the hospital, Decker speculated on how much longer they could hold out.

One wounded solder with a broken arm told Decker that the 200th Coast Artillery had been hit and every man lost. The guilt that every soldier feels, knowing that they have been spared when their comrades have been killed, tore at Decker's psyche. Two hours later, it was confirmed that the 200th had been hit. Though the area they were defending was badly damaged, only a few men were wounded. This good news lifted Decker's hopes that he would soon rejoin his unit.

At dusk, the number of arriving ambulances slowed. Decker took a shower, trying to wash away the stench. The hospital was overflowing with wounded, so Decker and the rest of the ambulatory men were moved down the street to the old Thirty-first Infantry Barracks. The young man from the farm country of middle Missouri was overwhelmed by the day's events. He struggled to comprehend his fate.

Bernard L. Anderson completed two years of college work before joining the CCC (Civilian Conservation Corps), rising to a company commander in 1940. In 1936, he enlisted in the Sixty-fourth Infantry of the Wisconsin National Guard. One year later he received a commission as a second lieutenant and after another year he became a first lieutenant in the Officers Reserve of the Fortieth Infantry. He was activated into the regular army at Selfridge Field in October 1940 and sent to the Philippines in May 1941.

Originally assigned to the Air Base Squadron at Nichols Field in the supply department, he was transferred to the Twentieth Pursuit Group after a couple of months, where he was assigned as the assistant adjutant. Less than a month before the war started, the unit activated the First Far Eastern Air Force which was destroyed on Bataan. It was later reactivated in Australia.

The construction of air fields and attempts at making the Army Air Corps an effective defender of the Philippines was a next to impossible task. In December 1941, that air force included an odd assortment of 311 different aircraft. Thirty-five were new B-17s; 103 were P-40s; and the rest PT-13s, B-10s, and an array of other old and reconditioned planes.

Anderson was on the Far Eastern Air Force's staff. The night before the Japanese hit, General George, Captain Eads, Colonel Allison Ind and Anderson were working in the top-secret room until about 2:00 A.M. They broke for some breakfast and Anderson walked about two blocks to his quarters and went to bed. It seemed he was no sooner in bed than his telephone began to ring. It was General George yelling to Anderson, "the Japs have struck Pearl Harbor!"

The force of B-17s was ready at Clark Field, as Anderson recalled, with "50 percent fuel and 50 percent bombs loaded."[10] They were awaiting General MacArthur's order to either top off with fuel or more bombs, if given the signal to strike enemy targets. The order never came and when the Japanese struck Clark Field they took the B-17s out of action.

Like the bulk of Americans on Luzon, Anderson was moved to Bataan, leaving Nichols Field on December 20, 1941.

John Boone was making a good living as a booking agent in Southeast Asia, booking shows wherever he could in Manila. When the Japanese bombed Luzon on December 8, he enlisted in the military in Manila. With two years of college, he was made a corporal in D Company Thirty-first Infantry.

Private Leon Beck, a five-foot-five Oklahoma boy, turned twenty as the war starts in the Philippines. He was in the Thirty-first Infantry and as the armies retreated ahead of the Japanese advance, the Thirty-first along with the rest of the Philippine and American units poured into Bataan.

Staff Sergeant Ray Hunt of the Twenty-first Pursuit Squadron was sound asleep on a camp cot at Nichols Field just outside Manila when he was interrupted by a horrendous racket. Bullets were coming down like hail, interspersed with bombs that shook the ground like a series of small earthquakes. He jumped into a half-finished foxhole just before a bomb hit not more that thirty feet away. It was Hunt's good fortune that the bomb was a dud. Nearby a friend was buried alive by another bomb burst, but fortunately he was dug out after a third man who'd been buried up to his neck yelled for help and both were rescued. Another soldier near Hunt had his canteen shot off his hip. Thus World War II began for Ray Hunt with a devastating shock.

Lieutenant Clay Conner, from East Orange, New Jersey, had trained with the Twenty-seventh Bomb Group in Louisiana prior to the unit being shipped to the Philippines.

On December 7, Conner, an officer named Cowert, and Rocky Gause had been to the jai alai fronton as was their usual recreation. About 9:00 o'clock the next morning, Conner rolled out of his bunk on the screened-in porch of his quarters and headed inside the house to shower. He noticed several men gathered around a radio which blared out something about Pearl Harbor being bombed. Conner continued to the shower, still numb from his long night, when he realized what he had heard.

After quickly dressing and running to the headquarters, he noticed hundreds of men hurrying back and forth in the large room. They were studying the air-warning table and listening to reports from stations over the Pacific.

Conner was ordered to gather all radio equipment from the Air Corps units and take them to the firing area and establish a communications depot.

For the next several days his unit established communications and then broke down the equipment moving to a new location until December 26. Then the unit was evacuated out of Manila and ordered to find any refuge to hide the equipment and to bivouac as they worked their way to Bataan.

First Lieutenant Donald Dunwoody Blackburn arrived in Manila on October 23, 1941. He was assigned to Fort McKinley, a pleasant post with beautiful acacia trees shading the asphalt roads around the golf course. His commanding officer Major Martin Moses, West Point class of 1929, is described as a man of slight build and medium height with a resolute chin jutting forth under muscular jowls. Moses assigned Blackburn to work as an instructor in the Headquarters Battalion, Twelfth Infantry, Philippine Army.

He found this a challenging assignment as there were no trucks, no radios, no field manuals and just one field telephone. He began his assignment not knowing that he would never get the opportunity to train his unit, due to the swift arrival of war.

On Monday morning, December 8, Blackburn and Shelby Newman were eating their breakfast when they were informed of the bombing of Baguio. Stunned, they cautiously took stock of their situation with the first confirmed wartime activity. Blackburn suddenly found himself battalion commander.

When the unit drove to San Juan on the Bocnoton River, they found the line of defense there was commanded by Major Arthur Noble, a classmate of Martin Moses, a cheerful, freckle-faced extrovert with a hearty sense of humor.

For the next three weeks, Blackburn was in one battle after another, blocking forces one day and ordering retreat the next. Finally, his unit was ordered into the Bataan peninsula and on January 1, 1942, the Eleventh Division covered withdrawal of all Luzon forces.

On December 8, Russell Volckmann was at Regimental Headquarters of the Eleventh Infantry, Philippine Army, where he had been reassigned, when Captain Robinson rushed into his office and exclaimed, "Hawaii has been bombed!"[11] That the war had begun was no surprise, but Volckmann was surprised at the attack on Pearl Harbor, some four thousand miles to the west of the Philippines. Most had expected that when war came, the Philippines would be the first place the Japanese would hit. It wasn't long after Captain Robinson left Volckmann's office before the steady drone of planes was heard overhead. Volckmann rushed out and counted sixty Japanese bombers flying south. Camp John Hay near Baguio was bombed at 8:30 A.M., and Clark Field was attacked a few hours later.

A few days later Volckmann found himself in command of a regiment of inexperienced Filipino troops, moving them into position to defend against a possible Japanese troop landing on the western coast of Luzon.

Volckmann knew that wartime waiting and idleness deteriorated morale faster than anything. For that reason, he pushed the officers and men to their limit in preparing alternate positions, overhead cover, switch positions, and improvised obstacles along the beach. At night, patrols were kept busy trying to catch flare-lighting spies. This threat became so great that Volckmann at last ordered all civilians to withdraw from the beach defense area between 6 P.M. and 6 A.M.

After a relatively quiet day, Doyle Decker awakened on December 10 to the sounds of machine-gun fire and exploding bombs. A small Japanese force had landed on the northern tip of Luzon and their air force was strafing and bombing various parts of the island to keep the Americans off balance. Decker and the other men in the barracks spent most of the day in a nearby bomb shelter. It was obvious that no one would be on a ship going home soon.

That evening Decker tried to convince an army doctor to release him to his unit. The doctor was adamant that Decker couldn't survive in the tropics. He told him that as soon as they could get a ship out of Manila, he was going home with the rest of the severely wounded.

Decker was astonished at the doctor's remarks and questioned his logic. He understood that there was no possibility for a ship to depart the Philippines without immediately being attacked by Japanese aircraft. He was determined to get back to the 200th.

Decker continued to hound the doctors, but to no avail. On December 23, the call went out for all able-bodied men to report to their units. Because the American fleet had been destroyed by the Japanese surprise attacks, relief would have to come from another location. The desperate situation in the Philippines called for all Filipino-American forces to move to the Bataan Peninsula. This would be the last stand against the Japanese advance.[12]

Every evening the men listened to "Freedom for the Philippines" on radio station KGEI in San Francisco. There were the usual promises of aid on the way and exhortations for the American and Filipino troops to hold out against the Japanese aggressors. The men took hope in the promises, but no additional supplies or troops arrived.

Badgering the doctors at every opportunity, Decker hoped they would declare him fit for duty and return him to his unit. Finally, on January 1, 1942, a Filipino doctor asked everyone wanting to return to duty to step forward. Decker almost leapt toward the doctor who told Decker that he shouldn't put him back in the field with his hospital record, but to sleep in his clothes and be ready to leave at midnight. The fires needed to die down at Pier Seven to allow a boat to come in from Corregidor. The next morning Decker was on his way to Bataan via Corregidor and a three-week odyssey to find his unit.

When Lieutenant Ed Ramsey of the Twenty-sixth Cavalry found out that Pearl Harbor had been bombed, he dashed back to his quarters, joining the general commotion. He threw some things together and rushed to regimental headquarters. There General Wainwright was huddling with the Commanding Officer of the Twenty-sixth while the officers assembled. Wainwright left as the men stood at attention, and the CO began issuing orders.

Ramsey's troop, G, was to move to the village of Bongabong, one hundred twenty miles to the northeast in the Sierra Madre foothills. Ramsey's mission was to relieve Captain Joe Barker's B Troop, and Barker and his men were to return to Stotsenburg. It was almost noon before G Troop had their horses loaded onto the trailers and their convoy moved out. Clearing the fort and turning onto the road toward Dao, they saw the first wave of Japanese bombers.

The men ducked as the planes dived toward them, but the target was Clark Field, and the bombers flew over their trucks and continued their attack. There were explosions, spewing fireballs into the air with the stench of gasoline and sulfur. The B-17s, which were being refueled and loaded with bombs, disintegrated, throwing debris across the airfield, igniting the depots and hangers. The noise unsettled the horses in their trailers. As they drove away, the Twenty-sixth was hushed, watching the U.S. air force go up in flames.

Vernon Fassoth had obtained permission to remain with his family until January 1. When the Fassoth family arrived at their home in Lubao they found the railroad station nearby occupied as an army supply depot for Mariveles, Bataan. Soldiers were using a house next to the Fassoth home while working at the depot. The following day, four more soldiers arrived to work at the depot, receiving supplies, ammunition, gasoline, food, clothes, and other supplies. The Fassoths welcomed the soldiers into their home as the house next door was full to capacity.

Martin Fassoth returned to the family home on December 29. That night Bill and Martin talked about how they had come to Luzon. Their father John had shipped to Hawaii from Germany at age 16. He first worked for a sugar company on Kauai and later owned a sugar plantation and sugar mill on Maui, known as the Kipahula Sugar Plantation. John had married another German immigrant, Anna Decker, and to this union were born six sons and a daughter.

Known as a shrewd businessman, John was elected to the Hawaiian legislature. Bill and Martin were born on October 2, 1890, in the little village of Waimea, Kauai. Bill had moved to the Philippines in August 21, 1913, to work for Americans in the sugar industry. He remained for six years and then at their invitation took a long-term lease on 1,120 acres of the Dinalupihan Estate, owned by the Roman Catholic Church, and 247 acres of private lands. Bill planted sugar cane for milling by Pampanga Sugar Mills in Del Carmen, Pampanga.

In 1915, Bill married a Filipina of Santo Tomas, Lubao, in Pampanga — Catalina Dimacali. They had four children, three boys and a girl who died at fourteen days of age.

Martin joined his twin brother Bill in September 1923 to help with the additional duties the sugar plantation presented. Martin, quiet and soft-spoken, remained unmarried until after the war.

Eighty Japanese ships entered Lingayen Gulf on December 22, 1942, challenged by ineffective fire from a few 155-millimeter guns. Unable to halt the advancing Japanese troops, the Eleventh Infantry withdrew and marched south on the night of December 24 and crossed the Agno River at Bayambang the next day at noon. Major Russell Volckmann had been reassigned from the Thirty-first Infantry in August to the Eleventh Infantry, Philippine Army, as senior instructor and executive officer.

As he looked over his maps and orders assigning the Eleventh Infantry to its defensive position along the south bank of the Agno River, Major Volckmann heard automatic weapons fire from the general direction of the river. Men began to run in all directions without seeking positions from which to return fire. Volckmann had the general alert sounded for the officers and soon had the unit in proper positions to defend their sector.

For the next several days, the Eleventh Infantry worked its way south, assuming defensive positions. At times it got cut off by Japanese units but it fought its way through to again take up defensive positions to slow the onslaught of the Japanese.

Defending the whole of Luzon was General MacArthur's original plan, but the successful advances by the Japanese troops had made it impossible to adequately perform. The U.S. air force of 277 planes had been wiped out, with only a few remaining P-40s available. Filipino-American troops were scattered all over the island. On December 24, MacArthur removed his headquarters to the fortress rock of Corregidor, and ordered all troops to back into a series of defensive lines, in what was known as WPO-3 or War Plan Orange, which would require the troops to slowly retreat into the Bataan Peninsula where they would make their final stand.

General Wainwright assembled four divisions of his corps, reinforced by the Twenty-sixth Cavalry, to direct the delaying action. Lieutenant Ramsey's troop hurried to join this battle, off-loading the horses at Bongabong and marching to Cabanatuan, the provincial capital, to rejoin the regiment.

An important supply depot, the troop hoped it would find rest and provisions at Cabanatuan. But on their arrival they found that the day before it had been bombed, and as the troop approached the town they could see the fires for miles across the rice paddies. The night sky was lit with oil drums exploding and ammunition crates thundering their contents into the air. Flashes pulsed beneath a black cloud bank that covered the horizon. Burning rice and charred meat combined with the smells of sulfur and oil to create a toxic stench. A million pounds of provisions meant for U.S. troops had been ruined. The cavalry troop had to continue without rest or food while the ashes of their supplies settled on their uniforms and horses.

That night and the next day the troop was followed by Japanese spotter planes, buzzing just out of range of their machine guns. Two or three times they scattered into the brush for cover as they were bombed and strafed by Zeros.

Ramsey's troop staggered into the village of San Isidro after their seventy-two-hour march, where they found the remnants of the Twenty-sixth streaming in. It was a skeleton of the regiment Ramsey had joined six months before. Showing signs of malnutrition, the men were haggard and the horses that were left could barely walk. Their remaining vehicles were riddled with bullet holes.

On the morning of December 29, Bill Fassoth was in his office at the plantation's rice mill when some U.S. Army officers arrived with part of their convoy of trucks, loaded with Filipino soldiers. The officers asked permission to park their trucks along both sides of the road running by the mill. They were waiting for the rest of the convoy to catch up with them. This kept the road open for other traffic on its way to and from Mariveles. Bill, noticing the men preparing to have lunch, invited the officers to have their meal with him. They got into one of the cars and drove about three hundred yards to Bill's home. The men were just getting out of the car when Japanese planes, flying in formation overhead, broke and made a bombing run on railroad cars loaded with ammunition, gasoline, and other supplies at the railroad station next to the mill. The railroad cars were only about thirty yards from Bill's home. The men and Bill's family ran to a dugout that Vernon had built with the aid of some soldiers two days before.

After the planes dropped their first load of bombs, the men left the dugout to inspect the damage, while Bill's family ran to another dugout farther away. The officers ran for their cars and trucks to get them moved farther down the road. The Japanese planes continued to bomb for another hour. When Bill walked out of the shelter, he could see Santo Tomas, Lubao, on fire. The mill was burning, and railroad cars were burning and exploding as Japanese fighters continued to strafe civilians.

That night, using bull carts to haul supplies and some furniture, several families from the barrio moved away from the highway toward the mountains to the northwest.

On January 1, 1942, some Philippine soldiers crossed the rice fields in retreat to the south, passing Bill Fassoth and several families watching from the jungles. With this discouraging sight, Bill and the rest of the group moved four more kilometers away from the highway. When the group stopped by the Porac River near the home of someone who worked for a friend of Bill Fassoth, it had become a large crowd, with many Filipinos following the food supplies. Here the people spent the night, with the women sleeping in the house and the men sleeping around a big haystack.

The group moved again after a man was brought in with a deep gash in his neck from a sword wound received from some Japanese soldiers not far away, and after learning that two other Filipinos had been decapitated. Traveling another three kilometers, they arrived in Barrio Santo Domingo. With help from some of the men, Vernon dug a big hole under a house and hid food supplies, medicine, and some ammunition for rifles and shotguns. Additional supplies of food were concealed in a dugout, covered with hay, at the side of the house.

Bill, Martin, and Vernon Fassoth began hiding during the day from prowling Japanese patrols that were going through barrios pillaging for food: pigs, chickens, etc. The Japanese were also raping women and girls. Wherever the Japanese found women and men in dugouts, they sent the men away and raped the women. Fifth columnists or pro–Japanese Filipinos were reporting those hiding to the roaming Japanese patrols. The men hid in nearby sugarcane fields during the day, having their meals sent out to them. The girls also hid during the day with the women, running whenever they were warned of approaching Japanese patrols. Volunteer guards were sent out to perimeters to warn of any approaching strangers. This system worked well in protecting the people. The patrols did not operate in the darkness, so all who were hiding could return at night. After a few days, the Filipinos in the barrio began to be afraid, concerned for their own safety because of the number of people with the Fassoths' living so near.

Chapter 2

Into Bataan

Louis Morton wrote in The Fall *of the* Philippines *that the defense of Bataan was conceived as a defense of depth. The first line, called the main battle position, extended from Mabatang, a short distance north of Abucay on the east, across Mt. Natib to Mauban on the west coast, a distance of twenty miles. A strong outpost line of resistance was established in front of the main battle position and defenses to a depth of several miles were prepared to the rear. Along the beaches on both coasts troops were posted to guard against amphibious envelopment.*

Bill, Martin, and Vernon Fassoth wanted to go into the Bataan peninsula to serve the American and Filipino armies fighting the Japanese, but on reflection had concluded that they were not military men and would be of little help.

On January 24, 1942, Martin and Bill left for the mountains bordering their sugar plantation at Dinalupihan, Bataan, leaving Vernon to care for the remaining family members. It took Bill and Martin a complete day to get to the foothills of the Pampanga and Bataan mountains. By avoiding the barrios they circumvented Japanese patrols. It took three days to select a secluded location for their first camp, away from any barrios and with a difficult terrain to avoid detection.

By mid–January 1942, Bataan had over a hundred thousand troops and civilians crowded onto a 400-square-mile peninsula. There was no more than a forty-day supply of ammunition, food, and forage for their animals. Every day brought new assurances that reinforcements and supplies were on the

Luzon with key positions (Courtesy Andrew Burton).

way. All they had to do was hold on until the relief convoy arrived. Given the destruction of the navy at Pearl Harbor, no such convoy existed or was possible.[1]

With numerous losses and the need to rest the troops, Captain Wheeler placed Lieutenant Ed Ramsey in charge of the first platoon of E Troop, composed of twenty-seven battle-drained Philippine Scouts. Ramsey moved in with the troop that night, and the next morning, before eating his own breakfast, he supervised the feeding and watering of the animals. At midday, General Wainwright drove into the camp in a dilapidated sedan. Always thin, he had become ghostly as he shared the dwindling provisions.

Wainwright was angry. He had come to chastise General Segundo for withdrawing the First Philippine Division from the village of Morong. Morong, he felt, offered a good defensive position along the river between the U.S. forces and the Japanese. He was adamant that it was a line the Filipino-American forces could not abandon, as it would connect with the Second Division defenses to the east.

Wainwright wanted Morong reoccupied at once, and he ordered Segundo to move his division forward. An advance guard was to rush to Morong to reconnoiter and secure the town until the division arrived.

Captain Wheeler and Ramsey were standing nearby while this conversation took place, and Wainwright caught Ramsey out of the corner of his eye. He ordered Ramsey to take his men as the advance guard. Ramsey saluted wearily and was about to start off when Wheeler spoke up, pointing out to Wainwright that Ramsey's troop had been on a long reconnaissance, and had just volunteered to stay behind since Wheeler didn't know the terrain. Could he send someone else? Wainwright shot an angry glance and denied Wheeler's request.

Wheeler walked Ramsey back to the troop, apologizing. The troop was ordered to mount, and Ramsey's first platoon was in the lead. Wheeler rode with the second platoon, followed by the third. Ramsey knew the coastal road by heart. It was little more than a jungle track with underbrush knotted up on both sides, making it was a dangerous place, a provocation for an ambush.

Ramsey formed his men in column of twos, spreading them out in a staggered formation to diminish them as potential targets. Four troopers took the point thirty yards in the lead, reaching the eastern edge of Morong after a six-kilometer march.

Three trails branched left off the road through Morong toward the sea. Ramsey signaled column left at the middle road, deployed the platoon in columns of eight men each, and commanded them to raise pistols. The platoon watched as the point riders entered the town. There was silence as they rode among the thatched huts. Ramsey then ordered the troop to advance.

Morong looked uninhabited. The huts were empty, the pens beneath them bereft of livestock. The only stone structure in the village was a Catholic church, closed against the advancing Japanese forces on Bataan. Beyond the village were thick groves of coconut palms leaning toward a swamp next to the sea, while to their right was the narrow Batolan River with a single wooden bridge, the area that Wainwright wanted to defend.

The troop moved watchfully toward the center of the village, the horses maneuvering head-high among the bamboo huts, the men watching for any movement. Ramsey observed the point guard turn in at the church square and vanish from sight, and then he heard gunfire.

Rifles and automatic weapons fired bullets from the center and northern end of the village, reverberating among the huts and sending jungle birds screeching in flight. Instantly the point men came galloping back to the troop, one of the privates bleeding onto his horse's neck and flanks. An advance guard of the Japanese army had crossed the river and had passed near the church just as the troop had entered the village.

Ramsey saw copious Japanese infantrymen firing from the village center, and behind them hundreds more were crossing the river and rushing toward the Batolan Bridge. He feared the main body would be surging across the river to retake Morong.

Over the noise of battle, Ramsey ordered his troops to position themselves, and he raised his pistol. A cavalry charge would be their only hope to split up the Japanese troops and to survive against their superior numbers. For centuries, the surprise of a mounted charge had proved overwhelming; now the situation and all Ramsey's preparation made it instinctual.

Ramsey brought his arm down and yelled "charge!" Bent prone across the horses' necks, flinging themselves at the Japanese advance, pistols firing, the men galloped at full tilt toward the Japanese riflemen. A few returned the fire, but most fled in bewilderment, some wading back into the river, others running frantically for the swamps. To the Japanese, the charge seemed an apparition from another century, horses pounding, ridden by cheering, whooping men charging headlong, firing weapons.

The charge broke through the advance unit and continued to the swamp, where the troopers dismounted and drew their rifles from their leather sheaths. Ramsey threw out a combat line of one squad along the river to keep the Japanese at bay, and led the rest back into Morong to hunt for snipers.[2]

The Ninety-second Infantry positioned on the right of the Eleventh Infantry was supposed to protect the flank, but Major Russell W. Volckmann, acting Eleventh Infantry commander, was uneasy about this arrangement. Recognizing the importance of the road and the vulnerability of his position, he shifted his line so that the troops of his Third Battalion were in position to guard the road. A roadblock was established where a platoon of tanks was positioned on the west side of the bridge across the Dalagot River leading into Zaragoza. The bridge was prepared for demolition, but the river was

Topical illustration of Bataan (U.S. Army Center of Military History).

fordable by foot soldiers. The organization of the roadblock was a wise precaution, for the Tarlac-Cabanatuan road had already been exposed on the east by the withdrawal of the Ninety-first Division.[3]

The Eleventh Division withdrew into northern Bataan on January 4, 1942. They rested in an area west of Balanga in a barrio called Boni. They were trying to rest when an American artillery unit fired its guns at the advancing Japanese forces. The big 155-mm guns belched long, rifled smoke rings and resounded with thunder as the shells left their captive tubes with lethal charges against the enemy.

The Eleventh was then ordered to defend the beach along Manila Bay from Abucay to Limay, and here they dealt the Japanese heavy casualties as the Japanese attempted to break through the defensive lines.

It was in the defense of the beaches that Donald Blackburn became acquainted with Volckmann, who had a reputation as a competent commander. He was short and slight with, deep blue eyes, brown wavy hair, a thin mustache and a pleasant voice belying his tough, no-nonsense nature.

The Thirty-fourth Pursuit Squadron left Orani, where they had been since just after Christmas, and moved further into the Bataan Peninsula to Little Baguio between Cabcaben and Mariveles. Here Earl Oatman and Hank Winslow, along with the rest of the Thirty-fourth were issued bolt-action, 30-caliber, 1903 Springfield rifles and steel helmets. Several older sergeants, who had infantry training, tried to teach the airmen how to break down their weapons, take care of them and shoot with some efficiency. The Thirty-fourth along with other Air Corps units were now part of the Provisional Infantry.[4]

On January 10 the men were loaded on a truck, moved to Agloloma Bay and stationed on the beach in a defensive maneuver. The men were now a part of the Seventy-first Philippine Division. For the next several days conditions on the beach were ideal, with warm breezes and beautiful scenery. Some men were assigned the job of obtaining fresh fish for the squadron and were proficient at securing the fish using dynamite in the tidal pools and collecting the stunned fish to supplement the unit's mess.

Bill and Martin Fassoth began working on the camp with the help of some Filipino boys they trusted to keep the location undisclosed. They had selected a beautiful setting below a small but high waterfall,on a stream with three pools one above the other. This would supply the camp with plenty of water for cooking and bathing. The stream was full of snails, small freshwater crabs and some eels. Erecting bamboo buildings took most of the week.

Bill then sent for his family, including his wife Catalina, Vernon, and his cousins Consuelo (17) and Carmen Tubo, (14), who were helping Catalina.

There was also Peaci, nicknamed "Peanuts" (5), whose mother had died in childbirth along with Peaci's twin, and Rose Shelledy and her two American boys, ages 12 and 9 who came with Vernon, Rose having no place to go and afraid of capture by the Japanese. Rose and the boys remained with the Fassoth family for two months before her brother sent word to have them sent to him.[5]

The camp had an outside kitchen with the stove built along a hill by the stream. A long table was built under the shade of a big tree for meals. It was the dry season, so the camp didn't have to worry about cover for a while.

Chickens were acquired from Vicente Bernia, a neighboring sugar-plantation owner. Vicente and Arturo Bernia had provided Fort Stotsenburg with chickens and eggs prior to the war. In fact they were trusted purveyors for the military. When Vicente had discovered sick chickens in his flock he had refused to sell them to the military until the infected birds were killed and the flock was free from further infection. The procurement department at the Fort was so impressed that they explicitly trusted the Bernias.

The Bernias' father was Spanish and their mother was a Filipina. Vicente arranged for all the supplies from Manila, as he had a truck and his brother Arturo had an automobile. They could travel to and from Manila, passing the different Japanese guards along the route by stating that the quantity of supplies were intended for their plantation in Gutad, Pampanga, and they were procuring extra supplies for the next rainy season. To add credibility to the story, many supplies were purchased from Japanese bazaars. This allowed the Bernias to show the receipts from the bazaars whenever they were asked about the supplies they were hauling. The provisions were then dispensed from the Bernia plantation to Fassoth's camp by packers upon whom Vicente could depend.[5]

Ray Hunt's working time on Bataan was spent repairing airplanes. Most were P-40 fighters, a few were old Seversky P-35s and obsolete but useful B-18 bombers; and others were B-10s, A-27 attack bombers, observation planes, and P-26s used by the Philippine Air Force. To keep the dwindling force airworthy, the ground crews worked day and night, in spite of oppressive heat and clouds of mosquitoes. The crews patched bullet holes and cannibalized disabled aircraft for any parts usable on other planes. Engines, even wings, were transferred from planes of one category to another. Somebody even figured out a way to alter gasoline-tank brackets on fighter planes to hold 500-pound bombs.

Early in the Bataan campaign it became apparent that most of the fighting would be on land. Since there were more pilots, maintenance men, and other specialists than the deteriorating air force needed, it was decided to make many of the men soldiers in the infantry. All the airmen needed were equipment and training. One day Ray Hunt was assured that his rifle was his best friend, and there he should treat it with tenderness and care. Hunt was not impressed, but eventually discovered that the advice was correct, as his rifle bailed him out of several difficulties.

In late January 1942, Hunt and several airmen were trucked to Aglaloma Point and deployed in a line across that small peninsula to fight a reported small group of entrenched Japanese. In the next several days, locked in combat in the dense jungle, Hunt learned a lot about some of the different kinds of men who people this world. In particular, he learned not to judge a person prematurely. Many a rear-area loudmouth fell quiet and cowered when he discovered a lethal enemy might be only a few feet away, entirely concealed. On the other hand, some of the most unlikely men calmly took initiatives and performed far beyond expectations. Hunt saw one young farm boy, praised for having killed several enemy soldiers, remark quietly that he had just done his duty, while another soldier of equally tender years cried and trembled and pleaded that he was sick.[6]

Private Doyle Decker spent his first night on Bataan looking for his unit along with several other soldiers who had come to the peninsula by way of boat to Mariveles. The men were welcomed to a navy hospital the first night and given a meal and blanket; they slept on the ground.

Bombing and machine-gun fire wakened the men the next morning and they all jump into nearby foxholes. Decker was the first in his foxhole and was nearly suffocated when several soldiers jump in on top of him. After regaining their composure, the men were fed two dry pancakes for breakfast and escorted by navy shore police to the front gate of the hospital and told to find their units.

Later that afternoon Decker spotted one of the 200th Coast Artillery Corps trucks and his old regimental commander. The 200th had been split into two units, the 200th and the 515th, to better support the various units on Bataan. The colonel wasn't sure where Decker's unit, Battery H of the 200th, was located, but took Decker with him and assigned him to one of the 515th units until Decker could rejoin his friends.

For the next three weeks, Decker was an air guard on an ammunition truck. He watched for approaching enemy fighter planes and knocked on the top of the truck to alert the driver, who then tried to find cover from attack. It was interesting work and Decker liked the men in his new unit, but wanted to get back with the men in his old battery.

He was impressed by the hard work and bravery demonstrated by an engineer battalion next to the 515th. The engineers worked through bombing raids as though nothing was happening. Japanese bombs made craters in the road and the caterpillar operators covered the large holes as soon as they were created, even while bombs continued to fall.

"How the hell do you have the nerve to work on the road while the Japs are bombing it?" Decker asked one of the grader operators, who replied, "either the bomb is going to hit you or miss. If it hits, you won't know what happened. If the bomb misses there's another damn hole to fill."[7]

Prior to December 8, 1941, Colonel Claude A. Thorp was the Provost Marshall at Fort Stotsenburg. With the withdrawal of troops into Bataan, he became the provost marshall of the Northern Luzon Forces under General King. On January 19, 1942, General MacArthur called Colonel Thorp to a conference. Since Thorp was unable to attend because of a bullet wound to his left leg, Captain David Miller was sent on Thorp's behalf. Thorp had previously proposed to General MacArthur that he be authorized to lead a group through Japanese lines north into central Luzon to organize guerrilla forces. Captain Miller returned from the meeting with the necessary authorization signed by Adjutant General Casey.

On January 27, the group assembled by Thorp left Bagac, Bataan, for Porac, with their ultimate destination the foothills of Mount Pinatubo near Fort Stotsenburg. There were four American officers in the group, Lieutenant Robert Lapham, Lieutenant Walter Cushing, Lieutenant Ralph McGuire, and Captain David Miller. With an additional nine enlisted men, some Filipinos, and two women, there were more than nineteen in the group. All were armed with Thompson machine guns or Garands (automatic rifles), Springfield rifles and pistols. Captain Miller was cut off from the group at Little Baguio and he was never able to rejoin the unit.

It took the group forty days to reach their destination, after many difficulties, including shortage of food, water and guides. After many encounters with Japanese patrols and after an ambush to secure food supplies, the group reached Timbo where they established their headquarters.

While in this camp, Colonel Thorp reorganized his staff, appointing Captain McGuire as his adjutant and Lieutenant Bob Lapham as his supply officer.

In late May, a Major Barber of the Intelligence Corps came to join the camp, bringing some soldiers and a radio set. Sergeant Alfred Bruce also came into the camp and was assigned to take command of a Chinese guerrilla unit operating in the mountains of Porac.[8]

Chapter 3
Little Food, Bad Ammunition

Even with the best of plans mistakes occur, and the hasty maneuver of troops into Bataan by the American and Filipino troops fostered many blunders. Due to bureaucratic rules and too little time to move necessary supplies into position, much of the food and ammunition were left in warehouses in Manila.

The conflict in the Pacific found two differing cultures at war. The Occidental and the Oriental had little understanding of the other. The surrender of the troops on Bataan sent a shockwave through both cultures, and to this day the resulting brutality is still being studied and psychoanalyzed. Powerful feelings about this tragic event continue to present internal conflict for those who experienced what came to be known as the "Death March."

The Second Battalion's weapons company had two mortars, one new 81mm and one old World War I Stokes 3-incher. The crews had only thirty-one rounds of the 81mm ammunition, so they fired the more numerous but less accurate 3-inch rounds. Sergeant Earl F. Walk, the mortar platoon leader, did not have much faith in the old rounds. "When we assembled the rounds," he recalled, "the insert that went into the body of the shell was red at one end and yellow at the other. If the colors were faded, generally the shell would not go off when it hit the ground, but we always hoped it would hit a Jap on the head. I believed one on the head would put anyone out of action."[1]

The Eleventh Philippine Army was in a poor defensive situation when the Thirty-first Infantry on its right flank was ordered south in defensive reserve. Major Volckmann did all he could to support his units in the field when a platoon from the Third Battalion was surrounded and captured. The Japanese tied all the men to trees and began questioning them. When they didn't get the right response, the men were bayoneted until all were dead except one man who survied eleven bayonet wounds and escaped to tell the traumatic story.

Firing broke out a few hundred yards from the Eleventh regimental headquarters on February 1. The Japanese had infiltrated the lines through the First Division sector on the left flank of the Eleventh. Mistaken as a small force, it took twenty-one days for three companies of the Eleventh and a battalion of the Forty-fifth Infantry to wipe out what turned out to be a regiment of Japanese.

On February 12 the Japanese unexpectedly retreated north from the battle of the "Big Pockets."[2] As the American and Filipino troops advanced into the area they were shocked at the carnage. The battle was a remarkable victory and morale boost for the Filipino-American troops. The Filipinos retrieved a generous sum of weapons and equipment, including an antitank gun which they used against the Japanese troops. An accurate tally of the Japanese loss of men and material was difficult, but Major Arthur K. Noble, Eleventh Division Intelligence Officer, counted 300 bodies and 150 graves in the Big Pockets. The Japanese had buried as many as six bodies in some of their graves. Lieutenant Bernard Anderson, Eleventh Engineers, in charge of burying the enemy, estimated 450 dead.

Toward the end of the campaign, when forage for animals was exhausted, the 250 horses of the Twenty-sixth Cavalry and 48 pack mules were regretfully slaughtered. Major Achille C. Tisdelle, a cavalry officer and General King's aide, wrote on March 15 that the Twenty-sixth Cavalry and other units had that day finished the last of their horses.[3]

On the night of April 2, two American antitank guns were placed on a defensive line to cover Trail 6. Private Leon Beck, Thirty-first Infantry, was in a crew that dug in, sandbagged, and camouflaged one of the 37mm guns. But the Japanese artillery destroyed both guns, along with trucks and kitchen vehicles farther to the rear under the ridge line in a defilade position across from the opposing barrage.

After three months of fighting the Japanese advance, with blocking actions and orderly retreats to new defensive positions, the outlook of surrender was assured. Lieutenant Don Blackburn, Major Russell Volckmann,

Major Martin Moses, and Major Arthur Noble chose to escape rather than surrender and sent a message to General Brougher.

Volckmann wanted to try to locate Colonel Horan who had a guerrilla group in Northern Luzon. Horan and his unit had not been able to make the trek into Bataan and had been organizing units of the Philippine Scouts and Philippine Army in his sector.

General Brougher acknowledged the request with an admonition about the dangers of surviving in the jungle, but agreed that their youth was on their side and gave his permission.

The temporary houses built by the evacuees at the Fassoth's campsite were kept neat and clean. However, malaria was prevalent and many of the evacuees died from the disease. Bill Fassoth estimated that about 70 percent of the people who died on Bataan succombed to malaria. There wasn't much medicine, and what little there was had such a high price that few could afford to purchase the drugs. Most resorted to the old methods of treatment for sicknesses, by looking for herbs, roots, and barks of different plants and trees. Rice was hulled by the old method of pounding the palay[4] grain in wooden bowls and cleaning by hand with different baskets or woven bamboo sifters and shakers. Everyone planted their own tobacco. Paper to roll cigarettes was scarce so young dried banana leaves were cut into thin strips as a substitute. Young boys made different tobacco holders out of bamboo, rattan, vines and reeds in the shape of horn instruments. Many of the pipes were eye-catching and fetched a good price at the public market.

One of the Filipino families that had moved and built a hut in Fassoth's camp helped Catalina and the men with carpentry. They had one daughter, eleven, who helped to look after Peanuts, and a son who was seventeen.[5] He helped around the camp and at night told bedtime stories to the children and girls. These stories were told in dialect that caused Bill Fassoth to laugh.[6]

Not wanting to attract attention of Japanese patrols, the people in the camp went to bed shortly after sunset, rather than light candles or lanterns. Mats were laid out on the floor of the huts and mosquito nets were erected to keep the pesky bugs from biting during the night. Lying down to sleep, the residents could hear the night sounds of the jungle. Animals, birds, and insects made their melodious sounds as each person found rest.

A swarm of honeybees made their appearance near the camp and about six weeks later a Negrito Bill knew appeared in the camp. Bill called out to him and the man agreed to gather honey for the camp. The little man took off his undershirt, and, with only a G-string around his waist, he gathered three dry boho[7] poles, tied them together and set fire to them, then put out the flames to create smoke. Climbing a tree, he placed the smoking poles ahead of him. Reaching the top of the tree, he gently pulled off the honey comb with some of the bees attached and brought it to the community wait- ing on the ground. Bill asked the man if any of the bees had stung him. "Only one," he replied as he pulled a stinger from his skin.

The honey was delicious. The Filipinos considered the unborn bees in the sealed wax of the honeycomb a delicacy.

The Negrito also brought the camp game. Early one morning, Catalina woke Bill and asked if he had heard the commotion that the chickens roost- ing in the trees were making outside the house. Bill lit a small oil lantern, started out the back door, and was attacked by bees. The bees did not like the light and attacked the lantern, causing Bill to jump under some mosquito netting.

The following morning at 4:00, the chickens again raised a commotion, but this time the offender was a big snake. A friend ran out with a shotgun and blew the snake's head off. The snake was clutching a chicken in its mouth, so the camp had snake and chicken for meat the next day. The python meas- ured over ten feet in length. The snake meat was cut up into chunks and cooked as adobo, braising it first, then simmering it with mild vinegar and spices until done, and finally serving it with a sour sauce sweetened with a little sugar. The snake meat tasted similar to chicken but had the consistency of fish.[8]

Bill Gardner was born on December 20, 1903, in the small town of Williams, Arizona, the son of William Gardner Sr. and Josephine Redstar, his Apache bride. Sid Jenkins spoke of Bill's heritage and early military serv- ice.

"Bill was an Apache — the blood of fierce fighting men who never gave quarter or asked for it. When Bill first enlisted [February 15, 1923] he went to the Thirty-first Infantry, which soon was sent to China. Duty in China was severe. Later he returned to the Philippines with the same regiment. He became a seasoned soldier, a noncom, and even learned to cook. To his com- patriots he was known as 'Chief' and, at the time of Bataan, [as] an 'old sol- dier' who in his stern way helped mold the recruits into fighting men." "He was awarded a battlefield commission to second lieutenant after the battle at Abucay Hacienda, January 22–24, 1942."[9]

Private Doyle Decker found Battery H after three weeks of riding air guard with the 515th. He had been replaced on the 37mm anti-aircraft gun, so he was assigned to the communications unit, laying and repairing phone lines. He observed Indians from Taos Pueblo working the phone lines as oper- ators. Afraid the Japanese might tap the lines, the Two-Hundredth had the

Pueblos speaking in their native tongue as code, as the Japanese were unable to understand the Tiwa language.

Not long after being reunited with his unit, rations were cut and the men then received two meals a day, with the evening meal served cold because of fears that a campfire would draw enemy attention.

Decker and another soldier in the "commo" unit, Ben Leslie, got the idea to warm their food on the hoods of the trucks when they had their motors running. With only two meals a day, the men in the communications unit let Leslie and Decker know they appreciated the extra effort.

The constant hunger and danger were relieved by occasional military success. Having been in the battery almost a month, Decker was accustomed to being awakened by a Japanese observation plane the unit called "Photo Joe." This was one of many observation planes so dubbed by various units. But this "Joe" got more daring each day, flying closer to the ground. One morning he got too close and Corporal Arthur Palmer shot the pilot down with a 50-caliber machine gun. Battery H saw the last of "Joe" when he disappeared into Manila Bay.

Just as he got used to his work in the communications unit, Sergeant Vickrey took Decker aside. He told him he had just received news that Decker was ruled unfit for combat duty when he was in the hospital. Decker was frustrated at the information. He didn't feel it made a lot of sense. He had been an air guard on ammunition trucks for three weeks and assigned to the communications unit for over a month. He felt he was fit for combat duty. Vickrey told Decker that it didn't matter what he thought. The army had its ways and Decker was now a cook's helper.

After a few days, Decker began to enjoy his new duty. He liked working in the kitchen and talking to the men as they came through the chow line. The mess sergeant, Clinton "Red" Wolfe and Decker hit it off.

There had been enough food to keep the morale high, but rations were again cut and the men could now only have half rations for their two meals per day. Spirits diminished as the men lost weight and strength. The shortage worsened daily and the only meat available was from horses and mules from the Twenty-sixth Cavalry. Cigarettes had become scarce and everyone, including officers, began to save cigarette butts. Some native tobacco was located and the men stripped the stems to make smokes. Though the native cigarettes tasted terrible, they were preferable to no tobacco.

The fighting continued as constant background to the hunger and discomfort. The big American 155mm guns were now firing all night. The latest poop was that as long as the big guns kept firing, there was nothing to worry about. Japanese aircraft intensified their bombing, however, blowing up several American ammunition dumps.

Morale continued to deteriorate as starving men were sickened by malaria and dysentery. Soldiers began to look like walking skeletons. Decker and Wolfe, troubled by the men's condition, roamed the hills near the Mariveles Mountains, searching for anything edible.

On April 3, a big push by the Japanese army commenced. The American artillery units pulled their big guns back from the Pilar-Bagac line to a position near H Battery.

Shelling was furious for the next five days as the men grew weaker and the rations were cut again. The American solders strained to do their work and operated their anti-aircraft guns with the little remaining ammunition.

Major Holmes's Thirty-third Infantry, numbering about 600 men, had begun its march west early on the evening of April 3rd along a section of Trail 429 which extended south of Mt. Samat. The men, many of whom had just risen from sick beds, moved slowly in the darkness, passing large numbers of stragglers pouring back to the rear. "Few had arms of any kind ... few even had packs," wrote Lieutenant Robert M. Chapin, third Battalion commander. "I asked several what units they were from, but they just looked at me blankly and wandered on."[10]

Doctor Paul Ashton, a captain in the Twelfth Medical Battalion, heard a sound in the roadside bushes and thought it might be Japanese; it proved to be Lieutenant Bob Chapin, whom he knew from the Thirty-third Infantry. Chapin was resting, obviously dead tired. He stated that on the afternoon of April 2, the Thirty-third Philippine Army had been ordered to head quickly back to a position west of Samat, now occupied by General Lim's Forty-first Philippine Army. The Japanese forces had proved too numerous and the Thirty-third was destroyed.[11]

On the morning of April 6, Lieutenant Clay Conner of the Twenty-seventh Bomb Group Communications was out on the road looking for food. When he got back to the area, he heard the receiver in the communications trailer blasting away. He ran in and recognized his friend's voice. It was Captain Bertram Bank of the Twenty-seventh, and he was shouting through the microphone, "This is Captain Bank! This is Captain Bank! We are retreating from the front lines! The Japanese have broken through! This is Captain Bank! This is Captain Bank! We're retreating from the front lines! The Japanese have broken through! They've broken through, and are scattering west and east of the main road! The Japanese are now almost to Bataan Field! Pull back! This is Captain Bank! The Japanese have broken through the front lines and are coming south! They are almost to Bataan Field!"[12]

Conner listened for another ten minutes. Bank kept repeating the same message, shouting desperately into the microphone. Conner couldn't believe what he heard. He walked over to the message center where Captain Mason and Colonel Gregg were sitting together, and asked them if they had heard the message that the Japanese had broken through. They had. Conner then questioned them about their plans. He was shocked when they replied that they weren't going to do anything. There was nothing to do. Then Captain Mason told Conner to gather his men and prepare to destroy all the equipment when they got the order.

The next morning, hundreds of men, having been cut off from their units, poured into the area. Most didn't carry a weapon. Their clothing was ragged and they were hungry, sick, and downcast.

Some told Conner that they were at the front when the Japanese overran their position. The Japanese had hammered a spot in the middle of their defensive lines. Day after day, night after night, the enemy planes divebombed the one location, until the Japanese drove a hole through the line. Then thousands of Japanese troops poured in with banzai attacks. Japanese with fixed bayonets streamed across the Pilar-Bagac Road south into the American lines, screaming at the top of their voices, "Banzai! Banzai!" They ran forward, hurling themselves into the face of machine-gun fire and onto the barbed wire, forming human bridges of dead bodies. Then the enemy soldiers behind that group would climb over the dead bodies of their own men. Finally, the bodies became such an obstacle that the Japanese moved their tanks forward and crushed the bodies so more men could pour through.

Day after day this had continued until they had at last sacrificed and thrown in enough men that the Americans couldn't hold them off any longer and had to retreat. The cost to the Japanese army, trapped in the cross-fire of the American machine guns, was beyond comprehension. The terrain was littered with humanity, impossible to cross without treading on bodies.

Amid the chaos of April 7, Colonel Vance was ordered to hold the Twenty-sixth Cavalry in position until General Bluemel arrived. Bluemel had found the two lost Thirty-first Infantry battalions and directed them toward the trail junction held by the troopers. A short time later, Bluemel came upon a ten-foot-deep bomb crater blocking a light tank, two scout cars, three trucks, and other vehicles, with an overturned tank lying by the side of the depression. The Twenty-sixth was 100 yards south on high ground and one kilometer north of the junction of Trails 2 and 10. Colonel Vance deployed Captain Joseph R. Barker's G Troop north of the crater, and G Troop commandeered as many fleeing Filipinos as they could detain, and had them work on filling the crater. Vance was single-minded about getting his two scout cars out of danger. A fight commenced when pursuing Japanese soldiers arrived at the crater. When Vance sent more of his men to the line, the gunfire increased and the Japanese began a flanking action around the right of G Troop and stopped the advance. Bullets landed around the Filipinos digging at the crater's edge and scattered the men. Furious Scouts grabbed a few of the fleeing Filipinos, but they were unable to retain enough men to finish filling the crater. Vance grudgingly ordered the scout cars destroyed and withdrew his men to a higher elevation south of the crater.

Meanwhile the First Squadron of E-F Troop, Twenty-sixth Cavalry, confronted the Japanese from hasty emplacements northeast of the trail junction. The position was open, with low shrubs and scattered mango groves, offering little cover. The Scouts found supply elements of the Fourteenth Engineer Battalion in the path of battle and ordered them out of the area. As the Japanese came upon the First Squadron, they sent flanking squads around both sides of the troopers. Simultaneously, Japanese dive bombers fired on the troopers at the crossroads, wounding Captain Wheeler, Commander of E-F Troop, and virtually wiping out the Second Squadron's two-squad rear guard. Under pressure of the flanking movement, the First Squadron began its retreat, experiencing the most severe shelling they had yet seen. The men crossed the area with short rushes in three- and four-man groups, suffering heavy casualties. Captain Jack Spies's B Troop was particularly hard hit — his men were unable to make the rendezvous — and an ambulance and two Bren Gun Carriers were destroyed. Bluemel, foreseeing the hopelessness of stopping the enemy at the junction, issued orders to repair to the Mamala River.

At the end of April 7, the depleted Thirty-third Infantry was all that remained west of Mount Samat. They had moved into position northwest of Mount Samat on Trail 6 early on the morning of April 4. At first light the regiment sent patrols north, east, and west, hoping to contact other American units and determine the locations of the enemy. Patrols sent to the west looked for Constabulary, those searching north looked for enemy positions, and those patrolling to the east tried to find the Twenty-first Division. But each patrol returned with the same information–none. No Japanese, no American, no Filipino units. On April 5, more patrols returned with no progress to report, but they had found twelve men from the 21st Division, in civilian clothes and without weapons, working their way toward refugee camps in the southern part of Bataan. "I advised them that they were forthwith attached to the Thirty-third Infantry," recalled Lieutenant Robert Chapin who commanded the Third Battalion. "Issued them hand grenades, and had them posted on the Catmon River on our left flank as a precaution against attacks from that quarter." When a man went to check on the new arrivals an hour later, they were gone.[13]

Eventually one patrol found a Japanese unit south of the regiment, between the Filipinos and the only route of withdrawal. The American officers took every measure to keep this information secret from their men, explaining that the Japanese on Trail 6 were a passing patrol, watching for the first signs of panic. By this time, many of Chapin's men were beyond panic, as they were dying from malnourishment. The presence of dead and dying soldiers in the foxhole line had dispirited the remaining men. The stronger ones tried to bury the dead and move the gravely ill out of sight.

Ray Hunt told a story in his book that illustrated one of the many hardships suffered by the troops on Bataan and in the tropics in general. He said that one day an old-timer told him that God had seen fit to create two kinds of mosquitoes for the Philippines: large, daytime mosquitoes that caused dengue fever, and small, nighttime mosquitoes that carried malaria.[14] Unhappily, Ray contracted both maladies. Malaria was worse than dengue fever, as it could be fatal. It induced severe chills, followed by vomiting, fever, and paralyzing headaches. Dengue fever did not have the accompanying chills, though it did cause every joint to ache and prevented a person from remaining in one position for more than a few minutes at a time. Rarely fatal, it just made people so ill that they *wished* they would die.

One burden was worse than disease: the threat of starvation. During the confusion that followed the onset of the war, a variety of snafus resulted in immense quantities of food remaining in warehouses in Manila instead of being moved to Bataan. During the maneuver of troops into the Bataan Peninsula, a large number of Philippine Constabulary troops abandoned their units, hid their guns, "resigned" from the war, and went home to plant rice. Lacking training, experience, and weapons they would have been of little use as combat troops. This helped the U.S. soldiers on Bataan, as the reduced troop numbers meant slower depletion of the skimpy stock of food. Unfortunately, the Constabulary numbers were replaced by some 20,000 panic-stricken Filipino civilians who fled into the peninsula and had to be fed along with the 80,000 or so assorted U.S. infantry, airmen, and sailors, together with Philippine Scouts, regular army and Constabulary remnants. Assembled on Bataan were about three thousand tons of canned meat and salmon, supplemented by inadequate supplies of rice. Combined, this constituted regular rations for 100,000 for a month. Because the siege of Bataan was projected to take much longer, the troops were put on half rations (approximately 2,000 calories per day) on January 8, 1942. This was cut to 1,500 calories on February 1 and to 1,000 calories on March 1 in conditions where men needed at least 3,500 calories per day to maintain health and strength.

When facing the lack of woman companionship, the average soldier would talk about women and sex. But the lack of necessary rations turned many soldiers' conversations to the topic of food and menus, so much that some men sounded like delegates to a convention of chefs.

After every animal and plant that could complement the rations was scrounged on the peninsula, the cavalry horses were slaughtered, including General Wainwright's favorite horse, Joseph Conrad, who ended his military career not in battle but on a menu. Toward the end of the Bataan campaign, the men were eating anything with feet, fins, and wings, and any plant that appeared to have edible leaves and berries.

Ray Hunt wrote that he hated to kill monkeys. It was bad enough that monkey meat was so tough and stringy that it seemed to grow right out of the animals' bones. The worst part was killing a monkey in the first place. He shot one out of a tree once for food. It fell at his feet, still alive, and looked at him in the most pathetic way imaginable, seeming to say, "Why did you do this to me?" Ray was not sure what it proved, but after seeing and experiencing the malice and ferocity of the Japanese soldiers, he could kill one of them without qualm, indeed he became eager to kill as many of them as possible, but he could never kill another monkey.[15] This feeling was conveyed by many men who have written about this terrible event in their lives.

A few days before the surrender, an event occurred that could take place only in the U.S. Army. Soldiers were asked if they wanted to take out $10,000 GI life insurance policies. Given the circumstances, most would have taken out $100,000, but $10,000 was the limit. Nobody argued about the premiums. The names of policy subscribers were then radioed to the States.

The men were also told that if they wrote letters to their loved ones these would be sent. Though not one letter got through, this brightened many men's outlook on the war. It was a good way for a fearful soldier to relieve some anxiety.

Though its members did not realize it at the time, April 8 was the last day of the Bataan campaign for the Twenty-first Pursuit Squadron. Ray Hunt helped to put the unit's last plane together, an old civilian Bellanca used to send several airmen and MacArthur's propaganda chief, Carlos P. Romulo, the short distance to Corregidor. The overloaded plane was able to get off the ground only after the men's luggage was thrown overboard.

The Twenty-first then retreated a short distance south to Mariveles Bay. There they threw away the firing pins from their rifles and stacked the disabled weapons to await the arrival of the Japanese army.

Though the men didn't know it at the time, when General King surren-

dered his U.S. Army troops on Bataan on April 9, some officers complied to
the letter, while others encouraged their men to escape, and still others looked
away, leaving the decision to each soldier. Most of the soldiers around Mariveles had no choice. They did not relish the idea of surrendering, and did not
know what to expect, but the Japanese had them surrounded. They could
only watch and wait as the Japanese dive bombers pummeled Corregidor.

April 8 found Sergeant Frank Bernacki and twenty-eight men of the
Provisional Air Regiment guarding the four bridges between Lamao and Cabcaben, when men began streaming across the first bridge going south. They
were from various Filipino-American units.

"All hell's broken loose!" an American sergeant shouted to Bernacki.
"The lines have broken just down the road! Get out!"

Bernacki hesitated. This meant the Japanese advance guard was rolling
down the east coast highway toward him. He finally got an officer on the
phone. "What should I do?" he asked.

"Grab your sack and take off."

"Shouldn't we fight?"

"Hell, no. Save your tail. I'm going to try and get to Corregidor."[16]

Bernacki assembled his men and drove buses onto the road and tipped
them over with the help of a dozen civilians, forming a roadblock with logs
mixed among the buses. As men fleeing from the front came through the
roadblock, Bernacki could occasionally hear the chatter of a machine gun,
but no Japanese troops appeared. Bernacki then put his men in a truck and
drove south to Cabcaben. The road turned due west and he continued past
Hospital Number 2 and up the hill to Hospital Number 1 which sat on the
right of the road at Little Baguio. The road became jammed as it joined a
network of others. When Bernacki reached the last town on Bataan, Mariveles, it was in chaos. A few boats were preparing to take the fortunate to Corregidor. Other boats were being towed out in the bay and sunk. Hoards of
confused troops from a dozen units waited at the sides of the boulevard.

Bernacki saw a brigadier general blocking the path to the docks. "No
one can go to Corregidor!" he shouted. "We've had it," he told Bernacki
wearily. "We're waiting here for the Japanese to kill us or capture us, if you've
got guns, tear them apart."[17]

Lieutenant Bill Gardner had talked with several men from his company
and others from the battalion. They were asking, "What are we going to do?"
There he was, the wise guy that had always been able to kid them out of their
troubles and find them a simple solution to their problems. Now there was
only one thing to say to them: "Go surrender yourselves."

Gardner and members of his company approached Mariveles where the surrendered forces were gathering. The town was filled with men empty of all hope or purpose, men who had broken down mentally, and were sick and exhausted. It was past 9:30 on the morning on April 9 and Gardner realized there was nothing more he could do for anyone. As for himself, he was going to try to get to Corregidor. He didn't know the distance from Mariveles to Corregidor but he was set on making it."[18]

On the morning of April 8, Red Wolfe and Doyle Decker walked a mile up the road from their camp in search of cigarettes and food. They had been told about a Filipino shack that had cigarettes. Reaching the hut, they bought a pack of American smokes and a few canned goods. They were walking back to the battery when all hell broke loose. Rifle and machine gun fire surrounded Wolfe and Decker as they ran, dodged and crawled toward their unit, finally reaching some of their group.

"The line's broken and we've been cut off!" shouted one of the men. "We're trying to find the battery commander and first sergeant!"

Sergeant Wolfe and Private Decker trudged south toward Mariveles until it got dark, making it hard to see. They took shelter in the roots of a banyan tree. Cold and hungry, they had only the clothes on their backs and .45-caliber pistols on their belts. After two hours of hiding, they heard two men softly calling. Wolfe recognized the voices as two GI's from B Battery. As the two soldiers walked by the tree, Wolfe and Decker reached out and pulled the men into the tree roots.

"Shut the hell up," said Wolfe. "There's too many damn Japs runnin' around out there." Private Nano Lucero and a staff sergeant were grateful to find friends and shelter. "The Japs charged our position and overran the battery," the sergeant whispered.

Several minutes later, they heard another man call out. All four answered in unison and then looked at each other in disbelief at their foolish act. A captain squirmed into the roots with the other four. "Our battery got overrun by the Japs. I managed to escape and have been trying to find some of the men."

They were all cold and miserable under the tree as the big guns on Corregidor shelled the area. Machine-gun fire and screaming filled the air as the Japanese forces continued to push toward the southern tip of Bataan. At midnight, with shells falling closer and closer to their location, the captain yelled for the men to move.

As they crawled out from the shelter of the tree roots, the moon broke through the overcast sky and lit their way through the jungle. The GI's approached a deserted outpost that had guns, ammunition, tents, food and other supplies scattered as though a tornado had hit the area. Each man picked up a blanket and canteen. The big guns on Corregidor continued to shell, with each explosion landing closer to the group. Five tired and frightened soldiers approached a riverbank, and as the moon went behind a cloud they stumbled over a small cliff. Not knowing which was worse, the shelling or the jungle, the captain decided to stay put until daylight.

The group had settled in for the night when an earthquake hit. The ground rolled and moved under foot. Trees swayed and a breeze seemed to travel with the quake. Decker wondered if God had given up on them.[19]

April 9 was the first morning that Ed Ramsey had not been awakened by Japanese bombing and shelling. He was ordered by Major Banning to take a squad to investigate downriver for a trail. The growth was so thick that the men had to crawl on their hands and knees. They had struggled a short distance when they heard the sound of troops. A hundred meters beyond their location they saw vehicles and a large body of Japanese soldiers marching toward Mariveles.

The Japanese now flanked them on three sides, front, left, and right. Their only relief was to their back, and the bank on the far side of the river was too steep for them to climb, so they began to wade upstream in search of a trail toward Mt. Mariveles. They hoped the higher ground would give them an observation point to determine available escape routes.

Each man crept into the murky river, staying close to the bank, and then worked his way upstream. So emaciated were the men that they had to stop every few minutes, and after they managed to pull themselves up onto the bank they collapsed among the rocks. Here they found Philippine army stragglers who had been cut off from their units the previous day. Some of the Filipinos joined them, but others, shocked and discouraged, continued toward Mariveles.

Ramsey's men slept on the riverbank that night, risking a fire to cook their remaining rice. Combined with some canned salmon, it was their first hot food in five days. Ramsey and Joe Barker combined their rations and cooked them by the river. They had spent the last days marching and crawling through the jungle and had discussed their situation. All pretexts were now precluded in their sorry condition. Ramsey had come to admire Barker's stoicism and courage.[20]

As they ate they talked about the lack of artillery punishing them on this particular day. Barker was exhausted and gaunt, his beard long and matted. His fatigues, like Ramsey's, were tattered and streaked with sweat from weeks of combat. Barker had become so skeletal that he was wearing his West Point ring on his thumb. They talked about the impending surrender. Neither thought they would last very long in a prison camp. After some more small talk they determined that rather than surrender they would try to escape from Bataan and work their way to the southern islands, then maybe New Guinea and Australia.[21]

Realizing that their chances were slim, they rationalized that they were still better off than trying to survive in a Japanese prison camp.

Captain Mason called Lieutenant Clay Conner on a land line and told him that the most recent decision was not to destroy any of their equipment. The American high command hoped that the cars and trucks would be used to transport the soldiers to prison camps, and that the valuable radios and transmitters would be used to communicate information to the States. The higher echelon conjectured that by turning the equipment over to the enemy, the Japanese would give their prisoners gentler consideration, and use the transmitters to let the United States (and soldiers' families) know that the Americans were still alive. This proved to be a poor decision. The Japanese told American families nothing, and not one man rode to prison camp. If a captive soldier couldn't walk, he was shot. Conner later wished that they had burned everything, destroyed every last vehicle, radio, and transmitter.

He learned however, that the Americans were going to blow up the ordnance dumps at 7 P.M., and that the communications unit was to clear the area because the dumps were only two of hundred yards from them, directly south, between the unit and the road. Captain Mason reported that the ordnance dumps were loaded with both heavy and small-arms ammunition.

Conner paid little attention to the order. He walked to one of the tents where they were receiving messages from men retreating from the front lines. Sitting on a bench, listening to the radio, he didn't notice when it was 7 P.M. Unexpectedly, a tremendous detonation and its shock waves blew Conner flat on his back. The blast blew the tent off its poles and ammunition flew through the area. Conner felt he was in the middle of a firecracker factory that was on fire. Confused by the noise, he didn't know if he should get off the ground or stay down. It seemed like the explosions lasted for an hour, as shells cracked through the trees, knocking down limbs, tearing through buildings, shredding automobiles, hitting against metal, with the flash of different explosions lighting up the sky like it was the fourth of July.[22]

On April 9 the Japanese seemed more intent on what they could confiscate than on collecting the American and Filipino troops for evacuation to prison camps. Corporal Gerald Wade was surprised by the appearance of the Japanese soldiers. Many had malaria and dysentery. Healthy Japanese had to push the sick ones forward.[23]

Chapter 4

Escape

"I see no gleam of victory alluring
No chance of splendid booty or of gain
If I endure — I must go on enduring
And my reward for bearing pain — is pain
Yet, though the thrill, the zest, the hope are gone
Something within me keeps me fighting on."
— Henry G. Lee, "Fighting On"

Of the nearly 12,000 American troops on Bataan, about 400 either did not surrender or escaped from the Death March. At the end of the war fewer than 200 of these were alive.

With the surrender of Bataan, four soldiers — William Gardner, lieutenant in the Thirty-first Infantry; William Gateley, sergeant in the 200th Coast Artillery; Arthur Hagins, private; and Bernice Fletcher, sergeant in the Quarter Master Corps — constructed a raft with a makeshift sail and attempted to sail to Corregidor. The ocean current was strong and they ended up in the China Sea. A Japanese cruiser came upon them and the commander asked, "Do you wish to surrender or be fired upon?" The answer was obvious and they were sent to a fenced area at Subic Bay Naval Base where they later escaped.[1]

When Thirty-first infantry Private Leon Beck, began the Death March, he had already made up his mind that he could not survive in a Japanese prison camp. Starving and feverish with malaria, he recalled some jail time he had done in the States. Seeing numerous dead bodies as he trudged along on the road repulsed any thought of prison life.

Picture of stop on Death March; notice men with hands tied behind their backs (National Archives).

For twelve days on the march Beck lobbied his friends to join him and make an escape; he didn't want make the difficult flight alone. Despite his pleadings, the response was always that the U.S. Army would be back in six months to retake the Philippine Islands and that it was useless to try to escape.

A few captured Americans had been put to work driving trucks for the Japanese. One of the American drivers informed Beck that he had to escape before the column reached the town of San Fernando where the captive soldiers were being loaded on trains that went directly to the O'Donnell Prison Camp.

Beck attempted to escape when the column reached the town of Lubao, ten miles from San Fernando. Locked in a warehouse for the night, Beck crawled out through everyone's legs but got caught by Japanese guards who beat him unconscious.

When Beck recovered consciousness and saw that the guards were carrying dead bodies from the warehouse across the road and throwing them in a mass grave, he crawled away again and hid in a nearby burnt-out building.

The next morning, barely able to walk, Beck rejoined the march with the next group that came along. Here were some men from his unit, the

Thirty-first Infantry. They offered to watch the guards, but did not want to escape; when they went by a row of bushes they told Beck to hide. He rolled off the road and hid in the bamboo thicket until dark when some friendly Filipinos found him and directed him to the Fassoths' camp.[2]

Frank Bernacki, formerly of the Air Corps, was tempted at the sight of the Zambales Mountains. Between Lubao and San Fernando, Japanese tanks with "Singapore" scribbled on their sides rambled down the road toward the marchers. When the guard's attention was elsewhere, waving to the tankers, Bernacki murmured to marchers around him, "I'm leaving. Anyone want to go with me? I hear Thorp has $50,000 with him."[3] He had heard that Colonel Claude Thorp had slipped out of Bataan two months earlier, with directions from MacArthur to set up guerrilla groups.

No one accompanied Bernacki as he crawled alone into the cane field. The leaves' sharp edges cut like knives in the suffocating growth. He crawled through the twisted vines and fainted.

Private Doyle Decker, Nano Lucero, Sergeant Red Wolfe, and the sergeant and captain with whom they were traveling were up at daybreak following a trail leading southwest toward Mariveles. After walking several hours they met Colonel Edgar Wright, who was traveling with two other soldiers. Wright told them that the Americans on Bataan had surrendered. He said their only options were to go to Mariveles and surrender or take to the mountains. His group was trying to get to Olongapo, a village on Subic Bay. He was familiar with the area and thought they could locate a boat and sail to Australia. He didn't invite the others to join them as eight men were too many for a small boat. That evening, the eight camped for the night together. Wright had a bag of rice he shared.

The next morning, the Decker group decided they would take their chances in the mountains. They bid Wright and his men goodbye, wished them luck, and walked north on a jungle path. They used the mountainous artillery trails, hacked and gouged through the jungle to allow placement of the army's artillery pieces away from the coastal highway where they would be exposed to the Japanese army. Because the artillery was often put in defilade positions to protect them from enemy observation or gunfire, the American positions were usually on the south slopes of the mountain ridges, while the Japanese positions were on the north slopes. The Japanese artillery used the American trails around the declining points of the mountain ridges and then branched off to positions on the northern slopes. By using the trails to traverse the ridges, Decker's group zigzagged through the mountains and pushed through the jungle growth at the upper levels of the ridges. The artillery trails made travel easier at times but lengthened the trip and placed the men in many bivouac and battle areas.

Daytime temperatures near 100 degrees Fahrenheit with high humidity made progress difficult, but because Bataan is a peninsula, the ocean and bay bordering the mountains cooled the night temperatures to the lower 50s. The men struggled and sweated during the day and shivered while sleeping at night.

The rice Colonel Wright had shared with them was depleted in three days. The men grew weaker as they struggled up one mountain ridge only to find another ahead of them. Water was not a problem, as each ravine had a stream. The available food consisted of small wild tomatoes and a few edible leaves.

The days dragged on and the men began to quarrel. The bickering bothered Decker, who had established a daily goal of climbing the next ridge. At the end of each day the men dropped into a fitful sleep, often dreaming of food. Decker dreamed of his sister Flossie's kitchen and the cherry pies baking in her oven.

The quarrels worsened and the captain and sergeant slipped off one night, leaving Decker, Wolfe and Lucero. The three decided that it was better this way. They were able to cope; the other two had been complaining and causing problems.

After eight days, having eaten only some wild tomatoes and leaves, the men were awakened by the crowing of a rooster. They found the rooster in a small pen and were surprised not to find a hut nearby. They killed the bird and boiled the meat in some river water in a bucket that Decker had found. As they finished their delicious meal, they heard some men coming toward them.

The three hid behind a large banyan tree and drew their .45's. Approaching them were three men wearing Japanese army caps. When the men entered the clearing, three pistols, cocked and ready to fire, confronted them.

"Don't shoot, don't shoot! We are friendly Filipinos!" the men shouted, removing their caps. The Americans slowly lowered their .45's and the Filipinos rushed forward to shake the Americans' hands, greeting them like long-lost friends. "Come, we have a home nearby, you eat with us."

When the group reached the hut, women appeared and began to cook. Decker watched with interest. The shack was typical for the area. It sat on stilts about three feet off the ground and was made from bamboo with cogon grass for the walls and roof. There wasn't any sign of a garden or other food plots. It was obvious that these people had very little for themselves, much less extra to share with strangers.

After the meal, Wolfe asked, "What day is it?"

One of the Filipinos replied, "It is April 19."

Wolfe realized that it had been ten days since they had anything substantial to eat.

The Americans thanked the Filipinos for the meal. The women returned their gratitude with proud smiles as everyone gathered in a circle to talk.

One of the Filipino men asked, "Do you have money?"

"I have ten pesos," replied Decker.

"If you give me pesos, I will go to barrio and buy sugar, rice, and cigarettes."

The other two Filipino men led the Americans into a bamboo thicket explaining, "You will be safe from Jap patrols."

The Filipinos fed the Americans, and the next afternoon the Filipino who took Decker's ten pesos returned with rice, sugar, and cigarettes.

With the provisions, the men didn't go to the house for food but stayed by the stream and cooked their meals. A drawback of camping by the stream and sleeping on the ground were the leeches. The little blood-sucking slugs crawled on the men as they slept or lay on the ground and had to be removed at least once a day to prevent sores from festering.

Decker told the others that he would be glad when they got somewhere so they could sleep off the ground. He didn't like picking the leeches off his body, afraid he would miss one and then be in a mess.

The following day Wolfe had a fever and cramps with vomiting. He told the others that it had been coming on for a couple of days and just hit him. The decision was made to stay in this location until Wolfe improved.

On one excursion in search of food, Lucero and Decker found an abandoned Japanese camp where there were mess kits full of something resembling rolled oats. Lucero thought they were compressed soybeans, as he had heard the Japanese ate a lot of soybeans and mixed different kinds of food with them. The strange food tasted good and was a pleasant change from rice. A further search of the camp and other bivouacs led to additional food supplies. Much of the food was odd to the men, but it stretched their rations. They had continued good luck when they found sugar and Japanese cigarettes.

The three learned to watch out for several plants as they searched the jungle. One was what the natives called the "wait a minute bush." It was the tacamura fern which has three fishhook-like barbs at the end of each stem. Negritos — short, dark-skinned indigenous people living in the mountains — used the fern to make fish traps, facing the hooks toward the back of a long cylinder with bait to attract fish. When the fish tried to swim back out of the trap, the hooks snagged them. The hooks were especially painful to unprotected skin. Decker would swear that every time he stepped off a trail the hooks in the ferns would catch his ears.[4]

Ray Hunt wasn't sure how many days he was actually on the March. But he escaped on April 21 after suffering near starvation and going days without water. His memories of the horrors inflected on the American and Filipino prisoners would haunt him for the rest of his life. The bodies of some soldiers were repeatedly run over by Japanese trucks until they looked like wet sacks of bloody mush. Men who hadn't had a drink of water for days would break for an artesian well beside the road and be shot or bayoneted by Japanese guards, without any reprimand by an officer. One minute the guards would seem rational and the next they would be ranting and taking their rage out on some poor soldier whose only crime was walking nearby.

Hunt watched both sides of the road and the guards. As he approached a bridge over a small stream near Dinalupihan, on the north border of Bataan province, he saw his opportunity. As he approached a deep ditch covered with dense undergrowth, he slipped from the right column to the center, then to the left. When a guard looked away he dove headlong over the bank into the ditch then lay there stiff and frightened. His heart was pounding so loudly that he was afraid the guards on the road above him would notice and recapture him. As the footsteps faded away he could hear a voice say something like, "Don't look. Do you want to get him shot?"[5]

After the column of prisoners had passed, Hunt crawled a short distance along the ditch and discovered two other escapees. They were too frightened to move. Only when Hunt spoke softly did one of them look around. It was Corporal Walter D. Chatham, Jr., of the Air Corps. Ahead of him, lying flat on his face, was Captain Winston Jones from an artillery unit. Hunt's leap into the ditch had terrified them during their own escape attempt.

Chatham, who had started the march from near Cabcaben Field, a few miles northwest of Mariveles, had been in a group hit by an artillery shell from Corregidor, intended for the enemy. It had struck in the middle of the assemblage, blowing bodies in all directions. A few days later, struggling with hunger, dehydration, and exhaustion, Chatham had grabbed at a bridge rail to keep from falling, and then a Japanese guard flipped him over into a gully forty feet below. Astonishingly, though he landed between two huge boulders, he was not killed. Two other Japanese guards appeared from under the bridge, but they were walking toward an artesian well to get water and overlooked him. Eventually Chatham climbed back up onto the road, reunited with another column and marched for another five days until he and Captain Jones dove over the bank into the trench where Ray Hunt found them.

Hunt wanted to leave their position, but the other two wanted to stay in place. Finally Hunt stood up and began to yell. Some Filipino farmers across the river heard him and one walked toward the three Americans. One Filipino stepped up onto a log, across the trench, looking as though searching

Death March: Between April 10 and April 23, 1945, on the road from Mariveles to San Fernando (National Archives).

the river for fish. Hunt asked if there were any Japanese nearby. The Filipino knew some English and told the Americans to stay down, and then he scurried into the underbrush. A short time later he returned and motioned for them to follow him. He led the men a short distance to a *bahay*, a house on stilts. It was close to the road, and through slits in the woven bamboo walls of the house they observed prisoners marching past. Hunt's sense of protection was lessened when he saw an American run through with a bayonet by a Japanese guard.

The house already sheltered another escaped American, a lieutenant named Kerrey.[6] After several days recuperating, the Americans accepted an offer by a Filipino to guide them to a nearby hacienda owned by an American civilian. The "march," they discovered, was not an unbroken string of marching men, but rather columns of one hundred to four hundred men, most with two guards, separated by two hundred yards to half a mile. This created opportunities for men to escape when one column had passed and another had not yet arrived.

The group with Hunt waited for one of these column breaks and at dusk began their journey. After they had passed a few sugarcane fields they were placed onto a cart with two solid wooden wheels, and were covered with rice straw. The cart, pulled by a carabao, traveled all night northwestward toward the Zambales Mountains. Hunt could not have made the trip by foot, as illness and hunger had exhausted his strength. At a later date when he saw his gaunt body he couldn't believe it was his own.

Three times on the trip the Filipino driver was stopped by Japanese who questioned him in English about escaped Americans. Because he could not speak English, he was able to answer only when the Japanese questioners had a Filipino interpreter who knew the Tagalog language. The Japanese never searched the cart, on the assumption perhaps that anyone who could not speak English would be unlikely to shelter Americans. At last they reached their goal, a cluster of grass-roofed houses under several shade trees. Here the Americans were fed, had their clothes washed, and were offered a haircut and shave. Hunt accepted both enthusiastically, but soon regretted his enthusiasm to be shaved. The barber was a Filipina who started by dipping her fingers into a coconut shell filled with cold water and patting Hunt's whiskers, then taking a straight razor that had obviously been used for projects other than shaving. It scraped at least two whiskers for every one it cut. Hunt endured the process with tears rolling down his cheeks.

It was here that Vicente Bernia entered the house. A muscular, bronzed man, he lived nearby and offered to guide the Americans to the Fassoths' camp where they could rest and recuperate.[7]

The Thirty-fourth Pursuit Squadron, now with the Seventy-first Philippine Division, heard about the surrender on the afternoon of April 9. They were ordered to destroy their weapons and to assemble on the main road at Kilometer 191. The first men to reach Kilometer 191 found the large cache of food that had been buried alongside the road earlier by the Seventy-first. Earl Oatman and Hank Winslow ate several cans of C-rations and put several more in their field bag. They had plenty of water and filled their canteens before leaving Agloloma Creek. They would later learn how necessary the water was for survival and saw many men die trying to obtain it on the march.[8]

When the Japanese soldiers reached the U.S. troop with whom Winslow and Oatman were traveling, they ordered the Americans onto trucks and drove them north of Mariveles. Before loading the trucks the Japanese searched the Americans for contraband. One took Oatman's gold high-school graduation-ring and his wristwatch. Anyone who resisted was clubbed in the head with a rifle butt, while those found with Japanese money or souvenirs were executed.

The Japanese soldiers were incredibly dirty, apparently not having a change of clothes in months, and their behavior mirrored their dress. They placed their captives in a holding area for three days. Mid-afternoon on April 12, they were herded up the main road and began walking towards Mariveles. Late in the afternoon as their column was directed to an area for the evening, Oatman discovered that he had left his canteen about a half mile back up the road. Realizing that his life depended on having the canteen, he walked back to find it. Fortunately, Oatman found the canteen where he thought he had left it, but on his way back to the group he had a close call. A Japanese soldier coming toward him lunged into Oatman with his shoulder and knocked him into a ditch. Neither man had said a word to the other. Oatman realized that he could easily have been killed by a Japanese bayonet. Safety in numbers would be Oatman's security in the future.

After having sat bareheaded in the sun for several hours, the men in Oatman and Winslow's column were moved out to the main road again, heading north. As they marched along, they occasionally saw the bloated, blackened bodies of dead soldiers lying alongside the road. If Oatman spotted a body he would tell Winslow not to look in that direction, and Winslow did the same for Oatman. After a time the bodies became so commonplace that they were overlooked, though the stench of the putrefying corpses was impossible to ignore.

The night of April 13 was spent sleeping on the ground, and the next morning the column was back on the road without having eaten in two days. Oatman's canteen was nearly empty, and as he marched near an artesian well he noticed several Filipinos getting water, so he walked over to fill his canteen. As he finished filling the container, a Japanese guard struck him in the back of the head with a wooden club, knocking him to the ground and lacerating his scalp. Though injured Oatman quickly caught up with Winslow and shared his water. The bleeding soon stopped, but Oatman had a headache as he marched down the road.

Oatman observed that stragglers at the end of the marching columns were harassed and beaten by the Japanese guards to make them keep up. Those too sick and weak to stay with the column were shot or bayoneted to death and left at the side of the road. Oatman told Winslow that the best place for them was at the head of the column with the officers. This made several officers unhappy, but Oatman and Winslow kept silent and kept marching. The column spent the night of April 14 at Balanga, sleeping on the ground as usual, then continued the march the next day, again without food or water.

On April 15 with more men fading, Oatman and Winslow heard sounds of beatings and the anguished cries of men as they were shot. At mid-afternoon the column was marched off the side of the road into a fenced-off open area at Orani. The ground was littered with debris, cast-off clothing, discarded gear, and human excrement from the thousands of Filipino-American POW's who had preceded them on the march.

The next day as Oatman and Winslow passed through sugarcane fields on both sides of the road, and as one of the guards dropped back to harass a straggler, they took the opportunity and darted into the field on the left and then lay down in the high cane stalks, two hundred yards from the marchers.

At dusk they worked their way out of the field and toward the mountains. They followed paths skirting the sugarcane fields and quickly found themselves in growths of bamboo where they laid down and slept the night of April 16. The next morning they were awakened by the voices of several Filipinos cutting wood with machetes. Apprehensive about making their presence known, they nevertheless walked toward the Filipinos and asked for food. The workers told them about two American cane planters who were living nearby, and without delay took them to Bill and Martin Fassoth's camp.[9]

Sergeant Earl Walk's platoon came by Dr. Paul Ashton's position in their weapons carriers. Walk told Ashton about his last shot fired in anger. They had tried to plug up a hole in the line made by Japanese bombing and shelling, and then they moved on behind the infantry. From there they were ordered to the rear, where they were given C-rations, the first they had seen since the start of the war.

Along the road near Lamao they received word to get rid of their weapons. They had one 81mm mortar round left, though there were some remaining in the weapons carrier. They set up the old mortar and fired our last round toward the north, hoping they might hit something. Then they dismantled the tube and threw away each of its removable parts at intervals as they moved back, doing the same with the 50-caliber machine gun. They slept that night somewhere near Mt. Samat. Walk slept so soundly that he missed the earthquake.

The next morning they went down the road to surrender. But Walk decided that he wasn't going to surrender, and asked if anyone wanted to join him. A corporal and another soldier agreed, so Walk started with them toward the foothills of the Mariveles Mountains.

That night they slept on the ground as usual. They had discovered several bivouac areas, but no food. All their C-rations were gone by this time. From the mountains they could look down on Corregidor. The island was a huge mass of smoke. A big fleet of Japanese bombers had flown over and blasted the island. They decided to walk north through Bataan and try to get back up into the Zambales Mountains.

Hiking all day and all night, they went to sleep in the jungle. Walk took off his gun belt first. He awoke the next morning and found that his pistol, holster, and gun belt were gone, along with the corporal. The other soldier and Walk trudged on, and during the day they found an old Enfield rifle that had been thrown away.

They came to a nipa shack (a bamboo hut) in the jungle at dusk. Looking around, they saw two chickens in a tree. Walk told his partner to take careful aim and not miss. "Just get those chickens!" He shot the largest chicken but the other bird flew away.

The next day Walk's companion decided to go down the mountain and surrender. Walk traveled on alone, and the following morning ran into a soldier named Joe Foley. They heard a lot of noise nearby and started to crawl through the undergrowth away from the sound, but it was so dense that they couldn't move. So they sat and waited about thirty minutes until the sound stopped, then backed out of the bamboo thicket.

After clearing the bamboo they climbed up a high hill from where they could look down into the lowlands, and they saw a sugar plantation and mill that they decided to visit. The mill was crushing juice out of the sugarcane and refining it to make brown sugar. The people at the mill gave Walk and Foley some of the thick brown syrup, a little bucketfull apiece, about a quart. They ate it all the way it was, raw. About three hours later the men had diarrhea.

The next day they came into a little barrio situated a half mile from the road that ran from Dinalupihan to Olongapo, connecting the road from San Fernando into Bataan. Walk had a malaria attack, so they stayed there for two days. After starting out again in the morning they ran into four Americans who told them about the Fassoths' Camp. About five o'clock that night they found the camp and were fed on their arrival.[10]

After the ammunition dump was destroyed, Lieutenant Clay Conner went to the Twenty-seventh Bomb Group Communications' Headquarters to see what had happened to Captain Mason and Colonel Gregg. Though the building had been blown to pieces, he found them still on duty. They were talking to Captain Bernard Anderson who was on his way through the area. Anderson was familiar with the region and the officers were talking about escaping through the mountains, and then through the front lines to the north to join Colonel Claude Thorp. Although he didn't really understand what Anderson intended, it sounded interesting to Conner.

Conner didn't know about Colonel Thorp and asked Anderson what he was proposing. Captain Anderson informed Conner that Thorp had been commissioned personally by General MacArthur early in the Bataan Campaign to escape through the front lines, and if successful, to return to the Fort

Stotsenburg area and pick up supplies, establish a headquarters and organize guerrilla forces to harass the Japanese from behind their lines.

Thorp been successful and was still at large. It was Anderson's idea to locate and join him. It sounded like an adventure to Conner. Anything sounded better than surrender.

Conner approached Captain Mason and asked, "Would it be all right if I wanted to go with Captain Anderson? Would you object?"

Mason replied, "No, I wouldn't object. Every man's for himself, now. General King has already been taken by the Japs. We just got the word, and officially you're on your own. You're no longer under command of the United States Army. We've been taken. We're through." But he added, "Let me tell you this. I've been in Bataan for many years on maneuvers, Clay. And if you want my advice, don't try it. You don't realize how rough, how rugged [it is], how many places that are absolutely impossible to get through in those craters and canyons and jungles of Mt. Mariveles. You will never make it. It's impossible. The front lines are mined, and the Japs are there. They'll be all through the area. Your chances are one in a million. It's safer to stay and be captured with the rest of the men. Remember, there's safety in numbers. They can't kill us all."[11]

At 3 P.M. Captain Anderson and his friends returned. Then they departed on their mission, a group of seven: Anderson, a captain, two lieutenants, two enlisted men — and Conner.[12] The group headed north from Little Baguio toward Mt. Mariveles.

The next morning Conner was sick and had diarrhea. His dysentery forced him to stop frequently, and his companions would wait intolerantly, giving sour looks when he complained about his stomach. A couple of times they refused to stop, and finding himself alone Conner forgot all vigilance and rushed after the group, clutching his pants and rifle, yelling for them to wait.

The second time this happened, one of the men turned on him with a snarl. "Look, Conner," he snapped, "these jungles are full of Japs. Every time you go hollering around like that, you're asking for all of us to get killed. Now get this: the next time you pull that, you're on your own." The rest of the group nodded in agreement. They would leave Conner, he knew it and they knew it.[13]

Two hours later Conner fell behind again. This time he was so sick he didn't care. But after a while the cramps left, he felt better, and he and Ernest Kelly, who'd stayed behind for him, then spent the day going down the side of a large gorge and up the other side. When they got to the top, they found that they were only a few hundred yards from where they had started. It took Conner and Kelly a week to reach the Pilar-Bagac highway.

Carrying their depleted rations and .45-caliber army-issue pistols, Barker and Ramsey were too weak from starvation and too exhausted to arm themselves with heavier weapons. A cloud of jungle mist hovered about them as they climbed up the crest toward the top of the four-thousand-foot Mount Mariveles.

The footing for Barker and Ramsey was difficult as they pushed through the undergrowth and gained altitude at a slow but constant pace. After climbing for an hour they came to a halt when they heard movement in the jungle ahead.

With pistols drawn, they confronted a young American infantry private, cut off from his unit and lost. Thin and gaunt, his uniform ragged, his scrawny arms and legs were covered with filth and bruises. Through dazed eyes he told them his name was Gene Strickland.

The three climbed higher as the air cooled and the terrain thinned, with fewer trees and bushes. They began to shiver in only their khaki uniforms, tattered and soaked with sweat, to ward off the chill. At dusk they decided to make camp below the summit.

That night, with a small fire for warmth, they shared the last of their rations with Strickland, and then took turns standing watch and maintaining the fire. The fire was all the comfort they had in that foreign, unsympathetic place; their only shield against the night air and whatever populated the mountain slopes.

Strickland told them he had been with the Thirty-first Infantry at Limay on the extreme right flank of the defensive line when the Japanese had attacked.

"We were already starved," he said as he licked the rice grains from his dirty palm. "Some of the fellas couldn't even hold a rifle. They hit us with everything — tanks, artillery, planes. We never had a chance."

Ramsey asked how long he had been wandering in the jungle.

"Two, three days," he said, wiping his mouth with the back of a slender forearm. "A few of us were trying to get back to Mariveles, but we got separated. We thought that if we could get over to Corregidor the Navy might get us out." He gave a little laugh. "We figured that if they could get MacArthur out, why not us? Pretty stupid, huh?"

"Why's that?" Barker asked.

"Well, I guess they don't send PT boats to fetch privates, do they, sir? I mean, I guess that's the difference between us."[14]

They had no purification tablets and were concerned that the mountain streams were contaminated from the days of warfare. The next morning they drank as much as they dared from their canteens, resolute to make their supply last as long as possible, and continued their journey to the top of the mountain. The remaining few hundred feet to the peak was over loose rock and in the thinning air their lungs rasped for oxygen.

When they reached the top they saw jungle for miles in all directions. To the east was Manila Bay and the rocky island of Corregidor, where Wainwright was desperately holding out with a defense force of fifteen thousand. Far below in a crater's base a few wisps of smoke curled up.

For three hours they maneuvered around obstacles on the crater's rim, clinging their way along by grasping the thorny branches of scrubby trees. The exertion and the elevation were exhausting, and they lay breathless for a while beneath the rim, unable make further progress.

Realizing that the altitude was hindering their progress out of Bataan, they decided to go back down the mountain to the north. Ramsey got up on his hands and knees. As he struggled to stand, his eye caught something below him, a shape, a color, just inside the crater rim. Ramsey stared at it in a stupor, trying to make the image come clear in his exhausted mind.

It was an orchid, depending from a limb just a few feet beyond his reach. Ramsey had seen orchids before, in flower shops in Wichita and on the corsages of college girls, but this one was different, a delicate, pale green in color. It was the only living thing amid the desolation of that place, and its petals pulsed seductively.

It struck Ramsey as strange and exotic, gave him a taste he had not known through all this terrible time, and also prompted a recollection of why he had come here, and what he had expected to find. The reality had become brutal and had shaken him to his core, yet this sudden vision seemed to restore him.

Ramsey called Barker's attention to the orchid, and he too stared in wonder. Perhaps it was their weeks of enforced fasting, perhaps the sheer desperation of their condition, but for a long time they stood in silence, unable to take their eyes off the beautiful flower.[15]

They continued their descent toward the Pilar-Bagae Road, the main east-west connection across the peninsula. They knew it would be coursing with Japanese soldiers bent on completing their conquest. But crossing the road was necessary in order to escape from Bataan and get into the plains of central Luzon.

Walking hurriedly toward the mountains, Margarito Silva met Clay Conner and Ernest Kelly on April 21. A gunnysack hung over his back, and he wore a straw hat and short pants, but no shirt, or shoes. With a broad smile on his face he walked up to Conner and Kelly and shook their hands, speaking very good English.

"My name is Margarito Silva. I'm glad to see you. Would you like to join me? I have several Americans living with me, and I'm supporting them. In fact, I have just been to the lowlands, sir, and I have gotten food for them. If you will come with me, we will be glad to have you."[16]

Late that afternoon they arrived at Silva's hideout. It was a secluded spot, a short distance from a river. Because it was so well hidden, a person could go up and down the river and never see the place. As they turned from the river, the little shacks were visible only after they passed through underbrush. There were five shacks; each was two feet off the ground and large enough to sleep four or five men side by side on bamboo floors.

Silva told them that some Filipinos from the town of Orion had come there and built this little place to escape from the bombing, killing, and confusion of the war, and from mistreatment by Japanese soldiers. Silva hated the Japanese.

Conner and Kelly were introduced to two other Americans, Ray Schletterer and Hayden Lawrence, both with the Seventeenth Tank Ordinance.

When Conner awoke the next morning, he heard men outside talking. Silva had brought five more Americans into the camp: Frank Gyovai (a rough West Virginia coal miner) Pierce Wade, Eddie Keith, James Boyd, and Alvin Inghram, all also from the Seventeenth Tank Ordinance. These men had all escaped with Schletterer and Lawrence, but had split up, taking different routes.

Because of the number of Americans in the camp, Gyovai, Wade, Keith, and Inghram left after a few days and went up the Orani River and over the slopes behind the town of Samal. Here were some more grass shacks where a Filipino named Jimmy Espino was taking care of another group of Americans.

Hayden Lawrence had a bad attitude toward officers and was making life miserable for Conner. He was constantly complaining and making accusations about officers and Conner in particular. Finally there was a confrontation, and, after Lawrence had backed down, Conner left for Jimmy Espino's place. Not able to care for him, Jimmy sent Conner on to Francisco Silva until better accommodations could be found.

When Lieutenant Colonel Frank Lloyd of the Philippine Constabulary found his way to Tala Ridge in northern Bataan, he found three Americans living in a small house with a Filipino named Margarito Silva and his family: Lieutenant Henry Clay Conner, Sergeant Samuel Dawson and Private Howard Mann. Another American, "Panama" Pierce Wade was also living in the vicinity with Hippolito Sayas.[17] Silva took Lloyd to one of the houses and introduced him to a Mr. Filimeno, telling Lloyd that the Filipino would take care of him.

When Frank Lloyd's benefactor Placido brought supplies up to the hut the next week, he told Lloyd that the malaria epidemic in Bataan had spread to the Tala settlement. Three of the Americans in Tala had died of malaria and it looked like Lieutenant Conner, who was now being cared for by Francisco Silva's family, was going to be next. Some of the refugees had malaria, too, and there was no medicine available anywhere. The only two Americans who were not sick were the big man, Frank Gyovai, and Panama Wade, the medic.

"Last night," he said, "they go to Orani with Jimmy Espino. They go to the Japanese hospital to get medicine. They do it at gunpoint, if necessary."

Frank Lloyd was shocked, but impressed.

"Jimmy Espino was a Red Cross medic," Placido continued, nervously. "They have not come back — and they may bring the whole Japanese Army."

When Placido brought Lloyd's supplies the following Saturday, he reported that Wade and Gyovai had broken into the Kalaguiman Hospital at night and had stolen all the quinine and Atabrine they could find.

"They got back to Tala safely but there is not enough medicine to go around. They saved Leutenant Conner. But two of Francisco Silva's children are dead."[18]

With the invasion by the Japanese, the dikes and dams for the rice fields had been blown up, causing the area near the north coast of Manila Bay to become a swamp. The result was a breeding pool for mosquitoes, and when the winds blew from the north, the mosquitoes had infested Samal. They were like black clouds as the winds carried them aloft. Weakened by lack of food, shelter and medicine, a person, exposed to the assault of countless mosquitoes became fodder and the blood-sucking vermin carried malaria throughout Luzon. People died by the thousands. In Samal, where the residents had the shelter of their own homes, 2,000 out of 3,000 died. The mosquitoes were carried by the winds up the valleys, and by thermals into the hills. At Jimmy Espino's place two men died. At Margarito's, one of the men who had escaped the Death March died. The mosquitoes came higher up the mountains, and two of Francisco Silva's children died. By the end of the second month after the surrender on Bataan the number of Americans at liberty was reduced by half.

Conner lived, but as he remembered it was not entirely by his own power. He was saved by a Negrito, though he learned later that the drug that cured him could have killed him. Francisco Silva, living in the hills, had a lot of friends among the Negritos. They lived a primitive life in the most inaccessible hills of Luzon, most wearing only breechcloths or nothing at all, though a few, who lived on the edge of society and made friends with Filipinos for trading purposes, wore ragged pants. One of Silva's Negrito friends' came and squatted in front of Conner and made several guttural noises. Then he boiled an herb called dita, and gave Conner the tart fluid to swallow. Having everything to gain, Conner drank the liquid down. The Negrito then left a portion of the herb for Conner to brew for himself. In two days the chills and fever were gone and he began to move around under his own power.

Silva was suffering the death of his children, and his wife was ill. Frank Gyovai sent word to Conner to come help to bury his two friends. Silva needed help with the sick and dying at his house and Conner gave assistance as he was able.

He wanted to get more dita, but was cautioned against it by Jimmy Espino. Espino was a college graduate and had a brother who was a doctor and told him that dita, though safe enough for the Negritos to use, was likely to have a devastating effect on softer, refined peoples. In several instances patients taking the drug had become deaf, mute, blind, or dead.[19]

On April 9, the Eleventh Division was ordered to stack arms near the division command post with white flags of surrender hanging from several trees. The American officers gathered inside the bamboo stockade and waited, then without warning the enemy arrived and began shooting, with no apparent recognition of the white flags.

Volckmann nudged Blackburn and said, "This is when!" They slumped down and rolled over a bank into a dry streambed and then they crawled slowly away from the command post into the darkness and thick jungle growth.[20]

The Japanese disregard for the white flags dispelled any misgiving Blackburn had, and he fled the area with Volckmann, Moses and Noble, jumping an embankment, crawling across a road packed with Filipinos and plunging into the jungle.

An hour after evading the enemy, Blackburn and Volckmann couldn't find Moses and Noble. Deciding it was foolish to search for their friends who were probably as lost as they were, Blackburn and Volckmann struggled on, stumbling into a dry streambed, where they crawled under some tree roots along the bank and rested. Without warning, three men came crashing out of the brush and into the streambed. It was Filipinos just as frightened as the two Americans. The Filipinos offered their services as guides and interpreters, and after resting for a few hours the group began its trek out of Bataan.

This ragtag band found several deserted Japanese camps with discarded rations to supplement the meager supplies they had managed to scrounge before their escape. After a few days of dodging Japanese patrols and searching for more food, the Americans made contact with a Philippine Scout who had escaped. He offered shelter and food at a grove of huts housing Filipino families who had lost their homes to the war. On their way to the camp, the group ran into another escaped American, Corporal Albert Bruce from the Thirty-first Infantry.

While they ate, the Scout's wife washed their uniforms. Waiting for their clothing to dry, more Americans showed up, two Air Force officers, Bernard Anderson and Bert Pettitt.[21] They had seen Moses and Noble, and reported that they were well and working their way north out of Bataan.

The four Americans, with a newly acquired Igorot[22] guide named Bruno, continued their way north, encountering a number of friendly Filipinos who gave them shelter and food. Because some of the food was barely edible, Blackburn and Volckmann had several bouts of stomach complaints resulting in additional loss of weight and weakened condition. On May 20 they finally arrived at a plantation owned by a Filipino named Dempson, and where a Filipino named Guerro, who had managed the plantation before the war, cared for the Americans with his family.

Suffering from multiple miseries — dysentery, malaria, beriberi, mosquitoes and rats — the usual camaraderie became strained. When Volckmann and Anderson quarreled over the distribution of some rice supplied by their benefactor, Anderson and Pettitt hastily departed.

After another relocation to find better medicine, Blackburn and Volckmann were told of a refugee camp for Americans in the Zambales Mountains, a day's hike from their position. It was said that there were about sixty Americans in the camp with an American doctor and a nurse.

After discussing the possibilities of moving to the American camp, and while fighting jaundice, Blackburn and Volckmann had an unexpected visitor, Shelby Newman. He told them about his escape and of meeting Anderson and Pettitt. Newman had seen the camp run by Bill and Martin Fassoth with help from Vicente Bernia who paid Filipinos twenty pesos[23] for every American brought into the camp. After suffering another malaria attack, Blackburn and Volckmann followed Newman and a Filipino guide to Fassoth's camp.

There was a creek outside the prison fence at Camp O'Donnell. Before the war there was a dam at one end of the creek, but it had been destroyed in the retreat. The American doctors decided that they would use the murky river water to cook the rice ration, but not to drink. There was a well with a pump in the camp for drinking water. With men dying from thirst, though, and the well insufficient, Japanese and American doctors decided that the prisoners would bring water from the river. Gilbert Neighorn and Gerald Wade from the Nineteenth Bomb Group decided to get on this detail.

After the "Death March," Neighorn and Wade were so grimy that on their first trip to the river they threw caution to the wind and went in to take a bath. As they swam they noticed that the Japanese guards were downstream working on the dam. Wade saw his chance, so he and Neighorn swam across the creek. Afraid the Japanese would come after them with guns, Neighorn and Wade walked up another creek for three hours and then they broke out on flat land. Gerald Wade had his first malaria attack that night.

They lay in the field overnight. The next day, about noon, they saw a Filipino who gave them what was left of his rice lunch. Though he spoke no English, they traveled with him on a trail that took them to a clutch of huts in the hills, finding there a school teacher and a Philippine Scout sergeant who spoke English.

Wade and Neighorn talked about getting to Mindanao. Sometime the next day Neighorn decided strike out on his own and left Wade.

After a week's rest, Red Wolfe had improved and could travel. Japanese patrols had probed near the camp several times looking for American evaders. Wolfe, Doyle Decker and Nano Lucero decided they needed to move on as their capture would endanger the Filipinos giving them shelter. As the three prepared to leave, their Filipino friends brought another soldier to them. He introduced himself as Captain Charles Long. He had been dodging Japanese patrols and wanted to be with the fellow Americans.

There was a serious discussion among the three because of the previous problems they had with the captain and sergeant. After much give and take they agreed to let Captain Long come with them if he agreed that everyone was to pull their own weight. "No special privileges for anyone," stressed Wolfe. Long was so lonesome that he settled to the demands rather than remain alone.

The group of four continued north and passed through areas where battles had been fought where they found American and Japanese bodies intermingled. The carnage created a macabre scene that the jungle had begun to cover with a blanket of green and brown. There weren't any shovels or trenching tools to bury the Americans. Even if the tools had been available, there were an overwhelming number of bodies to bury.

Helplessness swept over the men when they smelled the pungent odor of decay and death. The stink was worse at night when the winds died down and the air was stagnant. The next three days challenged the men's sanity as they walked through the grisly scene. Bones beginning to brown in the open air protruded through rotting flesh. The process did not distinguish Japanese from American corpses. [24]

Decker and Lucero became experts at locating Japanese food stashes. It appeared that the supplies were stored in the event the Japanese retreated.

After hiking two more days through another battleground, Long began running a high fever and Wolfe had dysentery. To avoid Japanese patrols, a camp was made a hundred yards from the artillery trail. The next day, as Decker and Lucero searched for food, Decker found three American bodies that appeared to have been killed in battle. Having no way to bury them short of digging graves with their hands bothered Decker. He and Lucero could only cover them with some leaves and branches and stand over them in silent frustration.

The following day, Decker spotted a man who looked like an American Negro camped along the artillery trail north of Decker's group. He didn't recall any Negro troops assigned to the Philippines. The man seemed to be alone, but Decker hesitated to go into the camp by himself and decided he would bring Lucero with him the next day and make contact.

The following morning, Decker and Lucero set out to encounter the stranger. Lucero took a concealed position to cover Decker with his .45 pistol, but the camp was empty, the campfire cold. The mystery man had moved on.

Lucero decided to explore the far side of the area, while Decker followed the trail near a stream. He noticed that something had slid down the high bank into the water. As Decker neared the edge and peered over, his foot slipped and he slid down the bank, coming to rest between two dead American soldiers. Each man's head was split open, severed by a saber. Decker scrambled to his feet, trying not to vomit. Dog tags on the men identified one as a colonel and the other as a captain. Further identification was unattainable from the mangled tags. Scrambling up the bank, Decker told Lucero what he had found.

Wolfe and Long remained too ill to travel, so Decker and Lucero continued their search for supplies. After a few more days Wolfe and Long, though scarcely able to travel, felt they should move before they were located by a Japanese patrol.

The group encountered some strange men on the trail. One was a Filipino, sitting beside the trail with bags of rice piled about him, who refused an offer to join the Americans, Wolfe suggested that they move on hurriedly, commenting "I don't think this son of a bitch is dealing with a full deck."

The men quickened their pace. Further along the trail they saw a swarm of flies rising from some cut bamboo. Walking over to determine the cause of the swarm, the men were shocked to see bodies in an open trench, covered with oil and in a state of decay making it impossible to determine if they were American or Japanese.

Hurrying pace again to escape the ghastly sight they approached a large tree and encountered another man, who spoke English, but looked Japanese.

"I am Filipino. You like to buy some cigarettes?"

Haggling ensued and a price was agreed upon. The stranger produced two packs of Camels. Because Decker had given up his last ten pesos, Wolfe produced money for the smokes.

"I think we better get goin'," said Long anxiously. "I don't like all the strange people we've encountered today."

Reaching the summit of the next mountain ridge, the Americans looked back and saw a Japanese patrol. They counted eight soldiers snaking toward them through a clearing in the jungle a mile away. Not waiting to see if they had been spotted, the Americans disappeared into the dense jungle.

The rest of the day was spent putting as much distance between them and the Japanese patrol as their bodies could endure. Late in the afternoon Wolfe called a halt and they filled their canteens in a stream. Lucero and Decker cooked rice and opened a can of salmon they had found in the last deserted American bivouac. After eating, everyone lay down to sleep, but mosquitoes were thick and no one got much rest.

Wolfe and Decker took the lead the next morning as the group continued its trek north. At noon they reached a bluff overlooking the Pilar-Bagac road which ran through a saddle formed by Mt. Bataan and Mt. Natib. It was the only road connecting the east and west coast. The rest of the afternoon, while Wolfe and Decker watched the road and discussed their situation with Lucero and Long, they noticed that Japanese trucks traveled past every fifteen minutes. They had to cross a flat, open field about three hundred yards wide to get to the road. The men decided to cross after dark when the rate of traffic slowed.

That night, after crossing the road and walking through heavy jungle and up a steep ridge, they laid down to sleep. The next morning they discovered that they were only yards from where the road made several sharp turns in the mountain. They hurriedly got up and made their way north. Late that afternoon they came to another river where they filled their canteens and camped

The next morning Wolfe was running a fever and sick to his stomach, Long was weak with dysentery, and neither man could eat. The others felt sorry for Long, but there wasn't any medicine for his condition. He had been told that sitting in water would reliever his ailment; accordingly he spent the next three days in the river. The treatment didn't help, but it did keep him clean from the continual bowel movements.

With Wolfe and Long ill, Decker and Lucero searched for food. Lady luck smiled on them when they found a mixture of Japanese and American cans of meat and fruit. The Japanese meat was a mystery, but it flavored the rice and gave needed protein to their diet. Lucero also found a large cache of rice, pressed soybeans, sugar, and several cans of meat in an abandoned

Japanese camp. With an adequate supply of food and two sick men, the group decided to build a hut and wait out the rainy season.

One day while searching for food, Lucero and Decker observed someone who looked like an American, but they were unable to make contact. The individual appeared to be watching the two in their search for food, but as soon as Lucero and Decker began to approach, the stranger ducked back into the jungle.

Wolfe's health improved and he volunteered to help Decker find a suitable place to build the hut. A short distance upstream from their camp they found a small clearing with indications of another encampment. Five Americans emerged from the jungle and introduced themselves. They were Colonel Frank Brokaw, Captain Louis Dosh, Lieutenant Bob Chapin, Private Andy Roskopf, and a sergeant who mumbled his name unintelligibly.[25] Decker learned that the sergeant was the man that he and Lucero had observed watching them.

The colonel wasn't friendly and questioned the ability of his group to include four additional men. "Decker, I don't think these sons of bitches are looking for company, let's look further up stream for a site to build our hut," said Wolfe.

A short distance from the clearing, Wolfe and Decker discovered a large field. As they trudged across it they found scattered bones and counted ten human skulls. The bodies had left bare spots where they had first lain. Vultures and wild pigs had scattered the bones over the field. Paper money was strewn among the bones, fastened together with paper clips. Wolfe and Decker picked up the money, totaling three hundred and seventy pesos.

Decker and Wolfe discussed the scene and wondered what had occurred. It appeared from the clothing that these had been Filipino civilians. They guessed that Japanese soldiers had killed the people for helping American troops avoid Japanese patrols. It was obvious that they were not killed for their possessions.

After further search, Wolfe and Decker decided to build their shack on a bluff overlooking the river, a good distance from the trail running through the valley which Wolfe had dubbed "the Valley of the Dead."

Over the next four days, while Lucero searched for food, Wolfe and Decker built a hut from bamboo and cogon grass, modeled after Filipino huts they had seen. They cut down large bamboo stalks and used the poles for the corners of the hut. Splitting the bamboo for sub flooring, they tied the pieces together with rattan vines, using bolos picked up after the surrender on Bataan to split the bamboo stalks. Cogon grass was woven to make walls, and they tied the grass in bundles and overlapped them for a roof.

The four days of working on the hut weakened Wolfe again, and Long's condition continued to decline, leaving him too weak to even sit in the river. They remained in the hut while Decker helped Lucero hunt for food, storing as much rice and canned goods as they were able. The rainy season was getting worse, with nonstop downpours turning everything outside their hut into mud. The hut was damp from the high humidity and lack of sun to dry the structure. They knew there would be days when they would be unable to make forays. Craving fresh meat, Lucero suggested that he and Decker try to kill a deer or wild pig.

The next morning Decker and Lucero searched for game. They spotted a small deer that had long straight horns rather than a rack. After stalking it all morning, they were unable to get close enough for a good shot.

At noon Decker heard something grunting in a nearby cane break. He yelled at Lucero about the noise. Lucero yelled back that he thought it was a wild pig. As if on signal, Lucero ran around to the opposite side of the break, shouting and waving his arms, yelling at Decker that a pig was coming toward him.

Instinctively Decker drew his .45 and fired. The pig dropped at his feet, a bullet hole between its beady eyes.

"Wow! What a shot," yelled Lucero, running around the break towards Decker.

"Ever hear of a blind hog finding an acorn, Lucero? Well, you just saw a blind man kill a hog. I didn't even have time to aim. Talk about scared, I thought that pig was gonna eat me alive."

To get the pig back to camp, Decker walked over to the cane break and chopped a bamboo stalk about three inches in diameter. Then he cut the other end so the pole was eight feet long, and hacked several strips of rattan vine, each two feet long, and tied the pig's feet around the pole.

"You want the front or the behind, Lucero?"

"Don't make no difference to me."

Decker picked up one end of the pole. "I'll lead. Put the pole on your shoulder and try to stay in step with me."

For first two hundred yards, Decker and Lucero nearly beat each other to death, with the pig swinging wildly from side to side. Staying in step on the rough jungle trail was a tough proposition.

"You sure you know what you're doin,' Decker?"

"Hell, yes. It's my partner that's causing the problem," laughed Decker. "Damn it Lucero, don't you know your left from your right? Try the other left!"

Frazzled, Decker and Lucero wrestled the pig into camp.

Captain Dosh was there and saw Decker and Lucero carrying the pig. He watched as Decker skinned the pig and cut the meat into pieces and placed them in a bucket to boil. He was impressed at what Decker and Lucero had accomplished. He told them that the colonel and sergeant were both sick and that he needed to get back and see how they were doing.

The next morning the men felt the consequences of having eaten the fresh pork. Decker remembered that cooking freshly killed pork before it had a chance to cool could result in diarrhea. Wolfe was the first to hit the bushes. Lucero was close behind, with Decker in hot pursuit.

Later that morning Dosh came into camp looking haggard. He told the men that the sergeant had died that morning, that they had just finished with the burial, and that the colonel wasn't getting any better. Captain Long spoke up, telling the men that he was getting worse and wanted to go to the Filipino shack they had observed on the mountain as they made their way to the camp. He wanted to see if they had some medicine. Long left by himself, but Decker hurried after him so he wouldn't have to hike the half-mile alone.

The Filipinos didn't have any medicine, but promised to help Long, providing him with a shelter so he could rest out of the weather. Decker, Lucero, and Wolfe took turns daily walking up the trail to the Filipino hut to check on Long, whose condition however continued to deteriorate.

Three days later Dosh walked into camp, distraught. The Colonel had died the night before and Dosh asked for help to bury him. It had taken all the strength his camp had to bury the sergeant and they needed help with the colonel.

Wolfe, Lucero, and Decker returned with Dosh to his camp and found Chapin and Roskopf shaken. "How long can we exist if we don't get any medicine?" moaned Roskopf. Roskopf was a medic and felt helpless without any medical supplies.

The men took turns digging a grave for Colonel Brokaw, using their bolos and some large bamboo poles they had cut from a nearby grove. They lowered the body into the ground. Dosh read from a Bible and said a prayer. "God, we ask that you be with the colonel. He was a good man and we will miss him. And Lord, please be with the living. We need your help. We can't make it without you. Amen."

The words hit home. The men's eyes were moist and a cloud of gloom descended over the group.

Decker, Wolfe, and Lucero returned to their camp. The next morning Lucero and Decker were searching for food when they saw Roskopf walking up the trail with his head down, mumbling to himself. Lucero asked what was wrong.

"Dosh and Chapin are pickin' on me," Roskopf murmured.

Decker saw that the young private was upset and told him he could stay with them, that there was always room for one more.

Roskopf stopped and looked up. "You mean it?"

"Of course I do," replied Decker. "Come on, let's get back to camp."

That evening when they were finishing their meal, Dosh walked into camp. He approached Roskopf and talked with him for a few minutes. Then he turned and addressed Decker and Wolfe.

"We didn't mean to upset Andy. We were talking about having lost the sergeant and the colonel, and Andy got real upset. When I told him to quiet down, he took off. This has been a hard time for all of us."

Decker suggested that Roskopf be allowed to stay in their camp. They could use the help and Roskopf would have time to adjust.

Dosh thought for a moment and decided it was a good idea. He volunteered to come over the next day and go with Decker to see Captain Long, as he might feel better in the company of an officer.

Arriving the next morning, Dosh accompanied Decker up the mountain trail to check on Long. When they walked into the shack they were horrified at what they saw. Long's hair was completely white and he was lying in his own filth, unable to move. The Filipinos were afraid to help him because they thought he had cholera, which is contagious.

Decker grabbed a bucket and went to a nearby stream for water. Dosh picked Long up and walked him out to a stump, sat him down and pulled off his clothes. Decker poured water over Long and helped Dosh clean him and the shack. They took Long back inside and fed him some thin rice gruel that the Filipinos had cooked for him.

"Boys, I can't take this. I've sent word that I want to turn myself in to the Japs. I promise I won't say anything about you to them. And Decker, Dosh, thank you for looking after me. Tell Wolfe and Lucero I really appreciated what they have done." With tears in his eyes Long continued in a whisper, "You have been good friends."

Decker and Dosh stayed a few minutes to get Long comfortable.

"You get back to camp," said one of the Filipinos. "Japs come soon for Long."

Dosh looked at Decker. "He's right, let's get out of here."

With heavy hearts they hurried back to camp. Chapin was there when they returned. "Damn, everyone is over here. I thought I might as well join the group."

Dosh looked around. "If you don't mind, I'd like to stay here also. I know you don't need an officer. We have to agree on what needs to be done, but I'll pull my weight and I know Chapin will also."

A few days earlier a Sergeant Phillips[26], hungry and lonely, had found the camp. He had lost track of time in his trek out of Bataan and was shocked to learn that it was May 15. He had been alone over thirty days.

The day after Dosh and Decker visited Long, Decker and Lucero walked back to the shack where Long was staying, arriving just as a black sedan pulled away. They hid in the jungle until the car was out of sight and then cautiously approached the hut. The Filipinos told them that Captain Long had died the night before. The Japanese had hurriedly left when told that Long's hair had turned white. The Filipinos had buried Long in a shell hole north of the hut. They hadn't touched the captain, using long bamboo poles to move the body. They told the Americans that they had used words from the Bible after burying Long.

Fifty feet north of the hut, Decker and Lucero found a mound of fresh dirt with three large rocks covering the grave.

Decker swore. "Damn, we lost another one, Lucero. I don't like this place. There are too many dead people. Let's get the hell out of here."

When Decker and Lucero returned to camp they found Phillips and Roskopf were sick. It was decided the group would remain in place until the two men were better.

Two days later Decker and Lucero again visited the shack where Long had died to see what he might have left behind. No one had yet retrieved Long's .45 pistol. Arriving at the shack they found an old shirt and Long's pistol belt with an empty holster.

Lucero heard someone approaching and alerted Decker. They drew their pistols and decided that they would fight rather than be captured. They sat with their guns trained on the door of the shack. The men walking toward the shack were speaking a Filipino dialect that sounded like Pampangan. They entered the hut and saw Decker and Lucero with their pistols pointed at them. The strangers dropped their guns and yelled, "Don't shoot, don't shoot, we friendly Filipinos!"

Decker and Lucero holstered their pistols and the Filipinos came forward and shook the American's hands. "We on way to Bataan to search for guns and ammunition. We from camp up north, run by American sugar grower. Bill Fassoth, his brother Martin, and the Spaniard, Vicente Bernia. Lots of food and camp deep in mountains where Japs can't find. You meet us three days; we guide you to Fassoth's Camp." As the Filipinos left they again promised to guide all the Americans with Decker and Lucero.

Back at camp Decker and Lucero told the others of their adventure and the promise made by the Filipinos.

The men argued for two days about the wisdom of meeting the Filipinos. Decker, Lucero, and Phillips were resolved to make the rendezvous. Dosh, Roskopf, Chapin, and Wolfe had their doubts.

When they weren't discussing the wisdom of meeting the Filipinos, the two groups compared their escape routes out of Bataan. Dosh heard where

Decker's group crossed the Bagac-Pilar road and nearly choked. "You all crossed a mine field. I helped lay the damn thing and knew how to avoid the area. I can't believe four men crossed where you did without detonating a mine."

On the eve of the third day, Decker, Lucero, and Phillips gathered their gear.

"Hell, you ain't leavin' without me," snorted Wolfe.

"Well, if Wolfe's goin,' I'm goin,'" said Roskopf.

Dosh looked at Chapin, "I'll be damn lonely with just you and me, Chapin. We might as well tag along. Besides, it will be harder to overpower seven men."

The group gathered their gear, weapons, and remaining provisions and walked up the mountain trail for the expected rendezvous.[27]

Clay Conner made daily trips down the trail to the area where Frank Gyovai, Eddie Keith, Jim Boyd, Alvin Ingram and Pierce Wade were living. Some additional Americans, including Jerry Dunlap, were living further toward the lowlands.

The author (left) and Nano Lucero at Lucero's home in Florida, March 2003.

Gyovai, Keith and Ingram were living with Jimmy Espino. Boyd and Pierce Wade were living with Hipolito Sayas. All except Gyovai and Wade were sick at one time or another. Conner contacted dengue fever. On July 15 Jerry Dunlap died. The Americans in the area held a funeral service for Dunlap, and Clay Conner read from the New Testament.

Then Harry Porter, who was living with Conner, became very ill. He enjoyed Conner reading the Bible to him, especially Romans 10:9: "If you confess with your mouth the Lord Jesus, and believe in your heart, that God raised him from the dead, you will be saved." Porter would tell Conner, "Read that verse to me again."

On July 27 Porter died and the Americans assembled for his funeral. Clay Conner read Harry's favorite scripture and all took strength in its message.[28]

Late in the day the Filipinos returned from Bataan and met the seven Americans, Wolfe, Decker, Lucero, Phillips, Dosh, Chapin, and Roskopf, who had become anxious that they had been duped. Each Filipino was carrying three or four rifles and a large amount of ammunition. They told the Americans that after a short rest they would guide them to a friend's house for the night.

When the group approached the friend's house late in the afternoon, several Filipinos met them, talking in excited voices. One of the guides explained in broken English that Japanese patrols were looking for the Americans.

The assemblage continued their travel north at an increased pace to distance themselves from the Japanese patrol. They avoided the lower terrain near the sea, climbing up ridges and down into small valleys, crossing numerous streams along the way. The jungle foliage closed in, causing the men to push through the dense growth where the "wait a minute bush" tore at the clothing and flesh of those not mindful of its prongs. The humid, stagnant air of the jungle tired the men. They were grateful when they came to a small stream at sundown.

The Americans were exhausted. The guides cooked rice and roasted dried meat for the men to eat before they fell a'sleep. Decker thought he had just closed his eyes when he smelled coffee boiling. Arising, he saw the guides cooking rice and brewing coffee.

The men ate more than usual as they knew they had to travel as quickly as their weakened bodies could endure, and stopping to cook a meal took time. They would eat twice a day on the trail.

Late that afternoon they approached a stream near a deserted bivouac. The guides told them to wait there while they retrievd another American soldier.

Several minutes later the guides appeared with a giant of a man who introduced himself as Sergeant Coleman Banks. Banks was large-headed man with black hairy eyebrows and big flaring nostrils. Prominent black hair protruded from his ears and nose. His teeth were crooked and stained. His shoulders and upper torso were broad and muscular, but his hips and legs were small and thin compared to his body. Malnutrition had caused his skin to hang from his large frame. As he introduced himself to each man it was evident that he was amicable, kind, and gentle. It was as if Ichabod Crane had transplanted himself from Sleepy Hollow to the Philippine jungles.[29]

The growing assemblage followed the trail for an hour to another stream where the guides caught freshwater crabs and roasted them for the evening meal.

The next morning Phillips was sick and ate little breakfast. Decker realized that Phillips wouldn't be able to carry his own pack so he carried it along with his own, tying the two together. As they traveled, Decker kept an eye on Phillips. Phillips was grateful at the gesture, but Decker told him to not think anything of it and to keep putting one foot in front of the other. He was grateful Phillips wasn't slowing down the group.

At noon the next day they entered a deserted barrio containing several grass huts. On one side of the barrio the men saw twelve graves with white crosses. The guides didn't know what had happened, but conjectured that the Japanese had killed all the residents for helping some Americans.

That evening they entered another barrio where the residents had been expecting them and had prepared a meal. The men had just gotten to sleep when they were awakened by the guides who urged them to get moving as a Japanese patrol had been spotted nearby.

The next day the exhausted men were hidden in a grove of trees while the guides investigated a village further ahead on the trail. Deemed safe to proceed, the group went on to the village named Lubo, with only five huts, reaching it by evening. Here they found three other Americans who had been hiding. The three didn't introduce themselves, either too tired, scared, or both. At midnight a guide stood up and in a low voice said, "It is time to move. We walk in single file. No talking. No smoking. It will take four hours to cross to the foothills. If we run into a Jap patrol, everyone is on their own. Just continue north and we will find you when the danger is over."

The next day the group reached a clearing in the mountains where Bill and Martin Fassoth met them. Though they were twins, Bill was somewhat taller and muscular, with light brown hair and a commanding presence, while Martin had darker hair and was not as outgoing as his brother. Bill spoke first. "Men, welcome to our camp. I know you are hungry and tired from your trip. Please come in and have something to eat and get to know everyone here."[30]

Death March: Japanese photograph of burial detail from O'Donnell prison camp (National Archives).

Bill Fassoth Jr. had been captured and was in the O'Donnell Prison Camp near Capas. The Filipino prisoners were dying at a rate of four to five hundred a day. A prisoner on the burial detail could himself be buried the next week. There were three other sailors from Dinalupihan who had found one another at the prison. They had decided it would be better to be killed in an escape attempt than to die from disease in the camp.[31]

Many of the men who escaped from the Death March worried about their legal position. Lieutenant Ray Hunt had refused to surrender. He later joined Robert Lapham's LGAF (Luzon Guerrilla Armed Forces), but worried about what his legal position would be in the eyes of the U.S. and the Philippine governments at the end of the war. His guerrilla commander, Major Lapham, was in a similar situation but said he never worried about it because he could not imagine the government punishing an American for continuing to fight the Japanese. There were nearly as many different responses to Japanese overtures to surrender as there were Americans at large on Luzon.[32]

Chapter 5

Fassoths' Camps

Some people believe in angels, those shimmering entities from the Bible. But on Luzon the angels took earthly form in the personae of Filipinos who put their lives at risk helping and sheltering American soldiers who escaped Bataan and the Death March. Two of those angels were cane growers who sheltered over 104 Americans for nearly a year in the jungles of the Zambales Mountains. The rescued Americans owed their lives to Bill and Martin Fassoth, and to Bill's wife Catalina.

Bill and Martin Fassoth were from pioneering parents and their inherited German determination and fortitude helped the escaping soldiers who found their way into their camp. Their father, John Fassoth, was born in Bremen, Germany, in 1866 and emigrated to Hawaii, landing in Kauai in 1882 at the age of 16. He was employed at the Koloa Plantation on Kauai for two years and then worked at the Waimea Plantation for the next thirty years as a chemist, sugar boiler, chief engineer, manager and director.

John married Anna Margaret Decker in 1888. Anna was born in Germany in 1862 and had also emigrated to Hawaii. John and Anna had seven children, Hans, William, Martin, Joseph, John Jr., Paul and Conradina.

John joined William Williamson in 1914 and purchased the Kipahulu Plantation and moved to Maui in 1915. He served in the Kauai Legislature in 1914 and the Maui House of Representatives in 1920–21, and is known for having served both the Kauai and Maui legislatures simultaneously for a short time. A well-respected legislator and businessman, he died of a heart attack in 1923. It was from this heritage and business background that Bill went to Luzon in 1913 to buy and run his sugar plantation. He was joined by Martin in 1923.[1]

Bill and Catalina Fassoth in front of their home in Lubao, about 1946 (Fassoth Family collection).

Camp 1

On April 17, 1942, the first two American soldiers, Staff Sergeant Frank Bernacki and Sergeant Rudolph Wurzbach,[2] came into Fassoth's camp. They ate some snake meat and pronounced it very tasty. They were exhausted, but would be among the healthiest men to reach the camp. A Filipino army sergeant came into the camp later that same day. The following day many more soldiers found their way to the camp. Most of the men were starving and suffering from malaria and other diseases. Some were near death.

Bill and Martin Fassoth employed Filipinos, carrying notes assuring help, to explore the mountains for other American soldiers, and began building additional huts to house the increasing population of the camp. Because of the soldiers' deteriorated condition, the Filipinos had to haul many of them into the camp in bull carts.

There was a quantity of sugar in the camp and with the addition of coconuts, Catalina and Martin made plates of coconut candy that the men appreciated. It helped them to regain their energy. Occasionally when men came into the camp they would find the residents sitting down to hamburger steaks and platters of papaya and banana salad. After months on Bataan with starvation rations, this looked like paradise, as some of the men had been reduced to cutting down papaya trees and eating the roots and bark from the trees to get nourishment on their trek out of the Mariveles Mountains.

As the American soldiers kept arriving, curious Filipinos were drawn to the area, and traveling musicians serenaded and played patriotic and popular American songs on their guitars, mandolins and harmonicas.[3]

Ramsey, Barker and Strickland made it across the Bagac-Pilar Road and came across a friendly Filipino farmer. He took them to his village and, after feeding them, the Filipino told them about the prisoners the Japanese had marched and brutalized along the road. The Americans were stunned at the account.

The next day, the Filipino and two of his friends guided the three soldiers to the rugged area at the base of Mount Malasimbo. As they walked through many of the battlefields where they had fought in the past four months, Barker and Ramsey took turns helping Strickland. Trees and apparatus blown away by artillery and bombs were strewn among corpses lying entwined among jungle vines. They hurried past the somber scenes as fast as their weakened bodies could carry them.

Early that evening they arrived at the edge of Dinalupihan and turned west toward Malasimbo. Nearing the barrio that was their objective, they heard children's voices laughing and singing, an unexpected and warm sound. Three Filipinos and an American greeted them. The American introduced himself as John Boone, a corporal of the Thirty-first Infantry Regiment. Boone looked forty, but was in his late twenties. Malnutrition and illness contributed to his aging process, of which he made derisive jokes.

Boone explained that he had not gone into Bataan with the retreating

Filipino-American forces in early January, but instead stayed behind and helped organize a guerrilla opposition. His intelligence people knew that the three Americans were in the area, and he had hot food prepared. That evening while they ate, Boone told them about Colonel Thorp who was authorized to enlist any Filipinos and Americans who wanted to join a guerrilla force. Barker asked about Thorp's location. Boone told them that Thorp had a camp in the hills above Fort Stotsenburg. The Japanese controlled the lowlands, so Thorp directed everything from his headquarters in foothills.

Up to this time Barker and Ramsey had thought only of escape and taking care of Strickland. He was exhausted from undernourishment and dysentery, and had lost a disturbing amount of weight. Ramsey didn't think Strickland could make the trip to Thorp's headquarters, but Boone told them it might be their best chance since Thorp's camp was near a plantation owned by some Americans named Fassoth. They had food and medical supplies and they were helping escaped soldiers. Boone offered guides to escort them to the Fassoths' camp. It was a two-day journey over rugged country avoiding Japanese patrols, but his guides could make the trip.

It was decided that if Strickland was to have any chance to live he needed medical care. Ramsey and Barker would accompany him to the Fassoths' camp, then go to locate Thorp. They remained at Boone's camp for a few days to recuperate and then followed the guides to the Fassoth plantation in the hills above the village of Floridablanca.

Ten months before, Ramsey had made the journey from the luxury of the Manila Army-Navy Club to Fort Stotsenburg. Now he was a skin-and-bones expatriate of a conquered army, cut off, looking only to escape.

The war had stood the world on end. That it would be righted again Ramsey had no doubt, but how long that would take and how much suffering would transpire till then, none could begin to imagine.[4]

Catalina Fassoth prepared the first substantial meal that Earl Oatman and Hank Winslow had eaten in months. The steamed rice, vegetables, and tropical fruit were delectable and nourishing. Oatman and Winslow could not believe their good fortune. That night they slept on clean rice straw mats among fellow escapees from the Death March. Every day additional soldiers, both American and Filipino, were brought in by local Filipinos. At Vicente Bernia's suggestion, he and Bill Fassoth were paying the local Filipinos 15 pesos for each escaped prisoner brought into camp.

This camp was idyllic, set in the midst of large tropical trees along a creek originating from several small waterfalls from the Zambales Mountains. With the increasing numbers, though, it was apparent that larger facilities were needed.

Oatman had begun having chills by mid-morning each day, soon after he arrived in the camp. He would sit on a boulder in the creek, a rock heated by the sun, to try and get warm. Although the sun was hot, Oatman continued to chill. By the third day, Winslow was experiencing the same symptoms. They realized they had contracted malaria. Though they were given some quinine, it was too little and too late to stop the attacks. They felt fortunate to be among friends and to have ample food.[5]

Boone's guides led Ramsey, Barker, and Strickland north through the Zambales foothills, out of view of the lowland barrios and trails. Barker and Ramsey had recovered some strength at Boone's camp, but Strickland continued to deteriorate. He moved slowly, using a bamboo pole, and paused every few yards to gasp for oxygen. Food and water slid through him and he suffered bloody dysentery. Barker and Ramsey tried to reassure Strickland that medical attention was available at their destination. They pressed on, but it took three days to reach Fassoth's camp

Bill Fassoth told them the story of the suffering of those who had surrendered. Hundreds of Americans and thousands of Filipino soldiers had been killed on the forced march from Bataan to Camp O'Donnell in central Luzon. Those who had found safe haven at the Fassoths told of the cruelty of the Japanese. Men frail from malnourishment and disease had been driven with clubs and bayonets. Those who could walk no farther were shot, beaten to death, bayoneted, or beheaded. The distress of starvation, dehydration, the broiling heat, and the inhuman treatment by the Japanese guards drove many men to insanity and suicide. The few who had managed to escape told stories that were almost inconceivable.

Ramsey and Barker listened, unable to fully absorb the significance of what they were hearing, but thankful they had not surrendered. The reports made them resolute to escape the Philippines.

Bill Fassoth told them that Colonel Thorp had his headquarters on Mount Pinatubo deep in the jungle to the north where he was organizing his emerging guerrilla force. Barker and Ramsey decided to report to Thorp and leave Strickland at Fassoth's camp to convalesce. Strickland was frantic at being left behind. Insisting he could make the trip, that he just needed a little more time, he shakily pulled himself to his feet.

Barker put his hand on Strickland's shoulder and reassured him that the Fassoths would take care of him until they got back. Strickland shook his head no, determinedly; he wanted to stay with Barker and Ramsey.

Ramsey joined in the conversation and reaffirmed Barker. Strickland fixed Ramsey with his pale, sunken eyes. "Didn't we make it this far? You're not going to go off and leave me like MacArthur did?"[6] Barker and Ramsey absorbed Strickland's rebuke. He relied on them; they were officers, and though they didn't think he could make the trip, they took him along.

Bill Fassoth gave provisions and two Negritos to guide them through the Zambales trails to Thorp. Barker and Ramsey fell in behind the guides on either side of Strickland. The small natives had an understanding of the jungles and mountain trails, and Ramsey and Barker had difficulty keeping up with them, especially helping Strickland in his weakened condition. The heat sapped Strickland's remaining strength. When they arrived at the barrio Timbo, Thorp's base in the hills, Strickland was shattered. They laid him in a hut, shuddering with malaria, hallucinating from fatigue.

Colonel Thorp was organizing his headquarters at Mount Pinatubo to the north, so Barker and Ramsey sent him a communication and settled in to remain with Strickland. He lay shivering through that night and the next day, unable to eat or talk lucidly. On the following morning, April 23, twenty-one-year-old Gene Strickland died.[7]

Camp 2

Vicente Bernia had suggested to Bill Fassoth that a larger camp was needed and said he would assist in providing additional funds to support the camp in addition to procuring supplies from Manila.

Earl Oatman was one of several American soldiers to accompany Bill and Martin Fassoth to select a more secluded location to build what came to be known as Fassoths' Camp Number 2, in a district known as Patal Garland. They followed a trail five miles up the dense jungle slopes of the Zambales Mountains. Bill chose a sloping site bordering a small stream. The stream joined a larger river several hundred yards down the slope, insuring an ample water supply for drinking, cooking, and bathing. A half mile down the trail from the new camp was a treeless, cogon-grass-covered[8] area providing an excellent observation position for spotting Japanese patrols that might approach the camp. The new site was built in a stand of large tropical trees vaulting 100 to 200 feet into the sky, capped by converging canopies of leaves obscuring the camp from Japanese observation planes.

With the approaching rainy season, Bill and Martin Fassoth were aware of the consequences to men not protected from torrential rains. The building of the new camp began immediately. Bill returned to make provisions for transporting his family, supplies, and remaining American soldiers.

Filipinos were posted near different Japanese garrisons to keep the camp informed of their activities, and to guard the approach to the new camp.

Martin supervised the construction at the camp. The erection of the

Illustration of the Fassoths' Camp #2 (Doyle Decker collection, furnished by author).

buildings required exceptional skills as there were no nails, so rattan and wooden pegs were used to hold the framework together. After a week of hard work, the men returned to move everyone and all supplies to the second camp. Many of the stronger men carried more than their condition allowed and had to put down their packs after a short distance. The able-bodied men and women did all they could to help those who were sick and unable to walk.

Until the buildings were erected, everyone had to sleep in the open, but morale was good. The first building was the camp's main structure, a barracks for one hundred men.[9]

Earl Oatman in his book, *Bataan: Only the Beginning*, described the building of the camp in detail. All the work was hard physical labor done with very few tools. The principle tool was the steel bladed bolo, the blade being about twenty inches long, two to two and one-half inches wide, and about one-quarter inch thick. The single cutting edge was honed to razor sharpness. The handle of the bolo was wood and the bolo was carried in a wooden sheath with a thong (leather or rattan) tied around the waist.

The buildings' frames were lashed together with rattan obtained from a vine that grows in the tropics of Southeast Asia. The upright poles used for the framework averaged six to eight inches in diameter. The cross framework and roof-ridge poles averaged four to six inches and these were cut and prepared similar to the upright supporting poles. Boho, a species of bamboo that grows wild in mountainous areas of the Philippines, was used between the hardwood supports. The roof was covered with overlapping split boho, similar to clay tile roofing. The floor of the main building consisted of palm boards, each four to six inches wide and about one inch thick. These were split from the trunk of a species of palm that grew nearby. Double-tiered bunks were constructed of smaller, debarked poles lashed together with rattan. The slats used for the bunk bottoms were of the same material that was used on the floor of the building. To provide a springy support for a comfortable rest when sleeping, the bed slats were narrower and not as thick. The barrack walls were constructed of split boho woven together in sections. These sections, fastened to the walls with rattan, overlapped at the edges to keep out the wind and rain. Windows, openings at regular intervals in the two longer outside walls, were covered with sawali, split boho woven together in sections, and hinged to the walls at the top of the opening using rattan. These windows coverings were propped open except in a heavy rain. A single open doorway was in a wall near one end of the building. A kitchen lean-to was attached, adjacent to the doorway, and was covered with sheets of corrugated iron packed in from the lowlands by Filipinos. Its floor was dirt. A rectangular cook stove was built; with rock sides and covered with a sheet of iron, its two ends were left open to insert wood for the fire.

The main building was completed in less than two weeks and the kitchen was added as additional Americans arrived in camp, just in time for the start of the rainy season. Because the building was erected on a slope, one side was high off the ground and was enclosed for storing supplies.

As numbers grew, Bill Fassoth arranged to have several of his trusted Filipinos build an open-sided, rectangular building for use as both a mess hall and recreation hall. Additionally, they built two small houses above the main building. One was for Catalina Fassoth, several nieces, and the nurse Hipolita San Jose. The other building was for the two Filipino men who helped in the kitchen.[10]

Vicente Bernia had brought Miss Hipolita San Jose, a trained nurse, to the camp to attend to the sick. She had been helping Doctor Layug who had been working with Colonel Claude Thorp at his guerrilla camp at Mt. Pinatubo. Thorp's camp had been disbanded and relocated near Tarlac. Catalina had looked after the sick men prior to Hipolita's arrival and appreciated the professional help.[11] She had been near exhaustion from nursing the sick soldiers and overseeing the food preparation.

There was always cereal, made from lugao, very soft cooked rice, served with sugar and milk or cocoa added, which the Filipinos called "samporado." There were hotcakes made from rice floor and served with syrup or jelly, and coffee. At noon and evening meals there was usually boiled rice with fish and meat courses, vegetables, and bread made from rice floor. This was hard work for Catalina and the women and Lebrado girls that worked in the camp.[12]

Bill Fassoth hired four additional Filipino girls to launder the soldiers' clothes, in addition to washing pots, pans and dishes. He also arranged for an army cooking range, which had been left by American troops in the Dinalupihan area when they withdrew into Bataan, to be hauled to the camp. Other cooking material, left by occupying Japanese soldiers, was collected from the Fassoth plantation.

The men dug a slit trench about 100 feet below the main building. This -military style trench served as a toilet for the men. The women had a separate, small toilet and shower area above the building. Drinking water was piped from small streams above the buildings to one corner of the mess hall, using lengths of boho split in half.[13]

Bill organized trusted Filipinos from his and Vicente Bernia's plantations to provide the new camp with rice, sugar, and other food supplies. For the next six months, the mechanics and expense of maintaining the camp was almost overwhelming, as several hundred Filipino-American troops passed through Fassoth's Camp. There were between 50 and 100 men in the camp at any one time. It was not established as a military or guerrilla camp, but was a place to rest and regain one's strength before moving on to other locations for whatever purpose the men desired.

Oatman was one of the men who went with Bill Fassoth to the lowlands. They traveled to a small nipa house at the edge of the foothills, where Bill had arranged for the delivery of raw sugar. Some Filipinos were unloading 132-pound bags of sugar from the back of a truck. The men formed a line behind the truck where a bag of sugar was placed on their backs to be transported to the camp. Wanting to be helpful, Oatman got in line and soon received a bag of sugar. It was the heaviest load he had ever tried to carry. He gritted his teeth and managed to lug the load to an open area where the bags were being piled. In his weakened condition, still recovering from malaria, he decided he wouldn't go for another sack, but watched in awe as the Filipinos, averaging 5 feet 4 inches and 150 pounds, finished unloading the truck. It appeared that they carried the loads with ease. The Americans were given a half a bag of sugar to carry back to camp.[14]

Vicente Bernia took many Filipino soldiers to his farm and fed them and let them recuperate.

Bill had some medicine on hand and obtained more from the drug stores of Lubao, Guagua, and Dinalupihan. These supplies were transported to the foothills by bull carts traveling at night over back roads and trails to avoid Japanese patrols, careful to keep the supplies dry from the rains and when crossing swollen streams. The supplies were then hauled to the camp by men from Fassoth's sugar plantation.

Bill also arranged for a man to supply the camp with fruit and vegetables, another for milk, chickens and eggs, and another for pigs and carabao for meat. It took all day to make the trek and the packers were fed a meal on reaching the camp. As many as seventy-five packers were employed at a time.

Another arrangement was made with the owner of two hundred cows and steers of semi-wild Brahma stock, and notification given to the corral man in the hills who was watching the herd. The stronger men of the camp were sent on the expeditions with some Negritos who shot the cattle. The Americans would then pack the beef back to camp. On the first trip for beef, a Negrito was given a Garand automatic rifle, something he had never fired before; when he pulled the trigger, he emptied the clip of shells before he could stop, shooting five cows.

Fish was procured from ponds and eaten fresh and dried. They also ate dried shrimp and bagong — small raw shrimp heavily salted and used to make a sauce.

Corn grown in the hills by the Negritos was exchanged for rice. The Americans would sometimes visit the Negritos who lived near the camp and roast ears of corn. As matches were scarce, the Negritos always kept a log burning, the corn roasting on the coals. Because they slept near the fire for warmth at night many Negritos, men, women, and children, had deformed legs, arms, fingers and toes from being burned by the hot coals.

Bill and Martin paid the Negritos for all the food and materials they brought to camp. In addition to meat, the Negritos brought rattan for binding the building materials.

Bill Fassoth was always scrounging materials for the camp. He usually took one of the American soldiers with him on his trips, but never more than one and always a different person. On one of his trips to the lowlands, he took a soldier who had a severe toothache. They found a woman dentist who came up to the Dinalupihan plantation to pull the tooth. Fortunately she had some novocaine, but wanted ten pesos for the extraction. Bill paid her three pesos.[15]

As the number of men increased, work details were assigned to carry out the daily camp functions. Earl Oatman was assigned to the firewood detail. Since were cooked on a wood-burning stove, the men were kept busy cutting and carrying wood to the kitchen. During the rainy season, the men cut and split the wood between heavy showers and stacked it underneath the barracks to dry out before being used.

After all the dead wood within a reasonable distance of the camp was collected, and live trees were cut for firewood, using two-person cross-cut saws, sledge hammers, steel wedges, and axes. One large hardwood tree provided enough wood for several weeks.[16]

In early May 1942, Lieutenant Arnold Warshell, an army doctor from the Twelfth Medical Battalion Philippine Scouts, came into camp. Prior to Dr. Warshell's arrival, a Filipino named Doctor Lupus, who was working with the guerrillas in Bulacan, had made two trips to the camp to attend to the soldiers. Bill Fassoth considered the camp fortunate to have only lost three soldiers, two by sickness and one through an accident.

Lieutenant Bob Reeves from the ordinance department, who Bill described as a very good and well-educated boy, was one who died. The other American to die from sickness was Corporal Owen Keiper of the 228th Signal Operating Company. Bill had brought Keiper into camp on a carabao, resting every two hundred meters due to Keiper's weak condition. Keiper only lived three weeks after his arrival. The third soldier to die was Larsen,[17] who also required help into the camp. He died when he got up one night and fell, striking his head on a boulder. All were given burials and funeral services. Scripture was read from the Bible and sacred songs were sung. The graves were marked with crosses and lined with big stones. To locate the graves after the war, nearby trees were marked.[18]

Bill Fassoth solicited clothing from several sources, receiving some from Manila, and bought some from a friend in Lubao who had in turn procured them from Bataan. The men laughed at themselves, as American clothes that fit before the war were now several sizes too large. The taller men wore suspenders, looking like secondhand clothes dealers, while the shorter men looked like dwarfs.

To pass the time, the soldiers played poker, betting with cigarettes and cigars. The camp was kept in tobacco with everyone sharing equally, except for the poker players.

Bill managed to get three radio sets and kept one operational. With the radios were three batteries, which had to be transported back and forth from the lowlands for charging. Eugene Zingheim, a private first class with the 194th Tank Battalion, Company C, Salinas unit, looked after the radio and kept it running, receiving KGEI from San Francisco. This gave the men welcomed entertainment and news from home.[19]

Walter Chatham, Winston Jones and John Kerrey were part of the group who came into the camp with Ray Hunt in early May. Vicente Bernia brought Hunt in on a horse. Hunt was too weak to walk and Vicente had to hold him on the horse as they walked.

Hunt spent the next five months recovering from his debilitating diseases and malnourishment. He was then able to be of some assistance when the move was made to the second camp.

Hunt found the new site to be an improvement over the previous sanctuary. Besides the running water piped into the camp by lengths of bamboo, a shower was provided by a nearby waterfall. However, the new camp had one fault. To conceal the camp from enemy observation aircraft, the men had cleared out all the undergrowth, while leaving the large trees to hide the settlement from view, but this still left the habitat of mosquitoes largely untouched.

When the rainy season commenced, the mosquitoes were given a breeding ground, and while the rains helped kept the enemy at bay, the biting and disease-carrying little insects furiously multiplied. The torrential downpours also made it difficult to secure food and medicine, and the increased population of mosquitoes brought the battle against malaria to a standstill.[20]

When Russell Volckmann and Don Blackburn came into the camp it looked huge to Volckmann, with its large main barrack with double-decker bunks made of bamboo and with several smaller buildings scattered about.

Food was a problem to Volckmann; he remembers eating a lot of rice and salt. In the morning he ate soft rice or pounded rice cooked like hot cereal.

Don Blackburn remembers waking up in a lower bunk and counting ten bunk beds on each side of the hut, enough to accommodate forty men. He was amazed at the sight. Having come into the camp unconscious, he cleared his head, got up, went out into the yard, and ran into Bill and Martin Fassoth.

Don remembered the brothers cursing each other constantly — "Listen, Martin, you silly son of a bitch." "God-damn you, Bill, you big blowhard." This was disconcerting at first until he got to know the affection that the brothers had for each other.[21]

Don Blackburn remembers his first breakfast at the Fassoths' camp as a rude awakening. Red Wolfe, a sergeant from the 200th Coast Artillery, had cooked the breakfast, and as Don was ready to eat, Red sat down and asked, "You and your pal are officers, aren't you?"

"Right, why?"

"I just want to warn you not to try and pull any rank around here. The war's over and in this camp there are no enlisted men and no officers. We're all alike. No rank. Take it or leave it."[22]

Nano Lucero, who came into the camp with Red Wolfe, Doyle Decker, Louis Dosh, Bob Chapin and Andy Roskopf, remembered how beautiful the camp looked, with buildings on stilts and facilities for cooking. He also remebered the latrines. There were slit trenches in the ground several yards from the sleeping quarters. Lucero couldn't believe that some of the men seemed too lazy or too sick to make it the few yards necessary to use the latrines, causing a mess in parts of the compound.[23]

Though Clay Conner was not in the large camp, he later came into Fassoth's third or fourth camp. He wrote in *True* magazine that Bill and Martin Fassoth had taken anything they could haul and moved back into the hills where they built a sanctuary for Americans and Filipinos. Of more than seventy Americans who had found haven there, most had escaped the Death March. The two brothers had Filipinos scouting for men fortunate enough to have fled the march, and guided them to their refuge. The Fassoths relied on many wealthy Spaniards and Filipinos donating money to supplement what the brothers were spending of their own funds to keep the camp supplied with food and medicine.

Dissension sometimes sprang up in the camp, as nerves were frayed by the appalling conditions men had suffered throughout their forced march. The Japanese patrols probing the area did not help the situation. The majority of the men were sick and feverish, with a multitude of diseases, of which malaria was the most prevalent. Scared and sick, the men were in no mood to deal with trivial irritations.

One point of contention was the matter of rank. There were some officers in the camp, from second lieutenants to colonels, but the largest group were enlisted men. Initially, many of the officers insisted on maintaining their privileges when it came to the burden of menial chores. The enlisted men built their own barracks and policed their own area. Special comforts such as lounging chairs, bunks and tables were built by the enlisted men with little support from the officers. Many of officers cooperated, but enough of them didn't to cause resentment toward all the officers. The enlisted men felt that they were all in it together, and that with the surrender of Bataan, the prerogatives of rank had ceased to exist. When they took the initiative to make others comfortable and care for the ailing, they thought they should get recognition for their work and have a say in the running of the camp. Instead, some were treated as though their resourcefulness was an outcome of their superiors' instructions, and were given to understand that they should be grateful for having intelligent officers. This did not affect a desirable outcome.

To the consternation of some of the higher-ranking officers, Bill and Martin Fassoth had decided that the purpose of the camp was rest and recuperation, not military operations. Jack Spies was one of the officers who pushed the idea of making the sanctuary a guerrilla camp. The members of the camp took a vote. Many of the men, especially the noncoms and privates, felt that the officers had surrendered them and thought that it should be the enlisted men's decision as to whether they would be guerrillas.[24]

Bob Lapham, who was never in the camp but who talked with several who were, told that there were quarrels among several in the camp at first. This was substantiated by other sources. Some wanted to organize and fight the Japanese, but others were satisfied to wait for the U.S. Army to liberate them. Many escapees, mainly lower-ranking officers and enlisted men, reasoned that military organization had ceased to exist and that everyone should be equal.

Another group, which was composed of Major Bernard Anderson, Captain Jack Spies, and Colonel Gyles Merrill, tried to convince Bill Fassoth to make the camp a military base and to place senior officers like themselves in command. Bill Fassoth emphatically refused this suggestion. He insisted that the camp belonged to him, not the U.S. armed forces, and that he had built it as a combination refuge and hospital rather than a military mechanism.

Arguments continued to ensue, with many becoming impassioned and prolonged. But over time the disgruntled left the camp.[25]

Bernard Anderson and Bert Pettitt continued their original plan of going to the southern islands of the Philippines to rejoin American forces which they were told had not surrendered.

Three days later they arrived at the Fassoths' second and largest camp, where approximately sixty Americans were recuperating. Here they met Captain Joseph Barker who described the guerrilla organization he and others were forming. Barker invited Anderson and Pettitt to join his unit. They told Barker they would consider his invitation and let him know their answer when they got to his headquarters at Timbo, Zambales.

Anderson and Pettitt left the Fassoths' camp and arrived at Timbo on June 26 where they again discussed guerrilla plans and organization with Captain Barker and with Lieutenant Colonel Thorp who was the commanding officer of the USAFFE (United States Armed Forces Far East) Luzon Guerrilla Forces. They decided to join the organization with the understanding that they would continue to the southern islands and further expand the organization as they traveled.

Anderson and Pettitt left Thorp's camp with Barker who was given command to the Eastern Central Luzon District, and with a representative of the Hukbalahap[26] organization. The Huk representative had been sent to Timbo to engage American officers to command the Huk guerrillas, numbering somewhere between fifteen hundred and two thousand men.

The group arrived at San Juan, San Luis, Pampanga on June 29 and spent a week traveling in the region trying to locate the military committee who controlled the troops they were to command. On finding the committee they had a three-day conference and discovered that the organization was socialistic and wanted to maintain the control of their troops and just use the Americans as an advisory council. Deciding that any advice they offered would be rejected, Anderson, Pettitt and Barker abandoned the mission.[27]

Doyle Decker spent several days resting and eating to rebuild his stamina. There were about forty Americans in theh Fassoths' camp, though the number varied, as some left when they were recuperated and others continued to find their way to the camp. Decker visited with many of the men and found that most had escaped from the "Death March." The information from the survivors reaffirmed Decker's decision to not surrender on Bataan.

Several men were planning to escape Luzon by boat and sail south, fifteen hundred miles, to Australia. Some wanted to form guerrilla units and use hit-and-run tactics against the Japanese. Others wanted to find an area free from the threat of capture and survive until American troops returned to the Philippines. All were confident it would only be a matter of time until their country would rescue them and take control of the islands from the Japanese invaders. Decker was reluctant to join any particular group until he had regained his strength and had time to evaluate his options. The monsoon season had started, but Decker had a dry place to sleep, a top bunk in the forty-foot-long barrack. He felt more secure than anytime in the last six months.

Nano Lucero and Red Wolfe had volunteered to help with food preparation. Lucero worked in the camp during the day, but feared a raid, so slept outside the camp at night. He had become something of a lone wolf and was alert to changes in the camp that might indicate trouble.

One morning as Decker was eating breakfast Bill Fassoth joined him. He was a large man with a booming voice.

"How are you doin'?" asked Bill.

"Great! I can't begin to thank you enough for what you're doing for us. What possessed you to build this camp?"

"Your last name is Decker? Correct?"

"Why, yes," replied Doyle.

"Funny, my mother's maiden name was Decker. Martin is my twin brother, but I'm older," laughed Bill as he related how the camp came into being. "I came to the Philippines in 1913 to run a mill for several American capitalists and after six years I took a long-term lease on 1,200 acres of the Dinalupihan Estate and 250 additional private acres of land. The Catholic Church owns the estate.

"Martin joined me to run the business in 1923 and we had a successful business going until the damn Japs messed things up. At the beginning of the war we lost our entire crop and had our house and the barrio where it was located looted and destroyed by the Jap bastards and their sympathizers."

As Bill continued his story, Martin walked up to him and Decker. "I think we need to build another barracks for the men," said Martin. "We're getting crowded up here."

"Hell, they can double up," replied Bill. "We ain't runnin' no Biltmore Hotel." Bill and Martin argued for a few minutes and finally Martin acquiesced. "Damn, Bill, I was only tryin' ta help the men. All you want to do is argue."

Bill laughed, "That's what Martin gets for bein' born second. I got all the best in me and he got leftovers."

"Yeah, but I'm not married and guess who gets his butt eat out every now and then." Martin looked smug at his retort. "Now, who's second?"

Martin walked off and Bill boomed out a big laugh. "We do this all the time. Don't pay any attention to us. It's how we communicate. Martin is invaluable to this camp and has great ideas for the men. Now, about how this camp came about...."

Bill related that his good friend Vicente Bernia, also a sugar planter, had visited them. He arranged for all their supplies from Manila, hauling them in a truck and an automobile his brother Arturo owned. They could travel to and from Manila freely, and when stopped at a Japanese checkpoint they would say the supplies were for their plantation in Gutad, Pampanga. Vicente bought most of the supplies at the Japanese bazaars and would show receipts so the Japanese would not question him very much. Then he would have the supplies moved from his plantation to the camp by men he trusted to keep the camp a secret.

When Bataan fell they conceived the plan of looking after American soldiers. Until the surrender they had not considered the possibility. The first two Americans who came into the camp were Frank Bernacki and Rudolph Wurzbach on April 17, eight days after the surrender. The next day a Filipino sergeant came into camp. The following day several soldiers were brought to them by friendly Filipinos. Most were starving and suffering from malaria or dysentery. Some were near death.

Vicente Bernia had helped make the camp a success; it was his idea to offer a fifteen-peso reward for every American the Filipinos would bring into camp. Vicente also had contacts in Manila with several wealthy businessmen who had established an underground network and were able to help with procuring additional supplies for the camp.

"I heard the guides mention a reward for finding American soldiers. Thank God we ran into your men when we did," replied Decker.

"It's a large undertaking and everyone is expected to pull their weight. When you're well enough, you will be expected to move on. There isn't enough room or food for everyone if they should stay."

"I can't thank you and your family and the Bernias enough. When I regain my strength I plan to move on. To be honest, I'm worried about how long this camp can go undetected."

Decker continued to rest for the next several days, and visited with several men, Including, Eugene Zingheim, the radio operator who had repaired a set so the GI's could listen to San Francisco station KGEI. From the news reports, they realized the Philippines could not expect relief any time soon.

Most new arrivals had little strength to work around the camp. And the increasing numbers of GI's caused a hardship in providing enough food, especially meat. Protein was necessary to rebuild muscle in emaciated bodies.

Vicente Bernia returned to camp from a trip to Manila to talk with Father Hurley, dean of the Ateneo de Manila, a college for boys, about a herd of cattle the owner had refused to sell to the Fassoths' so they could feed the Americans.

"What did Father tell you, Vicente?" asked Bill Fassoth.

Vicente grinned, "Feed my children."

Bill looked at Vicente for a moment and laughed. "Well the old son of a bitch had his chance. We will kill enough to feed the men. If the owner doesn't like it there are enough weapons in camp, so we don't need to worry about reprisal."

Bill asked for volunteers to pack meat back to camp from a hunt. Decker had sufficiently recovered and wanted to help. Having grown up on a farm and butchered cattle, he could be helpful on the packing trip. He, Earl Walk, Earl Oatman and five other men volunteered and left camp the next morning with two Negritos, who would kill the cattle.

At mid-afternoon, the group arrived in a valley southeast of the Fassoths' camp and discovered the cattle grazing. The Negritos quickly caught two bulls and cut their throats. The men tied the bulls' back legs with rope, threw the other ends over a tree limb and hoisted the carcasses head down. When the bulls were drained of blood, the men gutted and skinned the animals, cut the carcasses into quarters, then hanged them in the trees to cool.

The Negritos cut off the testicles of the bulls and ate them raw. The testicles were a delicacy they believed improved their virility. It made the Americans gag. "That was the most disgusting sight I've ever seen," said Earl Oatman.

The Americans salvaged the liver, and later roasted it for the evening meal. Earl Walk told Doyle Decker, "I can't believe I ate the liver. Hell, I don't even like liver. But it sure hit the spot."[28]

The men found a deep ravine and prepared a bed of freshly cut boho leaves. Earl Oatman ripped open two fingers on his left hand when he broke off some leaves from the bamboo. The cut bled profusely, but stopped after Oatman washed his hand in the stream, and wrapped his finger with a piece of shirttail for a bandage.[29]

After a sleepless night swatting mosquitoes, the men were awake at first light and each hoisted a quarter of the beef on his back for the trek back to camp. The weight of the beef and the jungle heat required several breaks for the men, and it was dusk when they were greeted by the smiles and hungry eyes of dozens of famished men. Those on the packing trip got double rations at the evening meal. One of the officers complained about this to Bill Fassoth. Generally in a good humor, Bill responded with a harsh look and a steel edge in his voice: "Look, I said everyone who went on the trip would get double rations. I didn't see you volunteer. If you want double rations, go on the next trip or keep your damn mouth shut." There were no further complaints and Decker's admiration for Bill Fassoth grew.

Decker never heard Bill mention reimbursement for what he and his family were providing. Many Americans would have perished if not for the Fassoths, Bernias, and other Filipinos. Decker went to sleep giving thanks for the Fassoths and for being guided into this haven of peace.[30]

Russell Volckmann recovered in late June and was able to help around the camp. In the middle of July he met Vicente Bernia. Bernia bubbled over with a contagious optimism that inspired Volckmann and Blackburn. His dark eyes flashed when he passed on whatever good news from America he had heard on the radio and told humorous stories about hoodwinking the Japanese.

From time to time the subject of guerrilla warfare would be brought up in the camp. Blackburn thought that most of the men who were not sick were apathetic and content to wait out the war.

Volckmann and Blackburn decided to continue their trip to the mountain area inhabited by the Igorot.[31] Meanwhile Vicente Bernia brought news from Walter Cushing, a guerrilla liaison officer who moved in and out of Manila disguised as a priest called Father Navarro. Cushing told of a West

Pointer named Pete Calyer who was organizing a guerrilla force near the town of Natividad, and this clinched Volckmann and Blackburn's decision to move out of the camp on August 15 to make contact with guerrillas.

Vicente guided the two to Shelby Newman's camp, but Blackburn came down with malaria, making the trip difficult. Vicente took the two to his home in Gutad, where a group of American officers were staying.

Doyle Decker raised with a strong work ethic, volunteered for jobs around the camp and gathered bananas, papaya, and other tropical fruits from the jungle. He also made two more meat-packing trips. On one endeavor he accompanied a Filipino to pick ears of corn for roasting. In addition to eating corn on the cob, the Filipinos roasted the corn until it was almost black and ground it, making a brew that tasted similar to coffee. They also brewed a beverage from scorched rice kernels.

As they approached the corn field, the Filipino motioned for Decker to stop and be quiet. Decker looked ahead and saw a family of monkeys in the field gathering corn in their arms. A baby monkey sat at the edge of the field and then began to wander away. It didn't get far when its vigilant mother dropped the corn she had gathered and grabbed the baby, gave it a scolding, bent it over her knees and swatted its rear end. The baby cried as the mother sat it down next to her and returned to gathering corn. The baby monkey looked around and, rather than wander away from its mother, began to pout.

The Filipino and Decker laughed, startling the monkeys who ran from the field with their corn and hid in the neighboring bamboo grove.

"Come, we gather corn. Then monkeys can finish their business," the Filipino laughed.

"These monkeys make their babies behave better than a lot of humans I know," said Decker.

The monsoons tapered to a couple of showers a day. Decker stayed busy around the camp making repairs to the buildings, and he helped with more food-gathering trips. The number of new arrivals straggling into the camp concerned him, and he believed it was only a matter of time until the Japanese located and raided their paradise. He made friends with several men; one he particularly admired was Jim Roulston. They spent hours talking about their families and religion. Jim was a Catholic from Boston, while Decker was a Baptist from Missouri, and although they came from different backgrounds and traditions, they respected each other and enjoyed comparing their families, memories, and experiences.[32]

Father Hurley, Dean of the Ateneo de Manila, sent two of his prize seminarians, both due for ordination to minister, to visit the men of the Fassoths' camp. The Americans built a big bonfire and gathered around for a sermon on the topic of the crucifixion, and then sang popular songs, duets and quartets, until midnight. Farther Hurley felt that in addition to the supplies he was helping send to the camp, that the men needed spiritual ministering.

The young priest heard confessions from the Catholics. One of the priests approached Decker and asked if he could be of any help.

"I'm not Catholic," said Decker abruptly. "I'm Baptist."

The young priest looked at Decker, tears welling in his eyes. "I'm here to help all God's children," he whispered, "not just Catholics."

The priest put his arm around Decker and whispered a short prayer for this child of God. From a box he had brought to camp he pulled out a Bible and gave it to Decker.[33]

"Here, this can be a comfort to you in the days to come."

The young priest also collected the names of the Americans in the camp. "We will try to get the names out by short-wave radio, so your families will know what has happened to you."[34,35]

In Doyle Decker's notes he listed the three deaths in the camp as taking place in a two-week period around the end of June 1942.[36] He described the men as having Christian burials. Russell Volckmann was described by Don Blackburn as presiding over one of the funerals. Decker described the mood in the camp after the deaths as depressed and anxious.

On several occasions, Decker was asked by John Boone to join his organization. Boone was described by Decker as a sniper who stayed outside the camp, only coming in for a day or two to rest and recruit men for his unit. "Come on, Decker," Boone would say. "I'm gonna form a group of men and organize the Filipinos into a guerrilla unit and cause the Japs a lot of trouble. Our tactics will be hit-and-run to keep them guessing as to where they will be hit next."

Decker hesitated, but he was uneasy about staying in camp. He discussed his concerns with Bob Campbell, a sergeant from Headquarters Battery, 200th Coast Artillery. They had a lot in common as they came from the same outfit. Campbell was also fearful about the future of the camp.[37]

In the late summer of 1942, Ray Hunt was bedridden with the chills and fever from malaria. Hoping that sunlight might help Hunt, Vernon Fassoth would frequently lug him outdoors. Beriberi, a vitamin B deficiency disease caused his hands, feet, and face to swell to such an extent that when they were touched indentations remained in the flesh, as though in putty. As if two diseases were not enough, Hunt also suffered from jaundice, causing him to urinate eight to ten times a night.

Filipinos had a lot of fascinating medical ideas and practices. Their effects varied from peculiar to fatal. Clay Conner had overcome a malaria attack by drinking tea made from an herb called dita, brewed by a friendly Negrito. Upon his search for more of the herb, he was told by a Filipino doctor not to try this, that only Negritos knew how to brew the plant.

In Hunt's case, one day a Filipino around the camp empathized with him and told him that if he wished to recuperate he should drink the blood of a black dog. The thought was disgusting to Hunt, especially since the blood was supposed to be obtained by cutting a dog's throat, but many Filipinos touted it as a guaranteed therapy. He was so frantic to recover that he was eager to try anything. When some of the revolting fluid was offered him in a coconut shell, he could gulp down only one swallow. After nothing useful occurred Hunt wondered if his faith was sufficient.

Next Hunt was told that work would help him. But even everyday camp chores seemed impossible in his weakened condition until the man who slept next to him, Lieutenant Bob Reeves of Ordnance, died. The camp rolled Reeves in a bamboo mat and held burial services. Soon three others died,[38] and it was obvious that more were in serious medial straits. Hunt resolutely went to work, putting his condition behind him. He would do a few duties, heave his previous meal and continue the chore. Hunt found his health improved, whether due to the work or his attitude he was not certain, but he was thankful.

Joe Barker returned to Timbo and sent Bernard Anderson and Bert Pettitt to a location fifteen kilometers southeast of San Miguel, Bulacan. Here they were in touch with a Mr. Gonzales, former-chief of police of San Miguel, and a Dr. Lapu, a professor of medicine at the University of Santo Tomas.

Anderson and Pettitt asked Barker for authorization to organize guerrillas in Bulacan, and Barker granted this. Establishing a headquarters, Anderson and Pettitt proceeded to organize the district, sending trustworthy men to the outlying provinces, investigating pro-Japanese Filipinos reducing banditry and other criminal activities, and helping settle disputes between individuals and organizations.

The work continued in this area until a Japanese raid at the end of August 1942. The headquarters was moved to Calumpit, Sibul Springs, Bulacan, where it remained until January 15, 1943, when the Japanese ordered all the area's families into Sibul Springs for an investigation and sent patrols into various localities to pick up those not complying with the order.[39]

Scouring for food and materials to maintain the camp took Bill Fassoth away for several days at a time. A meeting was held and the men elected an officer to act as head of the camp, another was in charge of supplies and yet another looked after the work-detail roster of men able to do chores around the camp, such as digging latrines, doing kitchen duty, gathering firewood, cleaning the area, and standing guard to watch for those approaching the camp. To give advance warning of Japanese patrols, an outpost was established on the trails leading into the site. The men at the outpost always had field glasses and weapons. They could look right into Manila Bay with their field glasses and even discern the number and name of ships in the harbor. Working two-hour shifts did not require a large part of anyone's time.

On a trip to the lowlands to visit his plantation at Pagalangang, Dinalupihan, Bill Fassoth received a note from a courier on his way to the mountain camp. Bill Jr. had sent the message and to his father's elation, Junior was headed for the camp. He was in Lubao, so Bill Sr. waited in Pagalangang for Junior's afternoon arrival, and then the two hurried back to surprise Catalina.

Bill Jr. had an interesting story to tell his family. He was on a ship that was sunk at Fort Hughes. The Japanese took all the survivors from Fort Hughes to Corregidor and then to the big prison camp in Tarlac, Camp O'Donnell. Here the prisoners were dying like flies at the rate of four to five hundred a day. Bill Jr. felt he was getting sick, so he and two other navy prisoners planned to escape and arranged to travel to Lubao. Bill Jr. and the two men had first dug and crawled under three barbed-wire fences. Whenever they heard the sentries, one of the escapees made the call of a young carabao calf calling to its mother, while another would pull the grass to mimic the calf eating. In one tense moment, Junior's shirt got caught in the wire and ripped just as the sentries walked by. Bill Jr. and his buddies began to make the carabao calls and rip the grass, which fooled the sentries.

At 3:30 A.M. they had run into an old man pasturing his carabao. He took them to his home and gave them a change of clothes, a sack, and a carabao to pasture the rest of the morning. Hiding the rest of the day, the three were put in a carretela, a buckboard cart, and transported that night to Angeles, Pampanga, where an old woman stalwartly maintained to the authorities that Junior was her son. Then the three were put into another carretela and hauled to Lubao, Pampanga, from where Junior traveled to the family plantation at Dinalupihan.

Through some influential Filipino friends, Bill Jr. was given forged papers with an assumed name so he could travel wherever he desired. He then became an additional source of food, material, and equipment for the camp.[40]

On July 4, 1942, Colonel Thorp issued his General Order Number One, setting forth rules and regulations for all authorized guerrillas to follow. A message to Australia was written and sent via a courier to Captain Ralph McGuire to be delivered to any submarine that might visit the islands, with the same message sent over the radio set in the camp. The message described the unit's accomplishments and gave recommendations for the promotions of officers and enlisted men.[41]

As the Fassoths' camp fill with escaped American soldiers, the men from the Philippine Army and Philippine Scouts were directed to Vicente Bernia's plantation. Vicente and his brother Arturo ministered to the Filipino soldiers and assisted their return to their home barrios.

Bill Fassoth estimated that there were between two and three hundred men who passed through his camp. There were never fewer than sixty American soldiers at any time from April 1942 to April 1943. The men were at liberty to hunt or go on hikes through the mountains to visit American officers and soldiers who had affiliated themselves with the guerrillas under Colonel Thorp and Captain Joe Barker in the Pampanga Mountains, or Captain Ralph McGuire in the Zambales Mountains. Most of the officers and men who joined the guerrillas were from the Fassoths' camp. They would meet at Gutad, at the home of Vicente Bernia and at times would have the luxury of drinking highballs made from alcohol obtained from fermented sugar or stolen from trains operated by the Japanese army.

In late July 1942, a written order was brought into the camp by Vicente Bernia designating the Fassoths' camp a military compound. Captain McGuire dispatched two groups of Filipino guerrillas numbering between seventy and eighty men through the camp. Many of the American soldiers in the camp did not want to be part of these guerrillas, and after a meeting the camp reverted to its rest-and-recuperation status.[42]

All was not sickness and depression in the Fassoths' Camp. On July 26, Lieutenant Arnold Warshell celebrated his birthday and gave Bill Fassoth twenty pesos to purchase a lichon, a whole roasted pig, which Catalina stuffed and prepared the night of the doctor's birthday. The men sat around while the pig was roasting and swapped stories and jokes and then had the feast at midnight. The food was rich and some ate too much, affecting their bowels the next day. But all the men enjoyed the party.[43]

One day Lieutenant Homer Martin came to Frank Bernacki and told him that he hadn't had a bowel movement in six days and wanted to know if Bernacki was having any problems. Bernacki assured Martin that not only was he not having a blockage, but like most of the men he was having too many movements. Martin asked if Bernacki knew of any native remedies for his situation. When Bernacki couldn't think of anything he suggested swallowing some soap. Martin didn't appreciate the humor in the proposal, so Bernacki recommended he see Dr. Warshell, who had some medications in his duffle bag. Martin approached Warshell and loudly, with obvious pain in his voice, said, "Doctor, I haven't shit in six days and I'm in terrible pain. Can you help me?"

Warshell, who could have a crude sense of humor at times, told Martin, "I don't have any medicine for your problem. Are you eating the same food as everyone else in camp?"

Martin replied that he was.

"My medical advice is to just keep eating," said Dr. Warshell, "you will either shit or explode."

Everyone in earshot started laughing, as Martin picked up a piece of wood and charged Warshell, spewing profanities.

Later on some of the men in camp boiled some leaves and roots provided by Negritos, and gave the brew to Martin to drink. The next day he crapped all over the mountain and was happy again.

In another incident, Lieutenant Dosh was suspicious that another officer was sneaking out of camp and eating some canned goods he'd stored in a duffle bag. It was agreed that when the officer took his usual afternoon stroll that the duffle would be searched, and sure enough they found cans of meat. Bernice Fletcher secured the bag. Dr. Warshell opened the 2.5-ounce cans of potted ham and distributed them among the men, including Lieutenant Martin and Bill Fassoth. Lieutenant Martin then hid the empty cans.

The next morning after breakfast it was time for the officer to take his usual walk, but he was heard shouting after he'd gone back to his bunk and looked into his duffle bag. "There's a thief in camp!" he bellowed, and he kept blabbering until Dosh told him what he had done. The officer continued to call Dosh and the rest of the camp thieves. Bernacki reminded the officer that the rule in camp was to share all the foodstuff that was found or brought into the camp. Bill Fassoth ended the commotion by stating that the rules were for everyone in camp and that they would be abided or those who had difficulty with them could leave.[44]

Leon Beck, after regaining his health, had found a small group of officers headed by Colonel Gyles Merrill. In an attempt to consolidate their guerrilla efforts, Merrill sent Beck with a letter addressed to the officers in the Fassoths' camp. The letter ordered the men to accompany Beck back to the lowlands and report to Merrill. The effort was met with indifference.[45]

Bill Fassoth's camp had grown considerably since Joe Barker and Ed Ramsey had visited it in mid–April. Now, in the early fall of 1942, nearly a hundred American soldiers were living at the camp full-time, men who had abandoned plans for escape and were waiting out the war. Ramsey had suffered a stroke while helping to organize Thorp's guerrillas, and had decided to return to the Fassoths' camp with Barker to get medical attention after hearing about the doctor in camp. The doctor about whom Barker had heard was Warshell, and he greeted Ramsey with a grimace.

After an examination, Warshell told Ramsey that he wasn't fit to travel for a few weeks. Though Ramsey protested, the doctor ordered him to shut up, reiterating the need for rest.

Though Barker was in a need of rest too, the doctor agreed that he could travel again in a week or two. It was decided that Barker would continue on to Manila and that Ramsey would join him as soon as his health improved.

Reluctantly Ramsey had to agree. The journey would wear further on him and he would be of little use to Barker. Drained physically and emotionally, Ramsey had ever regained the weight he lost on Bataan, and was now down to about a hundred and twenty pounds, well below his prewar weight.

By August 1942, Earl Oatman, without the benefit of medication, had survived malaria and regained his strength, thanks to the efforts of Bill and Martin Fassoth. Knowing he could not stay in the camp forever, Oatman had heard that the northern part of the Zambales Mountains was covered with dense jungle and except for the Negritos was largely uninhabited.

There were many stories about the dangers of the jungle. One that worried Oatman was about the club-headed python, said to grow up to thirty feet in length. The snake was said to kill its prey by hanging from tree limbs above the jungle trails and then, when prey passed beneath, striking with its head. Then the snake was said to drop to the ground and coil about the stunned prey, squeezing it to death.

Oatman wasn't sure he believed the story, but had learned that pythons were good to eat, having helped devour a 12-foot snake during the first few days he and Hank Winslow were in the Fassoths' camp. Oatman knew that wild pig, deer, and iguanas were available, provided he could persuade a friendly Negrito to hunt for him.

It was reassuring to know that the Japanese were afraid of the Negritos, who had killed Japanese soldiers patrolling in the mountains. Oatman reasoned that the Japanese were not likely to have as many patrols in the mountains, so they were a place to survive the war.

Winslow was not ready to leave camp, so Oatman left with two others for the northern Zambales. Bill Fassoth arranged for a Negrito to guide the three Americans over the Zambales mountain range to Zambales Province, where they could contact Filipino guerrillas to guide them farther north.

It took two days for the three Americans to travel to Captain Ralph McGuire's headquarters. After arriving and having a meal, they met with

McGuire and told him that they had come from the Fassoths' camp and were on their way to the northern area of Zambales Province. McGuire told the Americans that the region was very remote and that it would be difficult for them to survive, particularly if they were to need medical attention. He suggested they join his guerrilla unit, as he had safety in numbers. He would supply them with food, clothing, and medical attention. The other two accepted McGuire's offer, but Oatman was not sure he wanted to be a guerrilla and asked for time to give it consideration.

McGuire asked Oatman to spend several weeks with a staff sergeant assigned to a guard post on one of the trails leading from Iba, the capital of Zambales. The sergeant was recovering from a nervous breakdown and Oatman's presence might help his recovery. Oatman agreed to help the sergeant and was taken to the post the following morning.

The sergeant was living with a Filipino family near the trail he was assigned to guard. The sergeant told Oatman how McGuire's unit had arrived in Zambales Province. Near the end of the fighting on Bataan, McGuire was ordered to take approximately twenty men and work their way north to establish a guerrilla organization behind enemy lines. Near Olongapo, Bataan, they ambushed a Japanese convoy of trucks on the main road between Olongapo and Dinalupihan. The lead truck was blown up with explosives placed on the road. As the Japanese in the remaining trucks emerged, they were killed by rifle fire from American soldiers hidden on both sides of the road. The deadly ambush was a picture the sergeant could not erase from his mind.

Oatman ate well for the next two weeks while on guard duty with the sergeant. He especially liked the different tropical fruits that were available. The food and tranquility were tempting, but Oatman did not want to be a guerrilla. He felt that, in time, guerrilla activities would prove harmful to the Filipino families associated with the activity.

Oatman returned to McGuire's headquarters and informed him of his decision. McGuire suggested that Oatman return to the Fassoths' camp for further consideration of his position. Oatman declined the offer of a Filipino guide and traveled alone back to camp, soaked by intermittent and at times heavy rain. Hourly Oatman stopped and rolled up his pant legs to remove the leeches that had attached themselves while he walked on the wet trail. It was a loathsome experience, but one that had to be endured. After pulling or scraping the leeches off his skin, the area would ooze blood, attracting still more leeches, to Oatman's consternation.[46]

In late August 1942, Russell Volckmann and Don Blackburn were guided to Pete Calyer's headquarters by Vicente Bernia. They were surprised at the luxurious sanctuary provided by the Jingco family, wealthy Chinese-mestizo

Left to right: The author, Earl Oatman, Hank Winslow and Bob Mailheau, Riverside, California, September 1996.

rice planters whose daughters competed to see which one could cook the better food for their guests. Despite the lush accommodations, Volckmann and Blackburn were anxious to travel north and begin organizing the populace into a guerrilla force.

On their trek north, the two American officers stopped at Timbo, headquarters for Colonel Thorp, where they met Captain Wilber Lage, Thorp's adjutant, who in turn introduced them to Captain Joseph Barker. Barker provided the name of a contact at Mt. Arayat who could aid in their travels north through Japanese-occupied territory.

As Clay Conner regained his health, he wanted to do more than hide from the Japanese. He talked to Jimmy Espino about becoming active in guerrilla warfare. Jimmy told Conner that he had an uncle in the town of Samal named Pablo Aquino, who was one of the political leaders, and that the people followed him. He was pro-American, and he would do whatever they advised, if they cooperated with him. Frank Gyovai also wanted to investigate the possibilities of guerrilla life and joined Conner as he went to Samal to meet Jimmy Espino's uncle.

Fifteen men from Samal gathered together to discuss the potential of a guerrilla organization. They chose to call themselves the USAFFE guerrilla forces — United Stated Armed Forces Far East — and Conner was made commander.

A table of organization was prepared and men were assigned to lead companies and platoons. Conner trusted them, for they had nothing to gain by doing otherwise; their lives were now at stake. The Filipinos had more to lose than the Americans. Their wives, children, and homes, were at risk, as well as their lives. Conner admired them for their bravery, because their country was overrun with the enemy — a savage enemy willing to kill on the slightest suspicion of any antagonistic operation.

Conner and Gyovai discussed the implications of recruiting Filipinos into guerrilla warfare. The Japanese had gone through the area — every house — and they had forced people to put a paper flag in the front of their homes, a flag about eight inches square with a rising sun in the middle. On the flag, they had people list the names of everybody who lived in that particular house. The Japanese wanted a quick count of all the people in the area, especially the young men. The Japanese knew that guerrilla warfare was in its infancy and that the Filipino people were organizing against them. In flash raids the Japanese would come into an area, and then call the people in from the fields to see if everyone was present. If one of the young men was missing, they killed all the people in the house — men, women, and children. They would burn the house down and then leave, saying that the missing man was obviously in the guerrilla forces, and that he was a traitor to the Japanese Empire. It could have been that the young man was away in Manila. He could have been hunting in the mountains. But it didn't matter. The Japanese wanted the young men kept close to the area. They didn't want them traveling about, and they didn't want them organizing an underground.[47]

Doyle Decker had become restless; his intuition told him to move on. Several men in the camp had the same feeling. Bob Campbell, Henry Winslow, and Coleman Banks wanted to leave with Decker. The increasing numbers of Filipinos coming into and out of the camp made the soldiers nervous that a raid was imminent. Though John Boone had talked with them, none wanted to join his unit. They packed their few belongings, and early one morning in the middle of September 1942, they bid tearful goodbyes to the other men. Decker had been in camp two and one half months and it seemed almost like home. The other GI's were hard to leave behind.

Decker talked with Lucero and Wolfe. "Hey, why don't you go with us? We made it out of Bataan; we can make it to Subic Bay."

"Dammit, Decker, I'm not ready to leave," said Wolfe. "I damn near died on the trip to this place and I'm just not ready to leave."

"Me neither," Lucero concurred. "You know I don't sleep in camp, so I'm not worried about capture. I just don't want to make another trip."

"Good luck, Decker," Wolfe said softly, clearing his throat. "It's been good knowing you. I hope we see each other again when this gawddamn mess is over with." He walked away, unable to continue.

"I'll miss you, old friend," said Lucero, as he slapped Decker on his back. "God go with you." He hurried off to catch up with Wolfe.

Decker looked for Bill Fassoth, but he had left camp to look for provisions. Decker felt a void at missing an opportunity to thank Bill and tell him what the camp had meant to him. He knew he couldn't have made it this far without the help of the Fassoths.

The four GI's decided to go west over the mountains to Olongapo near Subic Bay. They hoped to find a boat and escape south to Australia. A long journey lay ahead as the four Americans trudged hesitantly into the mountainous jungle.[48]

Chapter 6
Raids

One thing Ray Hunt learned in war is that life is not a series of clear-cut decisions between good and evil: it is sometimes a succession of choices among alternatives that are disagreeable.[1]

In September 1942, a letter dated July 26 was received by various guerrilla leaders from Lieutenant Col. Claude A. Thorp's headquarters. In it he assumed command of all Luzon guerrilla units and assigned leadership to the various regions of Luzon, designating Captain Joseph R. Barker II as commander of central Luzon, including Manila; Captain Ralph Praeger as commander of northern Luzon; and Captain George J. "Jack" Spies as commander of southern Luzon.

The escaped American soldiers on Luzon were already in a chaotic state without any direction from higher authority. Then Thorp's organization was shaken with his capture in October 1942 and when Spies was killed on his journey to assume his command. According to Bob Lapham, Spies did not get along with Filipinos and was killed by unfriendly forces.[2] Barker began recruiting in Manila, having assumed command when Thorp was captured, but three months later, Barker too was apprehended, in Manila.

On September 9, 1942, Colonels Noble and Moses dispatched a native requesting a meeting at Barrio Benning with Russell Volckmann and Donald Blackburn. When they arrived, Noble and Moses were waiting. After catching up on their experiences, the men began thrashing out their future plans.

Moses and Noble had been with the Philippine Army three months prior to the outbreak of war. With only ten days of training the Twelfth Infantry was put to the test when the Japanese landed in North Luzon in La Union province and they rushed to meet the attack. When their defenses crumbled, Noble and Moses escaped and made their way to Baguio, where they joined Colonel Horan's retreat from the summer capital. Ultimately Moses and Noble rejoined the withdrawing USAFFE forces and commanded regiments of the Eleventh Division on Bataan.

Colonel Horan, the senior American commander in the north, had followed orders from General Wainwright and surrendered. Following Horan's example, many other officers also capitulated, but many of the units they commanded refused to surrender and continued to resist the Japanese onslaught.

Those commanders still active were Captain Ralph Praeger, Cagayan Province and Apayao, and Governor Roque B. Ablan of Ilocos Norte Province who had departed to the mountains where he had organized a guerrilla force.

Since Moses was the senior U.S. officer in North Luzon, Volckmann asked if he had assumed overall command. To his surprise, Moses answered that he had not, but was trying to recover his health and do some preliminary work. Volckmann responded that he and Blackburn were prepared to work under Moses and Noble's command when they assumed the necessary authority of the area.

The next day Volckmann and Blackburn were guided north by Herb Swick, another American officer working with Moses and Noble. After arriving at Bokod, they began to organize their area of operation. Three weeks later Moses and Noble came into the camp, having assumed command of northern Luzon, and authorized Volckmann and Blackburn to continue organizing guerrilla units in their area.

Per Dr. Warshell's recommendation, Joe Barker rested for a week before beginning his trip to Manila where he would begin organizing Filipinos. Barker and Ramsey agreed that after Ramsey's health improved he would go to Bataan and incorporate John Boone's guerrillas under their authority. With their hard work in central Luzon and Barker's trip to Manila, they would have consolidated half of the region Barker had been directed to command by Thorp.

Negritos lived in the Zambales Mountains and maintained a primitive way of life. The men wore G-strings and a few wore an undershirt. While the men loved to hunt, the women did most of the work. The women usually wore a dirty piece of cotton or wrapped themselves in rags. The most primitive Negritos, who lived in the most secluded part of the mountains, wore no clothing at all. Their children ran around, playing with sticks and stones. Raising barely enough to subsist, the short-statured, nomadic people traded corn for rice. Wherever the men went, the women followed with the children and their domesticated animals — dogs, pigs, and chickens. Some of the women came to the Fassoths' camp to pound palay for additional rice to feed their families.

It was through the capture of one of the Negrito men in the lowlands by the Japanese that the camp was raided on September 25, 1942. The Negritos had gone to the lowlands with some wooden parts for a Filipino-constructed plow. On rounding a bend on the river bank, one man walked into a company of Japanese soldiers who were searching for Filipinos carrying weapons.

The Japanese took this man prisoner and questioned him concerning Americans hiding in the mountains, and particularly about Bill Fassoth and his family running a refugee camp. A reward had been advertised for the capture of Bill and any member of his family. Additionally, there was a reward for Vicente Bernia, who the Japanese had connected with the camp.

The Negrito was taken by the Japanese to San Fernando, Pampanga, for investigation by the officer in charge of the local garrison. Through threats and torture with boiling water poured on his head,[3] the Negrito finally consented to lead the Japanese into the hills and locate the camp.

Bill was in the lowlands when the Negrito was captured and had been told of this by a runner. He dispatched the runner to the camp to give them advance warning, instructing the camp to break up, hide the supplies, and vacate the area.

Members of the camp took their possessions and moved in various directions. After not observing any Japanese patrols for a couple of days, some of the men thought that the camp would not be raided and returned. Bill was told that sixteen men had returned to the camp, so he sent another message to again vacate. The sixteen refused to believe the camp would be raided and so remained. So sure were these men that they were safe that they failed to place anyone at an outpost to give advance warning. The one person who was selected to watch the camp at night went to sleep on the job.[4]

When Earl Oatman reached the Fassoths' camp on September 23, 1942, he learned that Hank Winslow had left camp with Doyle Decker, Bob Campbell, and Coleman Banks.[5] There were now fewer than two dozen men in the camp, including several Filipino helpers. Bill, Martin, Catalina, and other Filipinos had left the camp.

The following morning, those in the camp discussed their options as it had been several days since the warning from Bill Fassoth. They decided to post additional guards and "sit tight" as there was plenty of food and they required additional time to plan their future. There were few choices; the most obvious one entailed joining one of the guerrilla organizations. Oatman had already rejected this option.

Late in the afternoon, several of the men went to the outpost guard station to observe the trail leading up from the lowlands, confident that if the Japanese raided the camp, they would use this trail. The surrounding terrain was too rough and densely covered to permit a Japanese patrol from any other direction. There were four Americans and several Filipinos who had been cutting trees near the outpost. They divided the night into two-hour shifts. The next morning they were relieved by several men from the camp who remained on guard during the day.

As the day passed, Oatman mentally rehearsed an escape plan he had devised to use if the camp was raided. He slept in the lower bunk next to the back door of the main building, the same bunk he and Hank Winslow had used when they first occupied the barrack. The door opened adjacent to the kitchen lean-to and was only ten feet from the corner of the building. From here there was cleared, even ground to the bank of a dry, boulder-strewn wash, six to eight feet wide. The far bank of the wash was covered in natural vegetation, and a short distance away was a steep slope leading to the jungle-covered mountain immediately west of the camp. Once Oatman passed the cleared area and wash, he would be protected from view and safe from pursuing Japanese. He was confident this plan would work as long as he had advance warning.

Before dusk, four men left camp to relieve those on guard duty. There was a full moon the night of September 24. As usual, the men sat and talked after the evening meal, and then made ready for sleep. The light from the full, tropical moon and the sound of nocturnal insects and geckos provided a misleading tranquility. Oatman was apprehensive though, as he removed his shoes and lay down, fully clothed. Another day had passed without the camp being raided.[6]

About two hundred Japanese soldiers were led to the camp by the Negrito and a Filipino who was led by a rope tied around his neck. The soldiers arrived at the foothills about 5:30 P.M. on that full-moon night. As the soldiers climbed the mountain trail they stopped at Filipino homes along the way and searched the residences, abusing the inhabitants and accusing them of aiding American soldiers. The Negrito delayed the arrival at the camp and gave the Americans additional warning, by leading the patrol to an outpost where two Filipinos were making paddles for canoes. The Filipinos were not connected with the camp, but on hearing the approaching patrol ran to the camp and warned the Americans. The men in the barracks tumbled out in every direction, with ten of the men escaping and six taken prisoner. The six were men too sick to escape and included Walter Chatham, Earl Walk, and Willard Smith.[7] Several shots were fired but no one was hit in the melee.

The Japanese also captured an old Filipino man and a small boy who were sleeping in the kitchen-helper's shanty. After searching for supplies and information, the Japanese set fire to all the buildings in the camp. They took the three Filipino men they had captured and bayoneted them. The little boy began crying and one of the soldiers decapitated the child with a sword.

One of the Filipino men, who the Japanese thought was dead, regained consciousness and crawled away. He was brought to the lowlands to a doctor for treatment. Bill Fassoth later came across this man who told of the harrowing experience.

The six American captives were taken to the lowlands by a different trail than the Japanese had used to find the camp. Upon reaching the lowlands, the Negrito was given some money and released. The Japanese then took the American prisoners to Dinalupihan and then on to San Fernando, Pampanga, by truck, where they were placed in the provincial jail. Those most needing medical help were moved to the provincial hospital.[8]

The six men captured at Fassoth's camp were put in one four-by-four cage. They were released from the iron prison once a day to take care of bodily functions. This continued for three weeks. Though only a corporal, Walter Chatham was the highest ranking man captured. The Japanese interrogated him incessantly about the Bataan operation, but there was nothing he could tell them. Infuriated, they continually beat him with a blackjack and a baseball bat. Then they shoved bamboo slits under his fingernails, and lit them. He passed out from the pain. The interrogators then drenched him with water, stepped on his bare feet with hobnailed boots, split his cranium with a baseball bat, and threw him down a stairway.[9]

Ed Ramsey had chosen to leave the camp with Dr. Warshell and Martin Fassoth who guided him to the hut of a Negrito high in the mountains. They remained there through the first week of October, and it was an amazing experience. Their craggy little host had three young wives, and he regaled his guests with stories of his sexual prowess and conveyed conjugal insight to his visitors. He was entertaining, telling his yarns in broken English, using the most elaborate assortment of profanity.[10]

Most of the Americans and Filipinos escaping the Japanese raid ran down a trail to a small barrio named Pita at the base of Mt. Malasimbo. The place was too small to accommodate all the people so they then split into smaller groups. Nano Lucero, William Coward and Raymond O'Conner went with Romana Romero and her children to Malabo. Coward and O'Conner then went on to Baruya.[11]

Ray Hunt felt that he owed his freedom and his life to the diseases that had nearly killed him, specifically to his kidney problems. When the raid occurred, he was on the opposite side of the barracks urinating for the umpteenth time that day and rolling a cigarette from home-grown tobacco. Carefully harvested and cut by Hunt, the treasure was carried in a small bamboo tube, something so precious that rather than run immediately Hunt fumbled to retrieve the tube before making a hasty retreat. Hunt then fell and lost his sense of direction. Too weak to run, he walked to the edge of a nearby creek, and stumbled over the bank. Then he followed the winding streambed and crawled out on the other side and into the jungle. As he pushed through bamboo thickets, he heard the sound of rifles in the camp.

Earl Oatman had just fallen asleep when something told him there was imminent danger. He quickly rolled from his bunk, grabbed his shoes, and "hit the floor running." He could hear Japanese shouting orders as he ran across the cleared area at the back of the main building and jumped across the dry wash. There were sounds of men running, rifle fire and Japanese voices. Without looking back, Oatman clawed his way through the brush and up the side of the mountain, avoiding large rocks and trees. Soon, the sounds and frenzied activity were behind and below him, and he was conscious only of his labored breathing. As he calmed down from his frantic escape, he became aware that his hands and feet were bruised and bloody from numerous cuts. He had lost his shoes and now walked barefoot toward the large creek that paralleled the trail to Zambales Province. Another twenty minutes of climbing and Oatman realized that he had escaped. Still moving cautiously, in the next clearing he came upon a Negrito hut where he could hear voices talking excitedly. He called hello to them in Tagalog (Apo), and identified himself as an American soldier. It was Oatman's good fortune that one of the Negritos had been employed by Bill Fassoth to hunt wild pigs for the camp.

Two Negritos emerged from the hut and began talking to Oatman in Tagalog. He could only understand a few words, but gesturing toward the camp, he told them about the Japanese raid and his escape. By this time the rifle fire had stopped, and by the glare from the burning buildings the Negritos understood what had happened.

One of the Negritos motioned for Oatman to follow him and then proceeded up the hill. When they came to the bank of the creek that flowed near the camp, the Negrito pointed upstream, saying in Tagalog that it was the trail to Zambales. Oatman tried to get the Negrito to guide him, but after a short distance the Negrito disappeared into the jungle. Oatman was now alone, but fortunately he had traveled the trail twice already, although in daylight. It was sufficiently light for him to stay on the trail, and he soon reached the summit and started downward towards the lowlands of Zambales Province.

Exhausted from fear and the exertion of the night's events, Oatman also was dealing with a left leg that had become numb and almost useless. Oatman had to lift his leg with his hands to step over a rock or log on the trail. It slowed his progress greatly, but at dawn he had arrived at a Filipino nipa house, adjacent to the trail and near the foothills. He told the occupants who he was and what had happened at the Fassoths' Camp. Oatman requested help getting to the nearest barrio. Because couldn't walk, the Filipinos placed him on a carabao, his long legs touching the ground on each side of the animal. The nearest barrio, Bujaoen, was a mile from the house.

Halfway to the barrio, the Filipinos passed a small hut on the left bank of a creek and fifty yards off the trail. Here Oatman was taken to talk with the barrio Lieutenant a man named Rodriquez. Captain Rodriquez turned out to be the local Filipino guerrilla organization's leader.

Oatman told Captain Rodriquez about the raid on the Fassoths' Camp and about his escape. He also requested a place to hide until he could contact other American soldiers. Rodriquez talked briefly with his mother and with other curious Filipinos who had gathered at the house. Oatman could not understand what was being said as they were speaking Ilocano, the dialect used in Zambales Province. Rodriquez then turned to Oatman and spoke to him in English, telling him that he would take him to a small nipa house hidden nearby and that food would be arranged for him. As they continued to talk, several Filipino men arrived and conversed with Rodriquez. He then told Oatman that some Americans were hiding nearby and that the Filipinos would take Oatman to them rather than hiding him in the nipa house.

Arriving at a hut occupied by the hiding Americans, Oatman was introduced to Colonel Gyles Merrill, Cavalry, U.S. Army; Lieutenant Colonel Peter D. Calyer, Thirty-first Infantry, Captains George Crane and Richard Kadel, Field Artillery; Major Roy Tuggle, Corps of Engineers; and Private Leon Beck. All had escaped the Death March before reaching San Fernando, Pampanga Province, and had lived with various Filipino families in Pampanga before crossing the mountains into Barrio Bujaoen. Beck had briefly been in the Fassoths' camp.

The officers had watched Oatman ride by on the carabao earlier that morning, but kept quiet and remained out of sight. When Filipino guerrillas from the barrio told them about the Japanese raid on the Fassoths' Camp and of Oatman's poor physical condition, the officers sent for him. At the time Oatman believed he was the only American to escape the attack.

Worried that the Japanese might follow him, Oatman told the officers that he had followed the same trail he had used several days previous on his return to the Fassoths' camp. He was told that the nearest Japanese garrison was in San Marcelino, nine miles west of Barrio Bujaoen. Any movement by the Japanese was quickly reported to Colonel Merrill through Captain Rodriquez's guerrillas.[12]

Ray Hunt was startled by a commotion in the underbrush. It was another survivor from the camp, a man named Mackenzie. Mac had some matches and tobacco, so they started the new day by smoking cigarettes and discussing their situation. Not sure of which direction to take, they nevertheless moved from the camp. The next day a crowing of a rooster woke them from a restless sleep. The sound of the rooster meant there were people nearby, so the two walked in the direction of the sound.

They found an old Filipino and a young girl who graciously fed them. Fearing that a Japanese patrol might be close by, Mac was adamant about returning to the lowlands, and departed, while Hunt decided to remain in the mountains.

The next day a typhoon, which the natives call a *baguio,* blew through the area with its troubled winds. It put out Hunt's fire, took the roof off the hut where he was taking shelter, and covered the mountain trails with fallen trees that looked from a distance like matchsticks. Now without food stores and fire, his feet deteriorating from the rocky trails, Hunt foraged and ate guavas and green bananas for the next four days.

Having rested, Hunt began working his way into the mountains when he came to a village inhabited by Negritos. They fed Hunt some camotes and green papaya soup, and then applied their primitive remedies to his feet. After he had rested, the Negritos guided him down the mountain to a Filipino family.

Another group of six escapees from the camp had set up an outpost with Martin Fassoth in another part of the mountains known as Isip in Bataan. Vicente Bernia and Bill Fassoth accounted for all the men remaining in the camp and moved to another location. Some of the men were placed with various Filipino families with promised payment for their services after the war. Upon the return of Vernon's group, Bill Fassoth counted himself along with Vicente and Arthur Bernia. There were now twenty-one men in the new camp.[13]

Camp 3

Bill Fassoth had all the members of his family with him as he began to build a new camp. Bill visited the men he had placed with Filipino families to ascertain whether they were getting proper care. These men often visited the camp to share stories with their friends.

As before, Bill situated the camp near a stream for water and bathing. The mountain stream was clean and there was plenty for drinking.

Bill made a trip to Isip to check on Martin and the men with him. On his way back to the new camp, Bill visited the camp the Japanese had raided. He found that the big American flag they had received from Father Hurley had been torn to shreds and draped over a tree stump. Radios and batteries were smashed into small pieces and the kitchen building was destroyed. Bill and a companion buried the dead.

Back at the new camp, Bill didn't keep a large supply of food on hand, prepared to move to avoid the Japanese patrols that continuously searched for guerrilla bands. Bill didn't allow Filipino guerrillas to stay near the camp, as many bandits disguised themselves as guerrillas and plundered and killed innocent people. There were many instances where bandits had accused someone of being a Japanese sympathizer, and stolen supplies, money, jewelry, and clothing. Now there were two enemies to dread, the Japanese and bandits.

Hipolita San Jose and Lieutenant Warshell traveled with Catalina from place to place, caring for the men who were sick and needed medical attention.

There were a lot of people helping supply the camps and it was decided to destroy any records and pictures that might identify these people from Japanese reprisal. Vicente Bernia had a photographer take pictures of everyone and everything in the second camp for future substantiation of their efforts, but Bill Fassoth decided those pictures would be dangerous in the wrong hands and had them burned.[14]

After the raid on the second camp, Bill Fassoth had begun to make arrangements for selected Filipino families to assume the perilous assignment of sheltering American. Ray Hunt was the ward of Mr. and Mrs. Louis M. Franco who lived in the village of Tibuc-Tibuc near Gutad at the extreme western edge of Pampanga province, ten miles north of the northwest corner of Manila Bay. The Francos could not speak English, but cared for Hunt as though he were one of their own.

They built Hunt a grass-covered hut near a small river that wound through a flat field. They supplied Hunt with food and other items by wading in the stream to avoid creating a path that could lead Japanese patrols to his location. Hunt was also given a 16 gauge shotgun pistol for protection. He was afraid to fire the weapon, fearing it might explode in his hands. Later Hunt was given a weapon he felt was more dependable, an Enfield rifle.

While Hunt recuperated, the Francos brought him books. Hunt read the books over and over, gaining knowledge of the history and geography of the Philippines. He also began to practice the Pampangano dialect of the area. As his linguistic studies progressed and his health improved, Hunt would periodically visit local homes and nearby villages where he could practice his vocabulary and make Filipino friends. He also gained insight about Filipino psychology and customs.

His Filipino friends did more than teach him their tongue and traditions. They also showed Hunt ways to supplement his food supply. They instructed him on how to make and set snares to catch wild chickens, and he watched his friends catch birds by throwing a seine over their roosting places in the tall grass. The same nets were used to catch fish from the river. The Filipinos were inventive, using a pile of rocks in the streambed where they were left for a week or so; then they would cover the rocks with a large net, weigh down its outer edges, then slide their hands under the net and remove the rocks one by one until only fish remained inside.

From time to time, Hunt would have an American visitor. One night a Japanese patrol was known to be nearby and Louis Barella was moved with Hunt into a large cogon-grass field. They were covered with a mosquito net secured at he corners by tying it to twisted stems of the grass. This thwarted the Japanese and the mosquitoes, but not a large rat that made its way under the net, but could not find its way out. The rat kept Hunt and Barella worried until Hunt, in frustration, lifted the net to let it scamper out. The mosquitoes exploited the situation. One thing Hunt learned in war is that life is not a series of clear-cut decisions between good and evil. It is sometimes a succession of choices among alternatives that all are disagreeable.[15]

Earl Oatman remained with Merrill's group for two and a half months. During this time he was well fed and he passed the time learning about the men in the camp. Colonel Merrill and Lieutenant Colonel Calyer were West Point graduates. Major Tuggle had been an engineer in the Philippines prior to the war and had been given a commission after the start of hostilities. Captains Kadel and Crane were artillery officers attached to Philippine Army units during the fighting on Bataan.

Early one morning Oatman was awakened by gunfire. Although startled and apprehensive at first, other men in Merrill's camp recognized that the gunshots were from American weapons. A Filipino guerrilla was dispatched to determine the cause of the shooting. Thirty minutes later a file of Visayan[16] Filipinos, led by Lieutenant Bill Gardner, Thirty-first Infantry, U.S. Army, approached the camp. He related to the officers what had just occurred. His squad of Filipino guerrillas had been ambushed by the eldest son of Captain Rodriquez as they approached the creek via a trail in the bottom of a ravine. During the skirmish, Captain Rodriquez's son was killed and several men on both sides were wounded.

It was not clear why Lieutenant Gardner's group was ambushed by the local guerrillas. When notified of his son's death, Captain Rodriquez was infuriated and demanded that Gardner be court-martialed by Colonel Merrill. The colonel told Rodriquez that he would investigate the matter. In the meantime Gardner and his men were kept inside Merrill's house to protect them from retaliation by Rodriquez.

Early the next morning, Merrill told Gardner and his men to leave the area immediately and not return. Although it was obvious that Gardner's men had been ambushed, the volatile nature of the situation dictated that they depart the area.

A short time later, Merrill's camp was alerted to a Japanese patrol. Merrill decided to move deeper into the jungle and away from Barrio Bujaoen. The men packed their few belongings and moved to a small, primitive shack deep in the forest, surrounded by huge tropical trees. The one-room shack was raised two feet off the ground and had one was open, facing a small stream. While Merrill's group was in this location the camp was hit by a typhoon. It was the first storm of this magnitude that Earl Oatman had experienced since he had arrived on Luzon. For more than twenty-four hours the hut was pelted with driving rain and strong winds that sounded like freight trains thundering down on them. All the men could do was huddle on the floor of the shack and watch the towering trees bend in the wind, hoping that none of the giants would fall on them. They could hear trees falling all around the shack, and feel the ground shake as nearby trees toppled. Eventually the winds calmed and the men thought that they were then in the eye of the storm. A few hours later the winds picked up again and they experienced another round of heavy rains and extreme winds.

Several days later the group was informed by the local guerrillas that they could return to the house near Barrio Bujaoen. As they walked along the trail they encountered huge trees lying across or parallel to their path. Some of the trees were more than 100 feet long and eight to ten feet in diameter at their base. If one of these giants had fallen on the shack all the men would have been killed.[17]

Doyle Decker, Bob Campbell, Hank Winslow and Coleman Banks were on the trail out of the Fassoths' camp when they saw a Japanese patrol. Rushing out onto the point of a ridge overlooking a shallow valley, they found sheer cliffs dropping thirty feet on three sides to the valley floor. Decker, noting the tall trees growing from the valley floor next to the cliffs, told the other three that their only chance was to jump into the tree tops and climb down to the ground below.

All made the jump and climbed down unharmed except for Decker who grasped for branches and leaves all the way to the ground, hitting with a thud. He jumped up, but had a severe pain in his lower back. He then raced to catch up with the other three as they avoided the patrol. Decker's right leg began to ache, but he was able to keep up with the group as they traveled down a new trail.

After several days of hiking and staying with friendly Negritos, the group was guided to a Filipino's house. He was amicable and welcomed the four Americans as though they were long-lost friends. He introduced himself as Leon and told the soldiers that his family had been entertainers in Manila before the war. They were from the Olongapo area and had moved back when the Japanese captured Manila.

At night Leon and his family brought out their guitars and sang. Winslow and Banks had good voices and joined in the singing, to the delight of Leon and his family.

During the ensuing weeks, the GI's found it hard to believe there was a war going on nearby. It was peaceful with Leon's family. The rest and the relaxed atmosphere helped the pain in Decker's leg subside.

Leon told the GI's, "We have heard rumors of American officers nearby, but no one knows their location." Other rumors filtered in about Japanese raids in neighboring villages. Decker thought this could be the local people's way of telling them it was time for their group to move on.

One morning a young Filipino delivered a handwritten message from an American colonel to Leon's house. The colonel wanted the GI's to move out of the area because he felt there were too many Americans in his vicinity and their discovery by the Japanese could put Filipino families in danger.

Leon told the soldiers that he had a Negrito friend who would take care of them. He guided the GI's farther into the mountains to his friend's hut. After eating with Leon's family, the first meal with the Negritos was a disappointment. Camotes (sweet potatoes) were the fare.

The next morning a three-day downpour began which meant that there was no fire to cook their meals. Without fire to cook rice, the men were hungry. To add to their misery, a typhoon hit and blew trees down around the hut. Finally the rain stopped and the sun appeared through broken clouds.

It was time to leave. The hut had been destroyed by the wind, and because the Americans came a day before the high winds, the Negritos thought the GI's were responsible. Their regard for nature led them to assume that the GI's had brought evil spirits with them.

Anxious to help the soldiers depart the area, the Negritos provided a guide to lead them back to Olongapo. Everywhere, trees had been blown down and mountain streams were flowing in torrents. A huge tree lying across one stream provided a bridge for passage. The men cautiously crossed the log, knowing that a slip might mean drowning in the swift waters. They clambered over fallen trees and traversed swollen streams until sundown when the guide led them to a Negrito hut where several fires burned. Decker sat down by one of the fires to dry his clothes. Happy to be dry and warm after the cold wet weather, he fell asleep. The guide awakened Decker after a short nap. They had to move on, as these people had heard that the GI's had caused the great wind, and they were uneasy with them in their home.

The next night a Negrito guide brought two Americans into camp. The two soldiers were unfriendly, and the guide was sick, coughing and spitting blood. As the soldiers obtained another guide and left, Negritos in the camp sent for a witch doctor. Soon a small, wrinkled Negrito arrived carrying a black bag. He paused to eat some food and talk with the Negritos who welcomed him.

Later, the four Americans laid down to sleep. Decker had drifted off when he was awakened by a yell. Thinking that the camp was being raided, he started to jump to his feet, but then he saw the sick man sitting near the fire and the witch doctor who had a rope lying across a wire stretching across one corner of the hut. Curious, Decker watched the witch doctor set one end of the rope on fire and then take brightly colored scarves, similar to those magicians use, out of his black bag and lay them across the shoulders of the guide. As he put the scarves across the guide's shoulders, the witch doctor mumbled and then shouted, jerking the scarves away.

Banks woke up, irritated at the noise interrupting his sleep. Decker told him to be quiet or he might get them killed. Banks grumbled and rolled over and went back to sleep. But Decker was mesmerized by the witch doctor and kept watching, certain the guide would be dead by morning. Finally the rope consumed itself and everything became quiet. The next morning, Decker awoke to find the guide sitting by the fire eating a cucumber.

When Decker asked how he felt, the man replied, "Much better." He had quit coughing at least. The guide stayed in camp for three days, improving each day. The next day the guide returned to his village. Decker couldn't believe what he had witnessed. Either these people knew some secret or he had just witnessed a miracle.

The GI's discussed their plight and agreed that four were too many to travel together. It put too much strain on the Filipinos and Negritos helping them. Meanwhile, Hank Winslow had an asthma attack and wanted the others to leave him and move on. He felt he would hold them back and he could wait where he was until he was better. Then he would try to find Leon and his family. The colonel shouldn't feel threatened by one soldier.

No one wanted to abandon Winslow. They decided to draw lots, with two leaving and the other one staying to look after Winslow. Banks drew the lot to stay. He was happy — he wanted to stay with Winslow and said that he wouldn't have felt right leaving him behind.

Decker and Campbell were both from the 200th CAC and felt camaraderie. With sad goodbyes, Campbell and Decker left with a Negrito guide. They abandoned the idea of escaping to Australia by boat. That would have been far too dangerous, as the Japanese would have been on the lookout and a boat hard to find. Instead, they decided to travel north toward Fort Stotsenburg and Clark Field to find Colonel Thorp.

Decker had heard about Thorp from many GIs, and speculated about his location. Decker knew it wouldn't be easy to find the camp as it was continually moved to avert a Japanese raid. From different men associated with Thorp, and who had visited the Fassoths' Camp, Campbell and Decker believed that Thorp's group was not far from the Fassoths. Having someone with authority to serve under would avoid the situation they encountered while living with Leon.[18]

A general conference was called and scheduled to be held on August 29, 1942, to be attended by all district commanders and squadron leaders, but on the evening of August 28, the headquarters at Timbo was raided by the Japanese. Warning of the raid almost came too late, resulting in a narrow escape to Mount Pinagalun. Colonel Thorp's Negrito barber, Captain Barker's servant and one of Eugenio Soliman's men had been captured by the Japanese—who'd interrogated them. Under intense pressure, they gave the wrong date for the meeting, allowing those in the camp to escape.

As a result of the raid, Colonel Thorp moved his headquarters to another location in Tarlac Province. Despite a warning from one of his Filipino officers, Colonel Pamintuan, the move was begun on September 2, 1942. Marcos Laxamana led them to a hideout which had no means for escape. When confronted about the inadequacy of the location, Laxamana discounted any fears as being unfounded. He assured Thorp that because of his connections they would have adequate warning of approaching patrols.

When Herminia Dizon got a letter telling her of the capture of her guardian by the Japanese, Colonel Thorp began to make plans to move to yet another camp. But on the evening of October 29 they were captured in a surprise raid by the Japanese. Those caught were Colonel Thorp, his secretary (and girlfriend) Herminia Dizon, Sergeant William Brooks, Dionicia Limpin, Private Magat, Fabian Franco, five Negritos and some other Filipino civilians.

After a few days of travel and interrogation the group was transferred to a Kempeitai (secret police) headquarters where Thorp made an impassioned plea for the release of the Filipinos and Negritos, most of whom were eventually freed. On January 22, 1943, Thorp was sent to Manila. Before he left, he managed to smuggle a letter to Herminia Dizon telling her of his suspicion that Laxamana was invovled in the raid, something that was later confirmed by the Japanese translator. The suspicion was reconfirmed when Laxamana himself confessed to a guerrilla leader in Tarlac shortly before his execution by the guerrilla unit.[19]

A few months after leaving Ed Ramsey at the Fassoths' Camp to recover, Joe Barker, wearing priest's regalia, was captured in Manila. Someone had given the Japanese information on his route of travel and plans.[20]

A few weeks later word was received that one of the Negrito *cargadores* (stevedores) had been captured by the Japanese and that the Fassoths' third camp was expected to be raided. Ed Ramsey decided to proceed to John Boone's headquarters near Dinalupihan. He further recovered from his stroke, assumed command of ECLGA (East Central Luzon Guerrilla Area), and began to organize Tarlac, Pangasinan, and later Bulacan and Manila.[21]

While at Vicente Bernia's, Vernon Fassoth was inducted into the guerrillas by Captain Louis Bell, as one of his bodyguards. Vicente had been educated by the Jesuits and was a good speaker with an ability to change people's views. Since Captain Bell did not speak the local dialect, Vicente was his spokesman. Vicente was so good at recruiting locals into the guerrillas that the Huks became upset and sent several men to meet with Bell and Vicente trying to recruit them into the Huk organization. Short of getting Bell's cooperation the men were to kill him, along with Bernia. About 250 Huk soldiers surrounded the Bernia home. Then discussions went on for two days in Bernia's home, with Huk commander Inman leading the negotiations.

Vicente told the commander that theirs was a USAFFE (United States Armed Forces Far East) guerrilla unit, that Captain Bell was the unit's commander, and that he didn't want to join a Filipino unit. He wanted his own unit. This upset the Huk leader and he began to bang his Japanese sword on the floor. This excited the men with Bernia and Bell, and they began loading their weapons. Some assumed they were going to die.

Vicente began talking, hardly drawing a breath. He appealed to the Huks' patriotism, their loyalty to the Philippine Islands, to their homes and to their families. By the time Vicente concluded his speech, there wasn't a dry eye on either side. The Huk commander was so overcome with emotion that he asked to join Bell and Bernia's unit. All the men then pledged allegiance to the American and Philippine flags.

The headquarters of the Hukbalahaps got word of the situation and dispatched another unit to kill the turncoats. After several months of hiding from the Huks, Inman was slain.[22]

Prior to the raid on the Fassoths' camp, a group of about forty men left Vincente Bernia's place and went into the Bataan Peninsula to gather arms and ammunition for their unit. As the group went into Bataan they were joined by many Filipinos also looking for arms, ammunition and any other supplies that had been left on the battlefields. By the time they reached Bataan, there were over 600 men in the group. After each man had recovered at least two rifles, they were told to go back to their homes and hide the weapons, then come back to Bataan. Louis Bell remained with Vicente, Arturo Bernia, radio operator Eugene Zingheim, Fred Stamper and Vernon Fassoth.

After the Filipinos left, the group began gathering more weapons and supplies, but a typhoon hit the island and the Filipinos never returned. The storm had obliterated paths in the jungle, and without paths to lead the way Bell and the men with him struggled to hack their way through the vegetation. After thirteen days with little food they managed to kill a dog. Though many Filipinos ate dog meat, it was not a desirable food. Then, Vernon Fassoth killed a hornbill bird with a lucky shot. Though a big bird, it was mainly feathers, but it tasted good to the starving men.

The group had gone to Signal Hill near Mariveles to retrieve radio parts so that Zingheim might repair the radio at the camp. The American soldiers living at Signal Hill had ample food supplies but refused to share any with the guerrillas. Providentially for the four at Signal Hill, the guerrillas did not retaliate. The Japanese had received information about the group and were guarding all the trails back into Luzon, but Vernon Fassoth and his group had intelligence reports about this and avoided the guarded trails on their return.

At this time Pierce Wade was found following Vernon Fassoth's group. He had been in the district, going back and forth trying to find other American escapees. Vernon asked Wade to join his group and go back to their camp.

The group continued its journey back to the camp, stopping at various homes to get food. The men were fed beef jerky and sugar, rice and bananas at one home, but they ate so much that after their long period without food,

Vernon Fassoth, sometime in late 1945 (Fassoth family collection).

they threw up the meal. After five or six days they came to a home that knew about the Fassoths' camp. The men were informed of the raid by the Japanese. Not sure they believed the story, the men continued their journey, but as they got closer to the camp they received confirmation of the raid. Eugene Zingheim was thoroughly disappointed that the radio parts he had recovered would not be used.

The men went to the now-destroyed camp and received word left by Catalina that she and Bill were at Bernia's plantation. They continued to Bernia's home and considered their future. Captain Bell decided to organize another unit in Tarlac, so Vernon Fassoth was transferred to John Boone's unit. Boone continued to organize in the upper Bataan area and Captain Bell was killed while organizing Tarlac.[23]

On the way back to the mountains, Conner and Gyovai had just entered the hill country when shots rang out on all sides. They were scared, though Conner doubted if any did more than blink.

Expecting the next rounds to kill them, they waited and became aware of men surrounding them. They couldn't see the men, but they could hear

Vernon Fassoth and John St. John, sometime late in 1945 (Fassoth family collection).

them. Then someone yelled an order, and a hundred men sauntered out from hiding. It was the Hukbalahap. Though he was afraid and upset at their tactics, Conner was delighted at the sight of the Huks. They were armed and liked to fight. After the apathy he had experienced in Samal, the Huks were like a refreshing splash of water.

Their leader was a man right out of the pages of Dumas. Never had Conner seen a man more fitted for the striking role of a guerrilla. In outward show and size he was the reincarnation of Pancho Villa that Conner remembered from old movie newsreels. The cocky, swaggering imp before him was Julian Palad.

Palad had heard through his Huk intelligence that the Americans were in region, and had staged the ambush to impress them. He expected that if Conner could be persuaded that he was no flash in the pan, then Conner and Gyovai would join his band, adding American status and an official authorization to his incursions. His demonstration was sufficient. Gyovai and Conner decided they would join him the next morning after leaving word with their fellow Americans at the hideouts. They also wanted to procure additional equipment.

The trip the next morning was a revelation. The Huks were well organized. When the men left the hills in the northeast corner of Bataan Province and entered the fields in the lowlands, Palad sent a messenger ahead to the first barrio on their path. Within half an hour the courier was back with one of the local Huk leaders, who had current intelligence about every Japanese patrol in his district. And the local chief had sent one of his own runners on to the next barrio to notify the leader there that a guerrilla force was coming through. From barrio to barrio the word was passed by this technique.

On this trip, the word was not good. Japanese were probing the district. Palad ordered his men to scatter into the jungle until dark. Gyovai and Conner took advantage of this to track down an American they knew through their own intelligence to be in the area, a corporal named John Boone. They found him, a tall, broad shouldered-man with a crisp blond Van Dyke beard and crewcut, living in a small barrio located less than half a mile from a large Japanese military camp. He had his barrio organized so well that the Japanese couldn't start a car without Boone receiving word. In return he had taught the Filipinos how to hide their food from Japanese patrols and what fabrications to tell in any given circumstances. He was pleased to see Conner and Gyovai, and invited them in for a chicken dinner.

Boone gave them the inside track about the Huks, of whom, up to then, Conner and Gyovai had heard only flattering stories. The rumors they had been told about the Huks had them as a branch of the USAFFE, but Boone told them his own ideas about the group.

"They're all right," he assured Conner, "but watch them. And watch Palad. As far as I've ever heard he's pro–American, but he's got a lot of screwy ideas. If he tries to tell you he's the leader, and starts issuing orders, bluff him down or you'll be sunk. But by all means go along with him. You can't learn the country in a better way, and if we're ever going to get going as guerrillas, the more country we know, the better."[24]

Boone wanted to go with Conner and Gyovai, but he had sent word of his whereabouts out over the region, and he decided to stay in the event that some of his old friends came by or sent word where they could be found. Conner told Boone he would be back in a month or so, and returned to Palad's band.

After more than two weeks with the Huks, Conner and Gyovai were despondent, as nothing had happened. They were making a lot of valuable contacts, and increasing their knowledge of the language, but as for harassing the Japanese, they hadn't even let the air out of a tire. Palad was willing, his men were willing, and the Americans were willing, but the Filipinos living in the area they wished to raid were not. The guerrillas wanted to burn some Japanese installations, but the scheme scared the local Huk leaders. The Japanese, they claimed, would move into their barrio, kill every resident, and burn every house. Since the guerrillas had to admit that they could not defend the local residents if a large Japanese force came to retaliate, they likewise had to admit it would not be righteous for them to strike and run, leaving the locals to suffer. Conner now recognized that the Japanese did not need large patrols to guard their food and equipment. They had a better guard than any human agency, and that was fear.

It was from Julian Palad that Conner learned more about Colonel Thorp's command and headquarters. Palad told Conner that Thorp was living at Timbo, about ten miles south of Fort Stotsenburg. Palad said the place Thorp was staying was a farm that had been owned by a man named Eugenio Soliman, an old Filipino. The old man had for years been the contact between the United States government and the Negritos, what little contact there was. Soliman was a homesteader back in the valley called Timbo. He had taken Thorp in and supplied his guerrilla force.[25]

By late October 1942, Conner and Gyovai had left Palad's group and were living in Barrio Delores with several Americans while they tried to organize the local Filipinos in a guerrilla unit. The Americans spent the majority of their time recovering from various illnesses and procuring food. Conner enjoyed the men talking about their homes. Frank Gyovai missed his mother's cooking. And he would talk about the hardships, the coal mines, and how the miners, were injured or trapped from time to time, how he'd been born in this area, and knew nothing but the filth of the coal mines of West Virginia.

Ray Herbert talked about Louisiana, and how he'd grown up fighting his way through the swamp areas, and how he'd won a scholarship in boxing to LSU. Bob Leyrer loved Wisconsin, his home, and told how he'd become interested in flying at a young age, and how he got into cadet school after graduating from the University of Wisconsin. Johnny Johns talked about all the girls he'd known back home. He was a likeable kid — always ready for an argument, and always ready for a laugh. He and Herbert had gone into the Army at the same time. They were both members of the Twenty-seventh Bomb Group. Conner didn't think they went ten minutes without getting into an argument. Johns would always end by saying, "I'm gonna punch you in the nose." And Herbert would say, "Well, you haven't done it yet!" And then they'd go on from there.[26]

Sergeant Alfred Bruce, formerly of Colonel Thorp's band, was led to the house at Delores. He was a husky fellow, about Frank Gyovai's build. He had a big beard — the rough kind, straggly — all over his face. He been with the MPs before the war, stationed at Fort Stotsenburg. Bruce was looking for Americans in the area to reorganize the Thorp group and get the outfit operational.[27]

Doyle Decker and Bob Campbell made their way back to the Fort Stotsenburg/Clark Field area with the help of several Negrito guides. They encountered many unusual people and situations in their journey. After they had crossed a river their last guide left them as she couldn't go any further. They saw a village and approached it cautiously, not sure how they would be received. The huts were deserted.

A little further they met an old Filipino who didn't speak English. Campbell tried to communicate in broken Spanish, and when he didn't succeed he used a few Tagalog words he knew. The old man wore a worried expression. Campbell and Decker gave up efforts to converse and continued down the trail. Suddenly, several excited Filipinos with rifles surrounded them.

The GI's stopped and evaluated the situation. The Filipinos raised their rifles as if to shoot and some began yelling and punching Decker and Campbell.

"You fools, drop your guns!" yelled a Filipina in Tagalog. "Can't you see these men are Americans?"

Marching into view was a gray-haired Filipina wearing two .45 pistols around her ample waist and carrying a Thompson submachine gun. With a stern, but pleasant smile she extended her hand and in perfect English introduced herself.

"I am Culala."

Decker had heard of this guerrilla leader. The Japanese had a high price on her head, higher than the 50,000 pesos for the capture of American soldiers who had escaped Bataan.

"It is dangerous for you to travel. There are several Jap patrols in the territory. Come with me and we will hide you until there is less activity."

Felipa Culala escorted the GI's to a nearby house.

"Stay here until I return."

Decker and Campbell spent a week at this hideout. They ventured outside for fresh air and exercise, but remained close to the house to avoid detection. A diet of green boiled peanuts wasn't appetizing, but it relieved their hunger pains.

When Culala returned she told them, "You can now travel safely. I will accompany you."

Late that evening they reached a barrio where two American officers, Lieutenant Ed Ramsey, Captain Louis Bell, and a few other GI's were living. Ramsey and Bell weren't friendly.

"You can stay the night but you must move on tomorrow," Bell stated bluntly. "We have all the men this barrio can take care of."

Culala bid Decker and Campbell goodbye. "This is as far as I have control."

Decker thanked her for her help, appreciative for what her band had done.

"Think nothing of it," Culala replied. "I hope you can find a suitable place to live. You will be okay tomorrow, just watch your movement."

The following morning Ramsey and Bell showed Decker and Campbell the trail to the next barrio. The trail was well traveled, and after a couple of hours they reached Barrio Banaba, located on the eastern slope of Mount Pinatubo and south of Clark Field. A Filipino couple, Mario and Cering Hardin, met Campbell and Decker and invited them to eat the noon meal with their family. They had two grown daughters, Maling and Pading, and a teenage son, Mario Jr.

Decker and Campbell spent the rest of the day with the Hardins. Though appreciative of the hospitality and conversation, they explained that they would like to find Colonel Thorp. Mr. Hardin knew a Negrito familiar with the area where Thorp was rumored to have his camp. Early the next morning the two GI's thanked the Hardins for their kindness and began the trip to locate Thorp.

That evening, Decker and Campbell found Thorp's camp raided and burned to the ground. Three huts were smoldering and what looked like a campfire was scattered about the center of the compound. Since there were no glowing embers, it appeared the huts had been burning at least two days.

"Looks like we got here too late," said Decker.

"Maybe we are lucky that we didn't get here earlier," replied Campbell.
An old Filipino walked out of the jungle.

"Where is Colonel Thorp?" asked Decker.

The old man shook his head back and forth.

Decker asked again, "Where is Colonel Thorp?"

The Filipino stared at Decker and Campbell and slinked back into the jungle.

Fearing the Japanese might return, Decker and Campbell spent the night a short distance from the camp, beneath a banyan tree. They didn't make a fire and took turns standing watch until morning.

Campbell and Decker returned to Banaba the next morning. As they entered the barrio they encountered a neighbor of the Hardins, Mr. Palo, who invited them to spend the night. Mr. Palo had a son-in-law named George who lived with him. Palo's daughter had died some months prior and George stayed to help the family.

Neither Decker nor Campbell could understand Mr. Palo's dialect, so George interpreted for the GI's. There was a warmth about Mr. Palo and a desire to help that transcended language. It was as if someone had sent an angel to watch over the Americans.

The next morning George told them, "My father-in-law has a hut in the mountains, not far from Banaba, where you will be safe."

Decker was relieved at the news because he was in a lot of pain from the injury he suffered when he and the three other GI's jumped into the trees to escape the Japanese patrol the first day they left Fassoth's camp.

The following day George guided Decker and Campbell up a thickly forested trail to a tidy and sparsely furnished bamboo hut with a view of the valley below. He enjoyed his new friends and spent several days with the Americans questioning them about life in the States, leaving only to retrieve supplies.

"You are so lucky to be born in America," George told them. "I want to someday visit your country."

Decker made a crude crutch from a tree limb and hobbled around the hut. George brought rice and warm buffalo milk from Mr. Palo and the Hardins, saying, "Here, this will help you regain your strength." Campbell combined these with wild tomatoes and mushrooms he found in the jungle and prepared a hearty soup.

A month later George arrived at the house and announced that he was afraid some other Filipinos had seen the Americans. He was not certain these particular Filipinos could be trusted, so he was moving Decker and Campbell to a banana grove on the other side of the mountain.

Here they built a hut from bamboo and rattan. And every few days for the next several weeks, with George's help, they moved to other locations to avoid detection.

At Thanksgiving, Mrs. Hardin and her two daughters brought a meal to the men and celebrated the American holiday. A week later George moved the men back to the Banaba area to a new hut Mr. Palo and George had built especially for Decker and Campbell.

The only approach was up a rock cliff. Decker's leg was still painful, but he managed the climb. The rock wall prevented anyone leaving tracks to the new location. The hut was beneath a huge tree, so only someone familiar with the location would be able to find the Americans. An ample supply of water flowed from a waterfall running through a crevice and fell a few feet before disappearing into another crevice.

Decker rested while his leg mended, passing time watching flying lizards and beautiful songbirds dart in and out of the tree over the hut. After a few weeks, Decker's leg was almost back to normal, and he no longer used his crutch. The new location felt secure, and Mr. Palo and the Hardins visited every few days. George was a liaison to the barrio and maintained a supply of food and news for Campbell and Decker.

The rainy season began and persisted from a mist to a downpour. George continued to supply rice, but there was little meat. Between downpours, Decker and Campbell took turns gathering mushrooms and green papayas to make soup, but they tired of this diet after a few days.

One day Decker looked out the hut and saw a Negrito with a gun. He held out the gun and indicated it was broken. With sign language the Negrito told Decker that if he fixed the gun, he would bring some beans and chicken for payment. With additional sign language, Pidgin English, Tagalog and Spanish, Decker told the Negrito that he need a square file and a prong from a beet fork to fix the firing pin on the rifle.

The next day the Negrito returned with a worn out file and a large piece of metal to fix the firing pin. Decker made signs that he would need a week to fix the gun and began to work on his project. He worked from daylight until dark every day and in six days the gun was repaired. Smiling uncertainly, he handed it back to the Negrito, hoping it would work but with no shells to test it.

The next day the Negrito returned with beans and a chicken. He took a shell from a pouch slung around his waist, and put it in the chamber of the rifle. He took aim at a nearby tree. Bang! It worked. The Negrito looked at Decker with a big smile, nodding his approval.

This started a new enterprise for Decker. Every few days, a Negrito showed up with a broken gun. Decker could usually fix the weapon and was paid in beans and an occasional chicken. But one appreciative Negrito gave

Decker a puppy. It was a wild dog he had caught, and it was so small that Decker could carry it in his shirt pocket. Though small, the female puppy was old enough to drink from a bowl. Every time Decker picked up the puppy she tried to bite him. After getting her ears boxed a few times she decided to quit nipping her new master. Because of her spunk, Decker named the puppy Firecracker. She was Decker's constant companion and wouldn't have anything to do with Campbell. She bit everyone who tried to pick her up except Decker.

Cracker was a small, white, short-haired dog and as she grew, she followed Decker everywhere. He talked to her as if she was human and she never talked back. The dog looked at Decker as he talked to her acting as though she understood every word.

Afraid she might bark and give away their location, Decker worked with Cracker and trained her not to bark by muzzling and scolding her anytime she started to yap. After she no longer struggled, Decker petted her and told her how smart she was. Cracker was intelligent and in a few days didn't bark, but her hackles rose and she muttered a soft but noticeable growl when anyone approached camp. Cracker seemed to either hear or smell Japanese soldiers from a distance, and by her demeanor Decker could tell if a friend or foe was approaching the hut.

Decker decided that Cracker was the best payment he had received from the Negritos.[28]

In October 1942 Millard Hileman encountered Margarito Agridano walking toward the hut where he and two other soldiers were staying as they recovered after their escape from the Japanese.

Agridano looked like a Filipino and spoke Tagalog and delighted in fooling the Japanese. He was of Mexican decent and was from Los Angeles, California. When Hileman asked about his time in the hills, Agridano was evasive. He wanted to get to the Zambales Mountains and join some American officers in the guerrilla movement. Hileman decided to join Agridano and they began their journey. After traveling several hours Hileman took a nasty spill, injuring his knee. When they reached a Filipino hut, a woman made a concoction of coconut oil and then used a candle to drip hot oil and garlic over the wound as she chanted. A few hours later the process was repeated and surprisingly the next morning the knee was healed and Hileman could walk without pain.

In early January Hileman and Agridano found Colonel Calyer and asked to join the guerrillas. They were assigned a Filipino family to feed them and were told they would be contacted when needed. This didn't sit well with the two recruits and they departed in disgust.[29]

By the end of October, Ed Ramsey was strong enough for the trip to John Boone's camp. His health had improved but he was still suffering the prolonged effects of his maladies. His malaria attacks were receding, and he was managing the dysentery with weekly injections of a drug called demetine, which the Manila cadres smuggled out to him. Underweight and subject to spells of weakness and fainting, Ramsey nonetheless made the journey. Joe Barker had written to Ramsey that he had begun to organize Manila. Barker's letter and improving health were invigorating to Ramsey.

Boone greeted Ramsey with the same impetuous smile Ramsey remembered from their first meeting, and before Ramsey asked, Boone offered to place his guerrillas under Barker and Ramsey's command. Boone's group had grown to several hundred men, and they were clearly attached to him. Ramsey accepted the offer and then promoted Boone, who was a corporal in the regular army, to captain in the East Central Luzon Guerrilla Area Forces.

"Captain," Boone repeated, savoring the sound of it. Then he gave Ramsey a disbelieving squint. "Can you do that?" he asked. "I mean, with respect, you're a lieutenant, sir."

"I'm deputy commander," Ramsey answered. "I'm acting on Joe Barker's authority and Colonel Thorp's." Ramsey reflected a minute and then added. "And General MacArthur's, too."

"Well, if it's okay by MacArthur," Boone drawled, "it's okay by me."[30]

Boone then asked Ramsey for a favor. Some months before, his troops had killed a local man for collaborating with the Japanese. To keep the location of the camp from the Japanese, the man's wife had been taken into the camp as a captive. This had posed a problem for Boone. He could not release her since she knew the position of the camp, but the attractive young woman in camp could cause trouble among the troops.

Boone then told Ramsey that he had fallen in love with the woman and she was in love with him. But morale would be further diminished if they lived together. He couldn't have one rule for his men and another for himself.

Ramsey thought the situation over for a few minutes and suggested that he marry them.

Ramsey was not sure that he had the authority to conduct a marriage, but he could not imagine who else had. Beside, Mao had written that the guerrilla commander must act as the sole legitimate authority in the country, and Ramsey supposed that included having the power to marry people. In any case, Boone jumped at the idea.[31]

Chapter 7
Capture, Surrender, Survive

The Philippines was the only country in Japan's Greater East Asia Co-Prosperity Sphere where they had a guerrilla problem. In British Malay, the Dutch East Indies, French Indo-China and the other countries in the Pacific, the natives had, by and large, welcomed the Japanese troops who helped them throw off the shackles of the European colonists. Among the Filipinos, though, it was surprising that so many still supported the old American government.

"These Filipinos," Major Nakai thought to himself, "who can figure them out?"[1]

In January 1943, guerrilla activity was causing the Japanese to expend an extraordinary amount of their time guarding various cities and commercial interests in the Philippines. Lieutenant General Shegenori Kuroda had taken over as the commander in the Philippines and the Imperial Headquarters was adamant that he curtail the guerrillas. He set about accomplishing his mission in two distinct areas.

He began by ordering a concentrated military clean-up of guerrilla organizations for sixty days. At the same time, he instructed Colonel Akira Nagahama, commander of the Kempeitai, to employ a new policy they named "Attraction." Attraction offered amnesty to any guerrillas or escaped Americans who surrendered during the sixty-day campaign. Those captured after the amnesty period would be executed. Kuroda increased the compensation to fifty pesos for any person who informed on escaped Americans or guerrillas.

For added impetus, General Kuroda declared that Japan would award independence to the Philippines when all of the guerrillas surrendered. The Imperial Headquarters was at a loss to explain why the Filipinos were supporting the guerrillas and especially the Americans. Since the United States had promised the islands their independence, to take effect on July 4, 1946, to give the islands independence at an earlier date seemed an astute move to Kuroda.

In Balanga, the provincial capital of Bataan, two Filipino brothers, both medics for the guerrillas, turned in an American major named Stanley Holmes and six other American soldiers for the blood money. When an American captain was captured near Orani with a Filipino refugee from a mountain refugee settlement named Tala, Major Nakai ordered Japanese soldiers to arrest every member of the village, which they accomplished, bringing every man, woman and child to the Japanese Army prison in Orani. The capture of the two officers had been a surprise — the only American officer Major Nakai was really looking for in Bataan was a colonel named Frank Lloyd.[2]

Several villages known to harbor guerrillas were retaliated against. Major Nakai's soldiers imprisoned and tortured numerous suspects. Convinced the villagers would soon tire of this action and turn in the guerrilla leaders, the tactics were amplified.

So successful were the Japanese actions that a Filipino named Ruben Bondoc exposed several of Major Nakai's own Filipino agents as guerrillas. The Kempeitai executed all of them.

In a bizarre turn of events, Major Nakai had received a menacing report. An American lieutenant named Henry Clay Conner was rumored to have recently arrived in Bataan or Zambales. The Kempeitai believed that Conner was put ashore by a submarine in advance of a planned American attack. Major Nakai sent a 300-man task force out to look for Lieutenant Conner.[3]

On February 22, 1943, the Japanese raided two camps on Mount Malasimbo, just north of Dinalupihan. The first raid hit the Fassoths' third camp, but the Fassoths' built another camp farther back in the jungle. The task force commander reported to Major Nakai that they had killed a number of Americans and Filipinos in the camp, but the two Fassoth brothers escaped. The reward was increased for each of the brothers.[4] The other raid was on a guerrilla headquarters located nearby, but most of the occupants escaped. Clay Conner and two other Americans, John Boone and Ed Ramsey, were rumored to have been there.[5] The raids resulted in thousands of arrests and Japanese commanders were sure that the guerrilla organizations would collapse.

A radio message sent by General MacArthur read as follows: GENERAL POLICY OF USAFIP IN THE PHILIPPINES IS TO LIMIT HOSTILITIES AND CONTACT WITH THE ENEMY TO THE MINIMUM AMOUNT NECESSARY FOR SAFETY. CONCENTRATE ON PERFECTING ORGANIZATION AND ON DEVELOPING OF

INTELLIGENCE NET. THEREFORE, UNTIL AMMUNITION AND SUPPLIES CAN BE
SENT, YOUR PRESENT MISSION AS INTELLIGENCE UNITS CAN BE CURRENTLY OF
UTMOST VALUE. NOTHING IS SURER THAN OUR ULTIMATE VICTORY. SIGNED
MACARTHUR.[6]

The bandit guerrillas[7] dug deep pits in the ground where they kept their
prisoners, including American officers, until trial. Sometimes the prisoners
were forced to do work around the headquarters prior to trial. Very few prisoners were released; most were shot after digging their own graves.

One evening an American soldier, Johnny Johns,[8] visited the Fassoths'
camp with a letter written by a U.S. Army captain to Americans hiding in
the mountains. The letter directed that the Americans surrender, stating that
no harm would come to them, that the food was good, and that medical and
dental care was available. Those who chose to not surrender would be shot
when captured. The soldier with the message was to deliver the letter to those
hiding in the mountains and to tell them they had seven days to make their
decision. If the soldier delivering the letter did not return in a certain number of days, the captain who wrote the letter would be shot. The soldier was
given seven pesos, cigarettes, and bus and carretela fare to perform his mission.

Everyone in the camp was given the opportunity to read the letter and
all declined to surrender. A few hours later a group of twenty Filipino
guerrillas came into the camp. Bill Fassoth asked them what they wanted. They
first claimed they were looking for building materials in the forest and happened into the camp. Not believing their story, Bill Fassoth pressed them
on their real intentions. The guerrillas then confessed that they had been in
Dinalupihan when the American solider had gotten off a bus and reported
to the Japanese garrison. They had followed him to the camp and were going to kill him as a Japanese spy. Bill explained to the guerrillas why the
soldier was in the camp and told them that to kill him would jeopardize
another American's life. This seemed to satisfy the guerrillas and they left the
camp.

The soldier spent the night and left the next day. On reporting back to
the garrison, the soldier told them that he had made contact on the trail, but
he did not relay the location of the camp.[9]

Ray Hunt expanded the story of Johnny Johns in his book *Behind Japanese Lines*, writing, "For unusual people, wartime often provides exceptional
opportunities to exhibit resourcefulness."[10] Ray Hunt met Johnny Johns in
the Fassoths' camp in the spring of 1943. Johns and Captain Shelby Newman
had been captured together by the Japanese. Johns had persuaded Newman

to write a letter persuading all the Americans hiding in the mountains to surrender. The Japanese assured Johns and Newman that they would feed and give good treatment to those Americans who turned themselves in, but said that those who remained fugitives would be taken into custody and beheaded. With the letter in hand, Johns approached the Japanese and convinced them to give him $7 in cash, some cigarettes, and a five-day pass, in return for him traveling to central Luzon and trying to convince American escapees to surrender. Newman was held hostage to guarantee Johns return. After five days Johns obediently returned to the Japanese but without having had success. He used his persuasive ability on the Japanese, convincing them that five days was not enough time to find and convince the Americans to surrender. This time the Japanese gave Johns an indefinite pass and he left on his mission.

Johns had somehow accumulated money before the war and had hidden it when hostilities began. Rather than searching for Americans hiding in the mountains, he retrieved his money and went to Manila where he spent his time at nightclubs and on women. Newman got wind of John's lifestyle and — fearing for his own life — began making plans to escape. The attempt succeeded and somehow, after his escape, Newman found Ray Hunt. Hunt was glad to have Newman's company, but the Japanese had learned their location and began probing near their position. Newman and Hunt decided they needed to split up and go in different directions. The Japanese had meanwhile found out that Johns was exploiting his position and arrested him, but Johns was slick and slipped away again.

On one occasion Ray Hunt had several visitors. They were Hukbalahaps, the Philippine communist guerrillas. Their leader had a parrot that he wanted to trade to Hunt for his rifle. The bird was beautiful but was no replacement for a weapon. Some of the Huks made signs which were easily understood and Hunt immediately gave the Huk leader his rifle in return for the bird.[11]

Having received information that Captain Barker was in the area, Bernard Anderson and Bert Pettitt decided that this would be a good time to make contact and report on their progress and discuss plans. On January 18, 1943, on their way to make contact, news was received of Barker's capture. Anderson and Pettitt returned to their camp and continued limited operations until February 23 when the camp was attacked by the Japanese.[12]

After recruiting cadres and appointing officers, John Boone and Ed Ramsey returned to Boone's camp at Dinalupihan in late January 1943. Mercado, an officer from one of their Manila cadres, was in camp with bad news.

General Baba had ordered a dragnet in Manila and hundreds of people had been arrested, with entire districts searched in a thorough sweep. The Kempeitai were torturing people for any piece of information that would lead to the capture of Joe Barker.

Barker had situated his headquarters in Tondo, a bandit-infested area overrun with refugees crowded in shacks. The Kempeitai was hesitant to enter this hostile quarter that was a core of anti–Japanese hatred. From this bastion of hostility Barker would venture around Manila dressed in the garb of a Roman Catholic priest. Since his arrival he had been talking with recruits, making speeches, appointing leaders, and amassing information.

Betrayed by a Makapili spy, a member of the pro-Japanese security force, Barker's bodyguard was captured in early January. After three days of incessant torture he told his captors the location of Alejandro Santos. On January 11th, Santos and most of his staff were apprehended. Under torture, one of Santos's officers revealed that the bodyguard worked for Barker and the Kempeitai began torturing him anew.

On learning of the sweep, Barker escaped from Manila to an isolated hill district northeast of the city. He stopped for the night at the home of one of his cadre, on his way to Porac. At daylight a heavily armed Kempeitai throng encircled the house, then burst in and arrested Barker who'd been sleeping. Barker was transported to the dilipidated Fort Santiago prison and incarcerated with Thorp, Santos, and dozens of others.

When Captain Joseph Barker was captured on January 14, 1943, the whole command of Colonel Thorp collapsed. Major Edwin Ramsey, second in command under the structure established by Thorp, proclaimed himself in charge of Central Luzon. Bob Lapham found Ramsey both ambitious and persuasive.[13] Ramsey had quarreled with the Fassoth brothers after he arrived in their camp for the second time, on July 5, 1942, when he'd attempted to sign up Americans in camp for his guerrilla unit. Forty-three men promised to join him. He worked hard to enlist Corporal John Boone, who had assembled a group of his own and had recruited the men in the Fassoths' camp. Finally, Ramsey created a unit near Orani in northern Bataan. Among its members were Pierce Wade and Frank Gyovai, with Lieutenant Clay Conner as commander, but the unit was barely organized when the Japanese broke it up. Ramsey and Conner then tried to reorganize near Olongapo, but the Japanese routed them again in August.[14]

In January 1943, Bill Fassoth took sick with malaria and was unable to gather supplies for about three months. Catalina kept the supplies flowing with help from her nieces and the able-bodied men in the camp. The Japanese patrols again probed the mountains trying to locate the camp. The men in the Fassoths' camp witnessed the Japanese raiding a nearby guerrilla unit only two kilometers across the ridge. The assault party used mortars and machine guns against the guerrillas' headquarters, and burned it to the ground. The guerrillas fled as the Japanese searched the surrounding area.

After watching the assault on the guerrilla camp Bill Fassoth and his group went into hiding by a small stream and when they returned that evening found it unharmed. The next night the Japanese again probed the hills and could be seen using their flashlights searching the hillsides, but again did not find the camp. While searching the Japanese did burn several Filipino shacks. The next day it was decided to abandon the third camp.

Camp 4

Vernon Fassoth left for the Isip camp, ten miles away, with some of the men. While the men whom Bill Fassoth placed with various Filipino families remained with them and others departed further into the mountains north of the camp, Catalina, Hipolita San Jose and the girls went to Dinalupihan. Still weak from his malaria attack, Bill took an entire day to make the trip to Isip with five men from the camp, while Martin took six men with him.

Martin contacted a family in Dinalupihan to bring supplies to the new camp at Isip. Bill had Catalina bring supplies from Dinalupihan as well. The group remained in this location about a month with plenty of food, and Bill's health improved under the care of Lieutenant Warshell.

Martin became adept at cooking pot roasts from wild hogs that a Negrito brought into the camp. An unusual animal called a musang, similar to a skunk but without the noxious scent glads, inhabited the area near the camp. Most Filipinos would not eat these animals. The musangs would come into the camp looking for food, and were aggressive. When a hatchet was thrown at one of them it hissed and wouldn't give any ground. No one in camp tried to kill a musang after that incident.[15]

While he was living with Colonel Gyles Merrill's group of officers, Earl Oatman was visited by his friend Hank Winslow. Winslow had left the Fassoths' camp with Doyle Decker, Coleman Banks, and Bob Campbell about two days before it was raided. Oatman had returned to the camp to learn of Winslow's departure and just in time for the raid.

After having left the camp and traveled to the area they were now located, Winslow had developed an asthma attack, so he and Banks had stayed put while Decker and Campbell had traveled back to the Clark Field area to find Colonel Thorp's unit.

Winslow made arrangements for Oatman to live with the same family that was taking care of him. Oatman moved with Winslow the second week of December 1942 to live with the Anton Barron family. Colonel Merrill had the authority to place enlisted men with individual families at government expense. The family was required to provide food and shelter to the best of their ability for a given amount of money, to be paid at the end of the war.[16] Oatman and Winslow were the only two Americans staying together with one family, as the Barrons had a large family and land holdings. The family consisted of Rufino, the oldest son; Espanacia, the oldest daughter; and two small children, a boy and girl.

Other enlisted men in the area were living with various families at Colonel Merrill's request. Millard Hileman, Coleman Banks and Bill Ostrander were living with families within a two-mile radius of Barrio Bujaoen. All of the men in the area had been in the Fassoths' camp except Ostrander and Hileman.

The Barrons' nephew, Joaquin Isidro, lived in a small nipa house thirty yards from the Barrons. Joaquin was about eighteen and he and Rufino spent most of their time together. Both spoke English and all the Filipino children in the area studied the English language in school. The Americans would converse with the children in English and they in turn would interpret for them with the elderly Filipinos. With Joaquin and Rufino's help, Oatman attempted to learn Tagalog so that he might converse with Filipinos and Negritos.

Oatman had difficulty with two things in his new home. One was betel nut, which the older Filipinos chewed constantly, staining their teeth and mouths black. The other was the Filipinos' uninhibited bathroom skills. It was unthinkable to Oatman for a man to just turn away from a group of men and women and relieve himself, or worse to squat down beside a trail to defecate. He and Winslow did eventually relent and would stand at the back of the Barron home and urinate with the other males before retiring for the evening.[17]

Millard Hileman and Margarito Agridano lived at the same farm, but their relationship was not one of amity. Hileman enjoyed visiting the Barron farm where Winslow and Oatman were living. They would talk about their homes, American food, the war, and their uncertain circumstances. The Americans were captivated by the simple lives and resourcefulness of the Filipinos in the vicinity. Winslow was particularly willing to experience the native culture. He took delight in relating one incident of their ingenuity.

Rufino Barron, Anton's son, had a painful cavity in a molar, and Winslow was grudgingly swayed into performing the dental work. A wire in a wooden handle was heated until it glowed. A wooden block was placed in Rufino's mouth and Winslow stuck the red hot wire into the cavity. Rufino jumped, but moments later the pain was gone. The process was successful.

On one of Hileman's visits Winslow passed him a bowl containing what looked like shredded coconut mixed with brown sugar. Hileman eagerly helped himself to a generous portion.

"What is this?" A sour taste coated Hileman's mouth.

"Fried ants," Winslow replied. He laughed at the look of distaste he saw on Hileman's face. The Filipinos considered the ants a delicacy, and Winslow dipped his fingers into the bowl for another helping.

Anton Barron went to the cockfights in San Marcelino every Sunday. Carrying two cages that resembled suitcases, he took his prize roosters and walked into town.

"I don't wish Anton any bad luck," Winslow said, "but I sure hope one of those roosters meets an untimely death. Then there'll be chicken on the table."[18]

The Americans shunned the barrios, but on one occasion Winslow, Oatman and Hileman went into Barrio Cinemar. Clinton Wolfe, who had been at the Fassoths' Camp when it was raided by the Japanese, had arrived at the Barron farm during rice harvest and went with them into the barrio. From the 200th Coast Artillery, Wolfe was a character whose flaming red hair had earned him his nickname, Red. Although in his early thirties, Wolfe had false teeth which, combined with a well developed sense of humor, had been the source of good-natured fun with the primitive Negritos. He had enjoyed their reaction at Barron's farm when he had taken his teeth out and clapped them together. The news about the mysterious feat spread quickly through the area. When they entered the barrio, Negritos excitedly pointed at Wolfe and expectantly began to follow him. Not one to disappoint them, he made a great show of the feat, thoroughly enjoying the attention and the amazement of the primitive people.

Another time Wolfe's hijinks brought no joy, however. Having taken to mocking Negritos in English, a language they couldn't understand, he approached a Negrito man one day and said with a smile, "You sure are a dirty little son of a bitch, Don't you ever take a bath?"

An unexpected response came quickly: "Sir, it is not my custom to take a bath, but I am not a son of a bitch."

His intended victim may have been the only English-speaking Negrito in the area. Wolfe turned as red as his hair, while his companions broke into hysterical laughter, seeing him at the receiving end of a joke.[19]

During the first two months that Earl Oatman lived with the Barron family, everything went well and life was enjoyable. He experienced new and interesting aspects of rural Filipino life. The Americans living in the area began to gather at mid-morning in an open area between large clumps of bamboo growing on a small creek bank near the Barron's home. They ate lunch and swapped stories about their past and speculated on their future. The Barron's furnished the rice and on occasion one of the other families would provide a vegetable, such as camotes or an eggplant to supplement the rice.

Early one morning there was gunfire in the distance and soon the other Americans came to the Barron home to determine their next course of action. They could distinguish the sounds of Japanese 25-caliber rifles and occasionally a Japanese knee mortar. As soon as the shooting started Rufino and Joaquin left to investigate, and after several hours they returned to report that Captain Rodriquez's guerrillas had ambushed a Japanese patrol as they crossed a river a mile from Barrio Bujaoen. The Filipinos were entrenched on one side of the river and the Japanese had retreated to the opposite side. Rufino told the Americans to stay at the Barron home until further notice.

When the shooting subsided, the guerrillas came and told the Americans that the Japanese had gone back to San Marcellino. One Japanese soldier had been killed and several guerrillas had been wounded during the battle. The number of casualties was extraordinarily low for the amount of gunfire.

While helping the Barron family harvest sugar cane, Oatman and Winslow had the opportunity to experience one of the country's alcoholic beverages. Several large clay jars were filled with freshly squeezed cane juice and a piece of fibrous, inner bark from a particular plant was added to each jar before they were sealed. Every few days the fermenting juice was tasted by Mr. Barron or one of his older sons. Finally, they announced that the fermentation process had come to fruition and the beverage was ready to consume. Oatman and Winslow were given a half coconut shell of the "basi." Oatman was not impressed, but Winslow seemed to enjoy his beverage. After he had consumed several shells of the juice, Winslow went with Oatman to their favorite spot in the creek bed, where Winslow sang cowboy songs and sipped more basi. He was inebriated and enjoying the moment.[20]

Clay Conner, Frank Gyovai and Ray Herbert moved from Barrio Delores back to Tala in February 1943. Because of the Japanese pressure against the guerrillas, many of the villagers had moved to the lowlands. The Americans still living in the area were concerned at having to find provisions for three more men.

Conner decided to move on to Moron on the western slopes of Bataan. To his disappointment, Gyovai decided to remain in Tala with Eddie Keith. When Conner and Herbert arrived in Moron, they were surprised to find that the town was patrolled every two or three days by the Japanese. The mayor explained that because of the town's isolation the Japanese reasoned it was a good setting for guerrilla activity. He told Conner that he would be better off going to a small barrio north of Moron.

The barrio recommended by Moron's mayor proved to be a friendly location and the villagers took care of Conner and Herbert's every need.

Ed Ramsey had come to Olongapo to check on the guerrilla operations and on being informed of Conner's location decided to contact him. When he arrived at the barrio he was surprised to find modern conveniences available. Ramsey wanted to stay a while and Conner was glad to have him.

Ramsey had been all over Luzon, contacted most of the Americans, and gathered a lot of information. He had heard a recent report by radio that the American troops were on their way back. Conner was doubtful. He hadn't seen any American airplanes for almost a year, and thought that if the American forces were on their way back they would have bombed Clark Field by then. True or not, it was good to hear.

Ramsey talked about the Huks, and Conner told him about the experience he'd had, and how the Huks were looking for him. This was no secret to Ramsey. He told Conner how he had also been captured by the Huks and about their intent to kill him. He had escaped through the Candaba Swamps and told Conner that Captain Barker had the same experience.

Ramsey told Conner about how this had all started. The year before, Colonel Thorp had given orders to Luis Taruc to organize USAFFE guerrilla forces. Luis Taruc was the mayor of one of the towns. Taruc had come to Thorp, like many other Filipinos, and pledged his loyalty, and Thorp had given him the authority to organize USAFFE guerrillas in his district. However, Taruc used his authority not to organize USAFFE, but to attract Filipino people who were pro–American, and who joined Taruc thinking that he was directly under Thorp, which was true. But Taruc organized these men with one idea in mind: gaining strength and arms under his command. He was only one of the men in the chain of command. There were men higher up, from Chinese communists on down. These men were divisive and they knew that in order to gain a following, they had to be on Thorp's team.

Hundreds of men joined Taruc and went into Bataan to find rifles, and ammunition. The Filipino people pledged their loyalty to Taruc because he was under Thorp. They gave him money, munitions, and food. They supported the men and worked with the chief of police of the barrios to release hundreds of men from the census the Japanese had taken, and in that way, gained a strong following.

This unit eventually changed its name to Hukbalahap, the "Huks." Luis

Taruc was one of the leading commanders. And the reason for the name change was that "USAFFE" was a very difficult name to use and it attracted too much attention. It was better that they use a Filipino name, one that was new and unknown. The people became loyal to the Huks. They thought this represented the pro–American/Filipino movement, but in truth it was the backbone of the Communist Party, which was to cause the Americans trouble.

Ramsey told Conner all the particulars, including some of the men's names, and everything he said checked with what Conner had discovered for himself.

The meeting proved informative. Ramsey stayed four days, and then he told Conner that he was going back to Manila. First, he was going to check with John Boone, and then he was planning to head north toward Lingayen Gulf, and there try to board a train for the capital.

Captain Louis Bell had already left for Manila, and they were going to reestablish the headquarters that Barker had formed. They intended to reorganize USAFFE, and try to gather the Filipino strength behind the American cause. It was quite an objective, quite a problem, and Conner wondered how long Ramsey could last.

Conner heard a year later that Ramsey had boarded the train in Lingayen Gulf, that the train had been sidetracked, and that Ramsey had been left aboard for over a week. He'd had some water with him, but it had run out. When he was picked up in the freight yard in Manila by faithful Filipinos who took him to a hiding place he was severely dehydrated and almost died. It was weeks before he was fully revived.

Ramsey was successful in organizing the area. Bell had died from typhoid fever[21] and Ramsey took over all operations.

In late February, Herbert and Conner left the Moron area and traveled toward the Fassoths' camp. After finding Boone's camp and talking with Ramsey, Conner had another malaria attack and decided to go to Bill Fassoth's camp located nearby. He stayed a short time, and visited with some of the Americans in the camp. He had known or heard of most of the men. Johnny Johns came over to the camp and during the evening got into an argument with one of the men, which turned into a fistfight. Bill Fassoth broke it up without much ado. With the men in such bad physical condition, their tempers were sometimes short and fights would break out. Bill could handle the situation and restore order.

The next morning Al Bruce and Tommy Musgrove arrived in the camp. They had been traveling through Pampanga and brought Conner the latest news. The Huks were giving Bruce a bad time, and the Japanese seemed to be increasing their garrison strength. Where there had been twenty Japanese soldiers in a town, now there were sixty or seventy. Bruce didn't know what was occurring, but he knew that the Japanese were putting a price on the Americans' heads. They wanted to clean out the guerrilla forces that were creating problems for the occupying forces.

Clay Conner and Johnny Johns left the Fassoths' camp a few days before the Japanese struck the shack near Boone's camp. It was fortunate they had moved because the Japanese had then targeted the Fassoths' third camp. The Japanese soldiers simultaneously hit Boone's hideout and the location where Bill Gardner and Ray Herbert were staying.

That evening Ramsey came over to Conner's location and asked if he would like to accompany him to the Lingayen Gulf area. Johns didn't want to leave, but Conner decided to join Ramsey. The two traveled just outside of the mountainous area into the lowlands, where Ramsey made contact with some friendly Filipinos. Here they stayed the night while Ramsey arranged travel to Guagua, where he had been previously — the home of the Jingco sisters.

Two days later Ramsey and Conner arrived at the Jingco's. The sisters were very pro–American, having helped Americans since the surrender of Bataan. There were four sisters and they were always happy — always smiling, moving, and taking short steps as they hurried about, knocking themselves out trying to help Conner and Ramsey.

They had a beautiful home, a mammoth, wood-framed structure with ten rooms. The home was well furnished with a lot of American imported furniture, rugs on the floors and mirrors. Not least, the home had a plumbing system.

The Jingco sisters fixed the men chicken, rice, and a lot of food that Conner had not seen in a long time. The sisters prided themselves in their hospitality; they would wait on the men, pouring more water, asking if everything was all right.

Ramsey told Conner that Colonel Merrill, Colonel Calyer, Major Tuggle, and Captain Kadel had lived with the sisters for a time. This was the place where they had organized Central Luzon guerrilla forces. But Ramsey and Conner knew they couldn't stay with the Jingcos. That would have been too good. The Japanese were saturating the area and it was dangerous for the men to be at the Jingco home.

On their way to Lingayen, Conner and Ramsey made contact with Bob Mailheau and Joe Donahey. Bob Mailheau had escaped from the Death March and had been given care by sisters in a Catholic convent in Santo Rita. Mailheau and Donahey decided to join Conner and Ramsey. The letter said he knew a family in a nearby barrio that would look after the two, Mauricio and Ciring Hardin. Ramsey wanted to leave Mailheau and Donahey at Barrio

Banaba and head north with Conner. Donahey agreed, as he didn't like walking across the rice dikes and hiding out in the sugarcane fields from the Japanese patrols.

The group visited the Hardins and the Lumanlans who were leading fig-
ures in Banaba. The Lumanlans' two sons, Democrito and Erting, joined the
group. Mr. Lumanlan was the lieutenant of the barrio — chief politician. He
was also a logger, going into the hills to cut logs and then bringing them into
the Japanese markets to sell.

As Conner and Ramsey traveled north the next day, they were directed
to two American soldiers named Wilbur Jellison and Charles Naylor who
lived outside of Fort Stotsenburg. That night after their meal the men enjoyed
sake.

The next morning Conner was upset by some comments he attributed
to Ramsey. Ramsey apologized for any misunderstanding, but Conner decided
to return to Banaba with Bob Mailheau, and Ramsey set off for Manila.

As Mailheau and Conner worked their way back to Banaba, they came
across Frank Gyovai and Eddie Keith. Gyovai and Keith had been dodging
Japanese patrols and fifth-column activities. They were elated to find Conner. Gyovai told Conner that Ernest Kelly and Howard Mann had been
killed.[22] For security reasons Gyovai and Keith had joined Pablo Aquino for
a short time. Aquino wanted the men to join him in the Candaba area, but
because of the problems Conner and Gyovai had previously with the Huks
in Candaba Swamps, they told Aquino, "No soap!"

The four Americans departed toward Concepion. The next day they
approached the little town of Lara. The men were tired and wanted to sleep.
They went into one of the Filipino homes where the people became almost
hysterical, telling the Americans that they could not stay, so the men went to
a house about a hundred yards further down the road.

Conner awoke early and saw four Filipinos sitting on a bench. He sat
up and asked if one of them was the mayor? "Yes," replied one of the men.

Conner yelled for the other men to wake up and get dressed. He knew
something was wrong and looked out the window of the hut.

The mayor began to talk about surrender, telling Conner that the Japanese would treat them well and give them food. Conner told the mayor that
the men would not surrender. The mayor was wasting his time talking about
capitulation.

The barrio's street was completely deserted. Gyovai then saw some Japanese and yelled "Japon! Japon!"

The Americans started to run in a northerly direction.[23] They ran through
the Japanese ranks, making for some rice paddies to get cover. In the melee
they got separated. Mailheau took off toward a river and spent the better part

of a day walking in the water beneath the riverbank to hide from other Japanese patrols. About the time Mailheau thought he had successfully made his escape he heard noises from another patrol. He looked down the river and saw a Filipino who had been fishing crawl back into some bushes on the riverbank. The Filipino saw Mailheau and motioned for Mailheau to come toward him. It didn't take any coaxing from the Filipino to get Mailheau to follow his directions. As soon as Mailheau got to the bush where the Filipino was hiding the Filipino reached out and pulled Mailheau in and motioned for him to be quiet. The Japanese patrol had reached the river and was starting to wade in the water toward the bushes where the two were hiding. The patrol went about a hundred yards and then stopped to look around and listen. For some reason their leader motioned for them to climb out of the river and head back from where they started.

The two remained in the bushes for a while longer, and when the Filipino felt it was safe he motioned for Mailheau to follow him to his home a short distance away. He and his family fed Mailheau, and Maiheau explained about his escape and wanting to find Conner and Gyovai. The Filipino told Mailheau that his teenage son would help him find his friends. It took three days to locate the others. They had linked up with Alfred Bruce and Tommy Musgrove. They were near La Paz where Bruce had been trying to get a guerrilla movement going in the region, without much luck. He and Musgrove agreed the group would have a better chance of survival if they could link up with Russell Volckmann and Donald Blackburn.

A couple of days later the group was about to journey north, when Japanese soldiers, who had word of five Americans in the area, ambushed them as they were leaving La Paz.

Managing to escape, after several days of close encounters, dodging, maneuvering, and running scared, Bruce and Musgrove decided they would settle near Tarlac and make it their base of operations. Conner, Gyovai, and Mailheau decided it wasn't meant for them to get north and headed back to the Banaba area where Donahey rejoined them.[24]

Bernard Anderson and Captain J. H. Menzano had proceeded toward the town of Angat to set up a camp in some mines north of Angat, Bulacan, where Bert Pettitt rejoined them ten days later.

With increased activities of the Japanese in this area, it was decided to move to the east coast of Luzon and reestablish intelligence contacts with the other parts of the island. On March 15, 1943, Anderson, Pettitt, and two of their Filipino sergeants traveled directly across the mountains toward Infanta, Tayabas, to their destination near Antinoman, Tayabas. They arrived at the barrio of San Luis, Mauban, in Tayabas on April 7, 1943. At this time

Anderson reestablished contact with their Manila agents and considered organizing the people in Tayabas who had not joined other guerrilla groups. Anderson and Pettitt then proceeded to Laganbyan, north of Mauban, and from there to locate and build another headquarters five kilometers north of Laganbyan on the Cabanabanan River. They remained here until January 1944, making frequent trips to the barrios north and south, with occasional trips to Babalete Island and barrios near Infanta and San Luis to obtain supplies and meet with agents carrying news and instructions to various individuals.[25]

In early 1943, Ray Hunt came across two men from the Fassoths' camp, Sergeant Hugh B. McCoy of the Fifth Interceptor Command and Sergeant Ray Schletterer of the Seventeenth Ordinance. An Igorot was with them, a man named Jose Balekow who had been a machine gunner with the Philippine army. The next day Fred Alvidrez, who had also been in the Fassoths' camp, joined the group. Alvidrez was of Mexican descent and could pass as a Filipino.

Many occupants of the camp had not liked Alvidrez. He would leave the camp for several days and upon his return brag about all the good food and women he had just enjoyed. Hunt reminded Alvidrez of an argument they had gotten into and Alvidrez's challenge to a fight. Hunt had been too weak at the time to take him up on it, but was now able to respond. Like two schoolboys, the men fought until they were both exhausted. After a short recess they again fought to a draw, neither admitting defeat, but too tired to continue the contest. Having exhausted their hostility toward each other, the next morning Hunt and Alvidrez resumed their trek northward with their group until they got near Camp Dau, just north of Angeles. After much discussion, the group split up, with McCoy and Schletterer leaving.[26]

On April 4, 1943, the Japanese ambushed Vicente and Arturo Bernia. Vicente came out of his shack with a Thompson submachine gun and killed several Japanese before he ran out of ammunition and ran. The Japanese shot him in the back and he died. Arturo was captured and trussed like a pig, with his hands and feet tied to a pole, and was carried down the mountainside to the San Marcelino airfield where he was questioned and then beheaded.[27]

Catalina Fassoth made a trip to Manila for supplies and Bill Fassoth was expecting her back on Saturday, April 4. Knowing Catalina would need help in packing the supplies into the camp, Bill recruited Martin and six other men, and started for the foothills to meet Catalina. Martin took the lead with their dog Chocolate. After traveling three hundred yards, Chocolate stopped, the hair raised on his back, and he began to bark. Martin rushed forward and observed Japanese soldiers at rest on the trail. Martin and Chocolate hurried back to the group and they all in turn made a hasty retreat back to the camp where they warned all to escape. There was only enough time to grab the guns, clothing and a few supplies, as sixty Japanese soldiers and twenty Filipino civilians followed the group into the camp. Fortunately, the Japanese did not see the men running out of the camp, which gave them time to hide.

Bill had Chocolate with him and held the dog's head and mouth shut to keep him from barking or growling. They sat by a big tree behind some small bushes on the hillside, and watched the Japanese soldiers search the camp. Some of the raiders passed within twenty feet of Bill and the dog. Another American escapee hid in some tall grass, four feet from the trail to the camp. The Japanese soldiers had bayonets attached to their rifles and poked into any suspicious clumps and bushes. Not finding anyone in the camp, the soldiers let the Filipinos who were with them loot the site and then set fire to the shacks.

After the raiding party left, the Americans salvaged some burned rice and one chicken that was tied to a bush. A few chickens running loose were also captured for food. That night the one chicken and some burned rice were all that twelve men had to eat.

The next morning after a breakfast of cooked rice and brown sugar, a council was held to discuss their situation. Some of the men wanted to go north toward Baguio and the mountain provinces. No one wanted to mention surrender or giving up to the Japanese garrison in Dinalupihan, but Bill addressed the men and suggested surrender due to their being continually hunted by the Japanese soldiers and the Huks becoming their enemies and a danger to the Filipinos aiding the camp. The lives of Bill's family were also in jeopardy. Most of the men decided that the idea of surrender was good. After breakfast, nine men started on the trail for the foothills of the mountains toward Dinalupihan. They left most of the medicine, guns and other supplies with the two men who remained at the camp.

At noon the nine men reached the hideout of an American civilian friend of Bill Fassoth, Eddie Hart. Bill made arrangements with Hart to dispatch a trusted Filipino, a relative of his wife, with a note to Catalina who was in Dinalupihan with the supplies. Catalina could not leave with the supplies to the camp in Isip because there were over a thousand Japanese soldiers in Dinalupihan scouting for Americans in the mountains. Catalina received the note telling her where Bill and his group were staying and saying that they were very hungry. She arrived at Eddie Hart's location about two hours later with what supplies she could put into a *carretela* (cart), in baskets, and sawali bags, which she and the girls hid under their voluminous skirts.

Because of a meeting that was to be held that Sunday afternoon by the

Japanese colonel in charge of the San Fernando garrison, all the roads leading out of Dinalupihan were guarded by the Japanese. The colonel was giving a speech to the Filipino people and had issued orders for no one to leave the town, especially the men. But this carretela with beautiful girls who gave the guards nice smiles was permitted to leave. The girls told the guards their destination was a barrio three kilometers from Dinalupihan, but in fact they were headed to the Fassoths' plantation. After passing the checkpoint, the carretela turned off toward Eddie Hart's home in the foothills.

When Catalina arrived, Bill told her of his intentions and asked if Bill Jr. was in Dinalupihan. Catalina said he was, so Bill asked her to explain the situation to their son and have him arrange surrender terms with the Japanese colonel, Susuki.

Considering the impending surrender of her husband, brother-in-law and American friends, Catalina made a lunch that was a feast. That evening Catalina and the girls went back to Dinalupihan and contacted Bill Jr.

Awaiting word from Catalina and not wanting to be captured, the men slept in the foothills outside of Eddie Hart's home. Bill could not sleep that night, thinking and discussing with Martin the story they would tell the Japanese. It dawned on Bill to tell the truth about the camp and to have the Americans do the same. Bill would shoulder the responsibility for the camp. After shaving and breakfast, Bill waited for his son who arrived about nine that morning. Bill Jr. had made all the arrangements with the Japanese colonel for the surrender.

After they had traveled to near Dinalupihan, one of the men who'd had an old Filipino taking care of him worried that his surrender might be detrimental to the Filipino, and decided against surrender. Another man who had been with a guerrilla unit that had killed a Japanese guard in Olongapo also decided against surrender.

Frank Bernacki was upset with some of the American officers who wanted to surrender with Bill and Martin Fassoth. Lieutenant Louis Dosh, Lieutenant Homer Martin, Dr. Arnold Warshell, and Bernice Fletcher all heard his words expressing disappointment. Bernacki confronted Dosh, and reminding him that he was a West Point graduate and that the army code is not to surrender if possible and if captured to take every opportunity to escape. Dosh told Bernacki with tears in his eyes that he just couldn't take it any more after being raided five times. Bernacki, undeterred, talked with the others, trying to dissuade them from surrendering, but with no effect. He asked Warshell to leave his medical bag, but Warshell told Bernacki that he wanted to use it to minister to the prisoners when he surrendered.[28]

When Bill and the group arrived at noon there were no Japanese soldiers at the outskirts of Dinalupihan. The Japanese had been ordered to remain in the town so the group could enter without being harassed by the soldiers. Bill Jr. left the group and called out to the Japanese officer in charge.[29] The officer arrived with two guards. There were now seven men surrendering, five military and two civilians. The Japanese officer asked if the group had eaten lunch and when told no, he dispatched a soldier to have food ready when they reached the garrison headquarters.

After eating and being well treated, the men were loaded on a truck and dispatched to San Fernando. Bill Jr. was allowed to bring Chocolate on the truck. Bill Jr. and the dog were then dropped off at Santo Tomas, Lubao, Pampanga, the home town of Catalina. The truck proceeded to the San Fernando garrison where the men were turned over to Colonel Susuki. The colonel asked who the two civilians were. After identifying Bill and Martin, the men were ordered into line. The colonel addressed the men, thanking them first for their surrender and promising that no harm would come to them. He further stated that Bill and Martin would be sent to the Santo Tomas internment camp and that the military men would be sent to the Cabanatuan prison camp. The colonel then asked Bill and his group to pose for pictures.

After the photos were taken, the colonel apologized for having to turn the men over to the provincial jail under the care of the prison warden, but said there wasn't a better place to put the group at that time. He issued instructions to the warden to give Bill and Martin extra privileges while in the jail, such as allowing them to see family and friends, receive food, money, or gifts, and to have liquor if they desired.

The jail was terrible. Their meal was a plate of steamed rice with a very small, thin, dried fish about a half inch wide by two inches long. Fortunately, Bill's family brought them food while they were in this jail.

There were four Americans already in the jail and a month later the number there increased to twenty-three. They all ate the food brought by Bill Fassoth's family. In addition there were many suspected guerrillas held there and they were treated badly.

Some of the prison trustees were convicts and were cruel to all the prisoners who failed to donate to the trustee's welfare. There was also no medication given to the prisoners, and Lieutenant Warshell had his medical supplies confiscated. He continued to minister to the sick and injured as best as he could. He was able to reason with the warden to send several cases to the provincial hospital for care and treatment.

All the men with Bill Fassoth were interrogated in the warden's office. They all told the true story of the camp. No one was implicated and the Japanese did not terrorize Bill's family in the hills. The men did not know the full names of the nurse or any of the other Filipino men and girls working for Bill, so none of them was identified.

After a month's confinement, all of the men were transported to the Cabanatuan prison camp. Bill Fassoth asked the warden to verify the order, as Colonel Susuki had promised that Bill and Martin would be sent to Santo Tomas. Bill was told the orders had come from headquarters in Manila. The warden dispatched a guard to Lubao that evening for Catalina and Bill Jr. They arrived at 10:30 P.M. and Bill asked for them to intercede the following morning. That was not allowed to happen. The men were trucked to Cabanatuan on May 9, 1943, where they would remain until a daring raid in January 1945.

Catalina continued to help the American men who were still in the hills and those who later surrendered and were in the provincial jail in San Fernando, Pampanga. She later had to go into the hills to hide as Vernon and Bill Jr. were working with guerrilla units. She remained active helping the guerrillas in the mountains until the return of American troops to Luzon.[30]

Nano Lucero and Romana Romero and her family had moved to Palacol where Romana had relatives. Nano was apprehended carrying a pistol and brought to Florida Blanco for interrogation. Able to convince the Japanese that he was Spanish, he was released and given back his pistol.[31]

In late April 1943, Hank Winslow and Earl Oatman received word that the Japanese had learned of the American soldiers living in the area of Barrio Bujaoen. Afraid that the Japanese might find them living with the Barron family, thereby putting the family at risk, Winslow and Oatman decided to leave the home and live further in the jungle in the foothills of the Zambales Mountains where they built a pup-tent like structure to shelter them during the rainy season. The Barron family continued to supply them with rice at their new location.

Without anything to read and not able to visit the Barrons or other Americans because of the Japanese patrols, living in the cramped quarters was difficult and monotonous. To help matters, Oatman made a set of dominoes out of boho, using his machete and making dots in the white inner wood with a lead pencil.

Because matches were scarce, a fire was kept burning continuously. Between episodes of rain Oatman and Winslow collected dead wood and piled it near their structure. The fire provided light, warmth, and a means of cooking.

Oatman explored up and down the creek, finding several young mango trees, and collecting the larger fruit from low-hanging limbs. He tried using the immature fruit in their rice and within hours they broke out with large, raised, white areas on their skin, the worse case of hives they had experienced. This stopped their experiment with the immature mangos.

Oatman's malaria attacks reoccurred. Mr. Barron showed him how to make a tea that was suppose to cure the malaria.[32] The tea was made by boiling the bark of dita, a tree growing in the area. The resulting liquid was as bitter as quinine. Oatman drank the concoction for several weeks, but did not find any relief from the malaria attacks. Eventually the attacks stopped without benefit of medication.

Four weeks later, the feared reconnaissance of Barrio Bujaoen having never materialized, Oatman and Winslow returned to the Barron home.

In May 1943, Hank Winslow left the Barron home and went to live with the family taking care of Bill Ostrander. Oatman wasn't sure why Winslow left, but thought he simply wanted a change.

One morning Oatman heard gunfire coming from the house where Millard Hileman was staying. He cautiously made his way to a higher elevation to determine what was happening. Hileman was firing from the nipa house where he lived. There was no answering fire, so Oatman knew the Japanese were not involved.

After several hours, Hileman came and told Oatman what had happened. The Filipino husband and wife who were taking care of Hileman had left early that morning to go somewhere and Hileman had heard a noise behind the house. Surprising several Negrito men stealing rice from a storage shed, Hileman had grabbed a rifle and chased them away, firing at them as they ran across a cleared field. To compound the situation, Hileman continued to fire occasionally while in full view of the Negritos hidden in the trees.

Although Hileman rightfully protected the rice supply of his host, the marauding Negritos could see that an American was firing at them with intent to kill. Inadvertently, Hileman had created a serious problem for the other Americans living in the area. Now if they had to temporarily leave their host's home to hide in the jungle because of Japanese activity, their safety could be impaired by revengeful Negritos.

The jungle-covered mountains were the Negritos natural domain. Neither the Americans nor the Japanese were safe if the Negrito disliked them. Fortunately, the aborigines generally like the American and hated the Japanese.

One morning in late May, Oatman and Coleman Banks decided to leave the Barron home and travel toward the Pampanga Province. They feared that their capture would lead to reprisals on the Barrons and knew they had been fortunate to evade the Japanese patrols. They arrived in an area a half mile from the Fassoths' second camp. All that remained of the nipa houses and outbuildings were wet ashes and pieces of smoldering bamboo from the Japanese raid.

Due to the late hour, Oatman and Banks walked a hundred yards from the area and lay down in the cogon grass. They soon discovered that they had made a poor choice of location, as mosquitoes swarmed the two men as they tried to sleep.

Arising the next morning, the two made their way to the foothills of the Pampanga side of the Zambales Mountains and started looking for a deserted nipa house in which to stay. They found one in a secluded area a mile from the edge of the lowlands. It offered protection from the rain and a hiding spot from Japanese patrols. There were two Negrito men and a woman living on the ground underneath the house.

One morning Oatman left the hut to find help and food. He saw a young Filipino boy tending a carabao at the edge of the jungle and followed the boy to his home. The men there told Oatman that a Japanese garrison was only ten miles from the home, but the soldiers usually passed on the other side of the river. They gave Oatman a small container of hulled rice and he returned to his hut where he found Banks lying on the floor wrapped in his blanket with chills from a fever. Banks told Oatman that he felt weak.

During the next several days Oatman scouted the area to find anything edible to supplement their diet of rice. Banks ate little and finally could not eat at all. Oatman left to find some carabao milk for Banks in hopes that he would be able to drink it. Succeeding in his mission, Oatman was stopped by some young men on his return to his hut and was invited to eat dinner with them. After eating, the men persuaded Oatman to spend the night, as the river was running full and would be dangerous to cross in the dark.

The next morning Oatman was awakened by the excited voices of his hosts. They told Oatman that a Japanese patrol had been seen crossing the river a mile below them, and the patrol had an American soldier and two Negrito men with them. The American and Negritos had their hands tied behind their backs and were strung together by a rope tied around their necks. By the description, Oatman knew that Banks was the American prisoner. One of the Negritos had a shotgun something considered a serious offense, and Oatman would later learn that Banks was executed on September 30, 1943, along with several other American soldiers. The Japanese commander wanted to make a show of stemming the guerrilla movement.

After several days with his Filipino hosts after the capture of Coleman Banks, Earl Oatman learned that there was an American soldier living nearby with ten Visayan Filipino soldiers. Since Oatman wanted to do something, and since it was too dangerous for him and his hosts to remain at this location, Oatman had one of the Filipinos take him to the American. This turned out to be Fred Stamper who also had escaped the Death March and had been in the Fassoths' Camp.

The Visayans were from the Thirty-first Infantry, Philippine Scouts, and were heavily armed. Stamper had also been with the Thirty-first, the only regular infantry unit in the U.S. Army in the Philippines when the war started. Oatman lived with the group for four weeks. Stamper told Oatman that the Japanese would never take him alive as long as he was capable of firing his gun.[33] The last time Oatman saw Stamper he was living with the Visayan soldiers.[34]

Chapter 8
The Summer of '43

All of the obstacles thrown at the guerrillas in 1943 were to set the stage for the success that followed in 1944. It was through the mistakes and survival techniques learned by the American guerrilla leaders that the arena was prepared for the return of the American troops to Luzon.

Russell Volckmann learned that Colonels Moses and Noble had been captured by Japanese soldiers northeast of Lubuagan, Kalinga, in June 1943. The Japanese had been active in the area and they were traveling south from Major Ralph Praeger's headquarters. Both Moses and Noble had taken ill and found a cave to hide and rest. One of their cadre went to a neighboring barrio to find some food, a Japanese patrol caught him, and he was tortured until he acquiesced and directed the Japanese to the cave. The colonels were sent to Bontoc, the capital of the mountain province. The Japanese commander forged an order by the colonels directing all guerrillas to surrender. The commander did not realize that the guerrillas would pay little attention to the directive.

Moses and Noble's capture was a blow to the resistance movement in North Luzon, because the colonels were greatly regarded by soldiers and civilians alike.[1] Volckmann had begun to control the Moses-Noble organization, though, months before the colonels were captured by the Japanese.[2]

On his way through a large barrio, one that he had passed through several times, Earl Oatman was stopped by a young Filipino acquaintance at the edge of the village. He discouraged Oatman from continuing through the barrio. He would not say why, just that Oatman should return to his hiding place.

As he could think of no logical reason to return to his hut, Oatman disregarded the suggestion and proceeded through the barrio. Halfway through the barrio, several young Filipino men stopped him and asked about his destination. Soon, several more joined the group and one of the men asked to examine the bolo Oatman had strapped to his waist. Oatman handed the bolo to the Filipino and the conversation turned to the presence of a Japanese garrison in the nearest town and how the Japanese commanding officer had given good treatment to recaptured American prisoners of war, especially those who surrendered.

The barrio lieutenant told Oatman that he had no recourse but to take him to the Japanese commander. Oatman decided that he was in a thorny situation and agreed with the barrio lieutenant's proposal. July 13, 1943, was the beginning of another chapter in Earl Oatman's life, one in which he was a prisoner of the Japanese.

Oatman was interrogated for several days before Japanese soldiers moved him from town to town, utilizing his mechanical skills to repair two of their cars, before sending him to the San Fernando prison. The Kempeitai had determined that Oatman had not participated in any guerrilla activities and would therefore not be executed.

One day at the prison Oatman noticed that in one area of the latrine there was a water faucet and a block of wood lying nearby. The block was four inches thick, six inches wide and two feet long. There was a curvilinear notch cut out of the center. An American staff sergeant and several of the Filipino workers told Oatman that the faucet and the block of wood were used by the Japanese for torturing prisoners, using what was called the "water treatment." The prisoner being interrogated was forced to lie down on the cement floor on his back, with his mouth directly underneath the faucet. While forcibly holding his head, arms and legs flat on the floor, the prisoner's mouth was forced open and the faucet turned on. To keep from suffocating, the prisoner swallowed the water. When his stomach was greatly distended with water, the notched block of wood was placed over his throat and pressed to the floor to prevent the water from being regurgitated. One of the Japanese interrogators then jumped up and down on the prisoner's stomach until he lost consciousness. When or if the prisoner recovered, he was questioned again. The process was repeated until the interrogator was satisfied that the prisoner was telling the truth, or until he died from the procedure.[3]

On August 7, 1943, Earl Oatman was taken to the Bilibid Prison Hospital with a case of appendicitis. He was placed in the execution chamber where twenty to thirty recaptured American POWs were temporarily housed. American naval doctors, accompanied by Japanese guards used a daily regimen to treat Oatman's appendicitis.

Hank Winslow and Bill Ostrander were also at the Bilibid prison. Winslow told Oatman that they had been recaptured about a month before he had been turned in to the Japanese. Winslow was being well treated, but Ostrander was severely beaten daily during questioning by the Kempeitai.

Oatman was subsequently moved to the surgical ward at Bilibid and had his appendix removed in October.[4]

In late June 1943, Millard Hileman and Bill Main had surrendered to the Japanese. They were imprisoned in the San Fernando prison and when Hileman was escorted to his cell he found he had three cellmates. Their appearance was repugnant to Hileman, with their scruffy beards and their worn out, dirty garb. Then he realized that he looked pretty much the same.

Hileman tried to introduce himself to the man nearest him, but the prisoner was unresponsive. One of the other men extended his hand, and commenced a conversation. It was Tom Rayburn whose first question was about Hileman's bridge playing ability. He was looking for a fourth partner.

Hileman replied that he didn't know the game and didn't want to learn. Rayburn didn't care about Hileman's response, tossed him a deck of worn cards, and told him he was his new partner. For the next few days Hileman played bridge, from the time he woke until the cell's dim light was turned off.

After five days at San Fernando, Hileman, Rayburn and several other prisoners were loaded on a truck and moved to Bilibid Prison. It was old, a remnant of Spanish colonization built a century before Admiral Dewey had come to Manila in 1898. Its outer walls formed a great square, in the center of which stood a round, domed office building. It looked like the hub of a great wheel with walls extending from it like spokes to the outer perimeter.[5]

Later that day as Hileman, Paul Vacher, and Bill Main were in their cell, sitting on the floor next to the electric chair, reviewing the day's events, they were joined by another American well known to Vacher.

"How you doing, Killer?" Vacher said. His question was directed at the newcomer, a skinny-looking guy with a week's growth of beard and a ready smile. An old straw hat was tilted sideways on his head. He sat down and rolled up a cigarette from some native tobacco he shook from a beat-up Union Leader can.

"Pretty damn good for an old Georgia hillbilly. These guys friends of yours?" he asked Vacher.

"Yeah, we came out of Bataan together."

Before he had a chance to introduce himself, someone called to him from outside and he left.

"That's Pierce Wade, the guy I met at Joe Cheeseman's just before the

Japs got us. He's the biggest bullshitter you've ever heard. He served in the Canal Zone before coming to the P.I., and when you hear his stories you'll know why I called him Killer."[6]

Among several other prisoners in Bilibid were Hank Winslow and Earl Oatman. Winslow and Bill Ostrander had been captured by the Huks, taken to San Marcelino, and then transferred to Bilibid.

Two others in the cell, Hugh McCoy and Ray Schletterer, had been taken from their jail cells and ordered to dig holes. They thought they were digging their own graves. The men were certain they would be executed when they finished digging. Instead, the Japanese filled the holes with garbage and marched the prisoners back to their cells.

The usual daily food ration was rice and seaweed soup given to the men two times a day. The men ate tiny bites to make the inadequate provisions last longer. Hot tea was brought to them in wooden buckets.

In the confined space of the prison cell, the men rarely talked about anything personal. With their starvation rations, food became the focus of their survival and conversations. Psychologically, food was the subject that symbolized freedom and dreams, and was something everyone could talk about without heartache.

The topic of conversation one day turned to pie. Each man began describing in detail their favorite pie. Some went so far as to describe the process of planting and harvesting the fruit, of preparing the filling, and recounting the taste of the finished creation. After all the others finished, Sill Herring spoke.

"Oh, hell; there ain't but one kind of pie." The compact, dark-complexioned man from Louisiana spoke with a decided southern drawl. "That's sweet potater pie!"[7]

The day after arriving at Bilibid, Main and Hileman were discussing their predicament. They were puzzled by their stay at San Fernando and speculated about what was next. As they talked, Pierce Wade joined them.

Wade asked them about their length of stay at San Fernando. When told that they had only been there a few days, Wade gave them advice on what to expect.

He told them that if they hadn't been interrogated at San Fernando they could expect intense questioning at Bilibid. Not only questioning but torture, with a lot of what they might think were stupid questions, such as where they lived in the States, what street they lived on and whether the street was paved or gravel. They could expect to be beaten no matter their reply. Wade told them that whatever happened they could not say anything about the Filipinos who had helped them, because the Filipinos and their families would be killed.

Because Wade had been through the interrogations, Main and Hileman listened closely, and during the next two weeks they gained more knowledge of the perils they would confront. Several Americans in the same prison had been executed. Not long before they arrived at Bilibid, Colonel Claude Thorp, who had led an ambush on a Japanese convoy before his capture in late 1942, had been shot.[8]

Another officer, Major Ralph Praeger, died a brutal death just after their arrival. Praeger had salvaged a radio transmitter and had been sending messages to Australia after the American surrender in the Philippines. The Japanese knew Praeger used the American code. Praeger was beaten with a baseball bat and then hung by his thumbs for forty-eight hours as the beatings persisted. The comatose Praeger, with a guard pulling each arm, was hauled into Hileman's compound and tossed into one of the solitary confinement cells. Praeger died from the continuous beatings, but never disclosed the American code. His courage inspired all the American prisoners and many speculated about their ability given the same circumstance.

Wade advised Hileman and Main to keep their stories simple, so they could remember them and tell the same story at every interrogation. The grilling varied. While beatings were frequent, occasionally Hileman and Main were treated well and were given pineapples or bananas. On other occasions the guard they called Golf Club, for his favorite tool of torture, gave one of them a cigarette, lit it, then snatched it from their mouths and ground it out with the toe of his boot, though once in a while they were allowed to finish a smoke. The behavior of Golf Club and the other interrogators ran the gamut from arrogant and brutal to smiling and superficially friendly. There was no predicting them.

Interrogators asked a wide variety of questions, most of them about Hileman's and Main's time in the mountains. They asked about the people who had aided them and wanted to know if they had taken part in any guerrilla activities. They were especially interested in the Fassoths' camp, but Main and Hileman had not been to the camp, so they did not have to lie about that aspect of their escape.

Everyone in the cells was tortured and interrogated, and, for the most part, all handled the repeated questioning well. The Americans were tough men who had shown bravery and enterprise in escaping, and after months of deficiency and adversity, most of them felt the Japanese could not top what they had already experienced. In many ways they felt superior to their captors and reinforced each other's morale. In one instance, however, a prisoner suffered a breakdown.

Dan Cahill was a big, tough-looking man whose world came crashing down on him one evening. He began to cry that he wanted to go home. Some of the men tried to shut him up and a few began to deride him. Then an unlikely voice emerged. It was Harold Todd Irving who began to recite Rudyard Kipling's poem, "If":

> If you keep your head when all
> About you
> Are losing theirs and blaming it
> On you;
> If you can trust yourself when
> All men doubt you,
> But make allowance for their
> Doubting too;
> Yours is the Earth and everything
> That's in it,
> And — which is more — you'll be a Man,
> My son!

Irving's words scored through the despair, and no one made a sound as he concluded the poem.

An interlude of silence was broken by Pierce Wade who parsed a few of Robert Service's poems of the Yukon with his own burlesque. The men alternated between hilarity and tears as the cadence of the verse and the amity it created brought comfort to all the men. Cahill gathered himself and one by one the men wafted to slumber.[9]

Many of the prisoners at Bilibid had ringworm and struggled to keep from scratching the infection. Medics gave them medication to treat the contagious fungus. It burned when applied, but after two treatments the rash usually vanished.

Pierce Wade had ringworm on his buttocks, which he had scratched with the sharp edge of a tobacco can lid. Lying prone on the floor, he asked Mike Slish to apply the remedy. Hileman watched Slish carefully daub it on, conscious of the stinging effect, but Wade's apprehension only protracted the torture. In frustration, Wade told Slish to pour it on the wound. Slish dutifully emptied the medication over the irritated area. The fiery red liquid ran down the crack of Wade's butt and swathed his scrotum with a blazing sensation.

Wade shouted as he jumped to his feet, asking Slish what the hell he was thinking. Slish sheepishly reminded Wade that he had asked for him to pour the liquid on the infected area. The men in the cell rolled on the ground in laughter.[10]

In September 1943, Captain Al Bruce, Lieutenant James Hart, Private Eugene Zingheim, Jose Raagas and Adelaida Villareyes were hiding out in a small hut in the barrio of Tapuak, Bamban. Bruce was forming a guerrilla organization. At five o'clock in the morning of September 3, their dog Daisy began making noise inside the hut, trying to alert the inhabitants to the approaching twenty Japanese soldiers, ten constabularies and four Filipino spies. Before the occupants of the hut could protect themselves, the raiding party opened fire, killing Lieutenant Hart, and capturing Villareyes and Eugene Zingheim, sick with malaria, while Bruce and Raagas escaped. Eugene Zingheim was bayoneted to death by the Japanese on September 30, 1943 in Capas. After nearly three months of confinement and interrogation Adelaida Villareyes was released and rejoined Al Bruce and his guerrilla unit.[11]

Crito Lumanlan brought the bad news of Hayden Lawrence's execution by the Japanese. He told Conner that Lawrence was captured in Angeles in a Japanese raid. Fearing that he was armed, Japanese soldiers had approached him cautiously. When they finally grabbed him, they knocked Lawrence to the ground and began to kick him, beat him, and jab at him with bayonets. He was taken to Angeles, where he was again beaten, and then picked up and knocked to the ground again to show the Filipino people that the Japanese were superior to the Americans. Then the water treatment was applied by taking a hose and shoving the nozzle up his rectum, bloating his intestines until they almost burst. Then they tied his wrists together, hung him to a tree by his wrists, and beat him across his stomach with bamboo poles until the water gushed out every orifice.[12] Then he was dropped to the ground unconscious.

Crito had tried to talk to Lawrence through a window, but the Japanese interrupted the attempt and Crito fled before he too was captured. Lawrence was exhausted, but he was hot-tempered.

The next day, when the Japanese resumed their torture, Lawrence shouted at the Japanese commander, Captain Tanaka, and challenged him to an honest fistfight, telling Tanaka that he was nothing but a coward. Tanaka unsheathed his saber and swung furiously right through the middle of Lawrence, leaving him to die in the marketplace square.

Crito Lumanlan had more bad news for Conner. Ray Herbert was dead. The Huks had taken him into custody in northern Tarlac, and had tried him for criminal action, convicted and shot him.[13]

Ray Hunt had information about Major Robert Lapham and his guerrilla organization in Pangasinan, Nueva Ecija, and parts of Nueva Vizcaya to the north and east, and extending into Tarlac, the province where Hunt had gathered a few guerrillas of his own.

Lapham was part of the group that came out of Bataan with Colonel

Thorp and was the inspector general before Thorp's capture and execution. He then took command of the guerrilla forces in Central Luzon.

As Hunt traveled to the north in the early fall of 1943, he sent one of his men to contact Lapham with an offer to place his small force under Lapham's command. Three weeks later Hunt received instructions from Lapham to contact Captain Albert C. Hendrickson, commander of Tarlac Province, and to serve with him. After several days of wandering and searching, Hunt found Hendrickson.

Hunt was elated to meet an American, and Hendrickson and he became good friends. They celebrated by hosting a dance near Victoria, Tarlac. The orchestra consisted of members of Hendrickson's guerrillas. That evening they relaxed, disregarded the enemy, imbibed liberally, and took pleasure in the moment.

Hendrickson appointed Hunt his executive officer and proclaimed him a captain. In their enthusiasm they engaged in numerous clashes with Japanese patrols. Little damage was done, but the Japanese, with their unfailing talent at mangling the English language, responded by putting out circulars calling for the capture of an American named Allen Ray (Al and Ray). Secret agents soon straightened out the confusion and Hendrickson had a price of 50,000 pesos on his head and Hunt 10,000 pesos on his.[14]

Late in the morning of Friday, October 8, 1943, Bilibid prisoners who looked out one of the windows overlooking the prison's stone-paved courtyard witnessed a gloomy sight. Most turned away, because to watch could attract retaliation from the guards. The few who did watch saw a line of twenty-six almost naked American and Filipino men, their wrists tied to a common length of chain, falter across the courtyard toward two trucks waiting at the main gate. The men had been undressed to their undershorts, or Japanese G-strings in some cases, and each man's head was covered with a *bayong,* a native bag made of woven palm leaves.

At noon on that cool, cloudy day at the La Loma Cemetery on the northeast outskirts of the city, one of the trucks unloaded its cargo. Japanese guards led fifteen hooded men, including Colonels Martin Moses and Arthur "Maxie" Noble, inside the walls. They closed the cemetery gates. Passersby heard a series of shots.

The other truck unloaded its cargo at the nearby Chinese cemetery. Five Americans, including Colonels Claude A. Thorp and Hugh Straughn, and four Filipinos, including Colonel Guillermo Nakar, were led inside. The guards stood them all in a line and removed the covers from their heads. Colonel Akira Nagahama, chief of the Kempeitai, read their death warrant to them. The guards then retied the covers over their heads, except Colonel

Straughn's, as the old gentleman refused to accept his. The nine men stood at the edge of an open, common grave, about four feet deep. They remained silent, except for Colonel Guillermo Nakar who shouted repeatedly that General MacArthur and the American army would soon be back.

A firing squad composed of Japanese prison guards shot the men. Anyone who was not dead from the first volley received the coup de grace from Colonel Nagahama's own pistol. Such was the case of Colonel Hugh Straughn who remained barely alive and kneeling at the edge of the grave. Colonel Nagahama walked up behind him with his pistol and blew his brains out. Guards kicked the bodies into the grave and Straughn's shattered glasses were thrown in on top of him. The bodies were then covered with dirt.

The next evening Colonel Nagahama dropped by Club Tsubaki, the Japanese officers' favorite nightclub in Manila. The proprietress, Dorothy Fuentes, born Clare Phillips, recognized the colonel, approached his table, and sat down to talk.

The morning newspapers carried stories of the execution of Hugh Straughn, and the American guerrilla commander was the main topic of discussion at Club Tsubaki that night. Claire Phillips had helped Hugh Straughn's guerrillas, and felt a certain kinship with him although she had never met the man. Hoping to learn more about him, she asked Nagahama if he had ever met Colonel Straughn. To her horror, Nagahama grinned broadly.

"See dis had?" he boasted. "Dis had dat used gun on him in Chinese cemetery."[15]

By October 1943, the Japanese had captured and executed virtually all the major guerrilla leaders on Luzon. General Kuroda declared that guerrilla resistance in the islands had ended, so the Japanese granted the Philippines their "independence" on October 14, 1943. Only Japan, Nazi Germany, and Spain recognized the new puppet regime.

Having fulfilled their promise, the Japanese now turned their attention to MacArthur's spies, their underground supporters, and the few Americans who still remained in the Philippines.[16]

In early 1943, the outlook for Luzon guerrillas was glum. Japanese patrols had increased. The Fassoths' camp had been attacked and burned in September 1942. Colonel Thorp was captured in October and Captain Barker in January 1943. By February, Thorp and Barker were in Fort Santiago awaiting execution. Captain Jack Spies had been killed on his way to assume command. Colonel Gyles Merrill was isolated in the Zambales Mountains. Russell Volckmann had begun to replace Colonels Martin Moses and Arthur Noble.

Captain Bob Lapham's domain was beset by problems and uncertainties, and Major Bernard Anderson was holed up in the mountains of Bulacan and Tayabas.[17] The Americans were coping with disease, despair, and organizational problems. There were many cultural systems to integrate and use to the guerrillas' advantage.

Chapter 9

Re-formation

The formation of guerrilla units was cumbersome at best. It involved on-the-job training, as no one had received instruction in organizing them. There were many units trying to survive and their first priority was procuring food. Some were more bandits and thieves than fighters. Some of the Huk units were more disciplined than others, submitting to Mao Tse-Tung's teachings, while many others who had joined the Huks were more concerned about killing the Japanese invaders than following communist doctrine. Of all the guerrilla groups, the Huks may have had the most experience in this type of warfare.

Some of the problems precipitated by guerrilla units led by Americans were lack of cultural understanding and desire for power and control. Lt. William Gardner, a noncom who'd been commissioned in the field, was leading the Visayans, a guerrilla group in Pampanga. He and the son of Rodriquez, the leader of a group in the Zambales Mountains, got into an argument, shots were fired, and Rodriquez's son was killed. This started a feud between the two groups. Eventually two Visayans, Lebrado[1] and Cebuano were killed in an ambush by the Zambales guerrillas, furthering hostilities. At times it was hard to tell who was the enemy, the Japanese or another guerrilla group trying to establish influence.[2]

In early 1943, Clay Conner continued his organizational efforts in the Clark Field and Fort Stotsenburg area. Frank Gyovai, Bob Mailheau and Joe Donahey had joined Conner in the Banaba Barrio. One dark, rainy night on his way back to Banaba, Conner convinced his Negrito guide to take him to Doyle Decker and Bob Campbell. Until this time no one would tell

Conner of Decker and Campbell's location, even though the Hardin and Lumanlan families were supporting both groups. Each was afraid that one of the groups might be captured and thus reveal the other members.

As Conner and his guide approached the hut, Cracker, Decker's dog, began a low growl and walked around the hut. Before they could move, the Negrito called out, "It's okay, I have a G.I. with me!"

"Come on in!" Decker yelled with relief.

Entering the hut, Conner reached out his hand and introduced himself. He explained that he had been on his way back to his camp, but because of the heavy rain he was seeking shelter and had convinced his guide, Humbo, to show him their location.

Humbo was one of the Negritos for whom Decker had repaired a gun. Before the war he and his brother Mario worked as servants for a wealthy Filipino, and they learned to speak English. Their ability with the language made them valuable guides and interpreters.

Conner was five foot eight, with dark hair and a glint in his eyes. Some would describe him as handsome. He had a no-nonsense attitude, with an air of confidence bordering on arrogance.

Decker reached for his pack and handed Conner dry pants and a shirt. "You can wear some of ours until yours dry." Water ran in streamlets off Conner and escaped through the bamboo slats to the ground below.

Conner told Decker and Campbell that they were hard to find. Conner's camp was just two miles farther up the mountain, and he had known of the other two Americans' existence for the last two months, but couldn't convince anyone to lead him to them. Conner commented that Decker and Campbell had made good friends with the Negritos and local Filipinos.

The men spent the night eating rice and talking about how each got to the Philippines, and about their units and their escapes. Conner tried to persuade Decker and Campbell to join his growing unit. He told them about the other three Americans in his camp, and left the next morning with assurances that Decker and Campbell would visit the camp in the next few days.

After the rains slackened, and following directions provided by Conner, Decker and Campbell hiked two hours up the mountain trail to Conner's camp situated on a beautiful plateau at the edge of a cliff. A spring flowed from the side of the mountain, running a few feet and then cascading down the cliff into a river below. When they walked into the camp they saw four men sitting around a fire.

Conner greeted Decker and Campbell, and introduced Frank Gyovai, Bob Mailheau and Joe Donahey. The men spent the rest of the day reliving their trials. The stories varied as much as each man's background. Decker observed the others as they talked about themselves.

Frank Gyovai was the first to tell his story. He was a young and excitable giant of a man who had quit high school to follow his father's vocation as a coal miner in West Virginia. "I saw the army as a way out of the coal mines," he laughed, "and look at me now." Decker noticed that Gyovai was totally devoted to Conner from the many stories he told of their exploits in recent months.

Joe Donahey, who at five foot nine was more Conner's size, told his story next. Thin, nervous, quiet, and intelligent, Joe had grown up in Iowa. He was an army careerist but preferred the security of numbers to the adventure of guerrilla warfare. "I don't think we can win out in a skirmish with the Japs," he mumbled at one point in the conversation. "I would just as soon stay in the mountains and out of sight."

Bob Mailheau introduced himself as a son of a Los Angeles Police Department detective. His six foot two frame was thin at 140 pounds, down from his usual 170 prior to his escape from the Death March. "You can't tell it by looking at me now," he joked, glancing at his chest and arms, "but I used to have some muscle on these bones."

The discussion turned to organizing the Negritos. Related to that topic, Conner didn't want Campbell or Decker to move to his camp. He wanted them to stay near Banaba, linked to the lowlands as an intelligence-gathering unit. They were to take orders from him, but couldn't expect any help with food or other provisions. They would have to rely on themselves, the Hardins, and Mr. Palo.

"Hey, that's fine with me," Decker replied. "I prefer bein' on my own."

The men all shook hands. This was the birth of the 155th Guerrilla Squadron. Conner used the squadron designation because he was an Army Air Corps lieutenant. Colonel Gyles Merrill, ranking officer after the capture of Thorp, later renamed the unit the 155th Provisional Guerrilla Battalion to more fittingly describe them.

As Campbell and Decker headed back to their camp, they discussed Conner's offer. Campbell wasn't convinced the plan would work. He felt that if they took orders from Conner, then he should help them. Decker reminded Campbell that they had made it own their own with help from the Hardins and Palos and that this would give them something to do, something with a mission and purpose. Despite his misgiving, Campbell agreed to the plan.

For the rest of 1943, the 155th continued to grow, as the Americans made contact with Negritos on Mount Pinatubo and Filipinos in the barrios and villages of the lowlands around Clark Field and Fort Stotsenburg.

All was not peace and happiness with the 155th. Mailheau and Gyovai had some conflicts, with one resulting in a fistfight. After this, Mailheau moved to the camp with Decker and Campbell. Campbell though, didn't like

Mailheau taking Decker to the lowlands to recruit guerrillas and another rift developed due to this. Decker, who liked both men and understood their different proclivities toward the war, tried to make peace, but Campbell finally moved to another area and built his own hut.

A few days after Campbell moved out, Humbo visited the camp.

"Clay wants Bob to come to camp for a report on his progress," said Humbo seriously, proud of his English.

Mailheau packed his belongings and headed up the trail with Humbo. He told Decker to keep his head down and watch his skinny ass. They had made enough trips to the lowlands for a while and he would be back in a couple of days.

The next day George, Mr. Palo's son-in-law, arrived with a thoughtful expression on his face. He had seen Campbell the day before. Campbell had moved in with a Filipino woman whose father was helping to feed them. George told Decker that Campbell was lonely and wanted Decker to visit his camp.

Late that afternoon, Mailheau returned to camp with a smile. He had a lot of news. Conner was happy with their work recruiting and organizing the Filipinos in the lowlands. He wanted them keep their camp near Banaba; in the event either camp was raided, the other camp would still be intact. Conner had contacted Colonel Merrill and the colonel wanted them to gather as much information as they could and continue to organize the local people. They were to avoid contact with the Japanese as much as possible. Their primary objective was to organize their forces as a blocking unit to prevent the Japanese from crossing the mountains to the China Sea when the American forces returned to Luzon. They especially wanted to keep the Japanese from using the old cavalry trail from Stotsenburg to Iba as an escape route to the west coast. Colonel Merrill also wanted them to find and map as many locations of Japanese units, prison camps, airfields, ammo dumps, and fuel dumps as they could.

In addition Conner had designated Mailheau to be in charge of intelligence and had promoted Decker to the rank of first lieutenant and Mailheau to captain in order to give them some credibility with the Filipinos and Negritos.

Decker looked up and said, "Hell, yesterday I was a private. Sounds good to me. Is our rank worth a damn?"

"It is for the time being. It's a battlefield commission. If and when the American forces get back, the commissions might not stand up, but for now we have the rank."

Decker laughed, "What did Conner become?"

"A major," Mailheau responded.

Mailheau told Decker that because Merrill was a colonel, Conner couldn't promote himself to be equal to Merrill. Merrill was hopping mad anyway, as there were men all over the island promoting themselves to colonel in order to head their units. In fact, Conner had shown Mailheau a communiqué from Merrill questioning him about his promotions. Merrill wasn't happy with Conner handing out promotions and making himself a major. Conner had gone into a long explanation to Merrill about the need for rank to have credibility with the locals. Another consideration — the Huks were running around with all kinds of rank trying to recruit additional people into their units, as the Filipinos were impressed with rank.[3]

On more than one occasion while they were out gathering supplies, Cracker saved Decker from ambush. The dog was friendly to few people other than Decker, but she hated Japanese soldiers. Whenever they were away from camp, Cracker ran down the trail ahead of Decker. When she smelled a Japanese patrol she would run back to her master, her hair bristling, her teeth showing, and a low growl coming from her throat. They would immediately move off the trail and take cover in the dense jungle foliage. Cracker wouldn't make a sound, but as the Japanese patrols passed by her hackles were up and she shook with emotion.

Decker was grateful to the Negrito who gave him Cracker. She meant more to him than anyone. He owed her for helping him to keep his sanity and for alerting him to possible danger.

One evening in late 1943 when Mailheau was at 155th headquarters, Decker was drifting off to sleep when an agitated Cracker began to walk around the hut growling. Immediately Decker rolled out of the back of the hut, dove into a ravine, and hid in the bushes, a move he had practiced in case the hut was discovered by the Japanese. Cracker was right behind him, and no sooner had they taken cover than the Japanese riddled the hut with gunfire. One of the soldiers walked to the rear of the hut and shot several bursts of gunfire into the ravine with a staccato rat-tat-tat and a whump-whump-whump as the bullets hit the ground. The shells barely missed Decker and Cracker who both could smell the sulfur from the muzzle burst. There was shouting and commotion for several minutes. When the Japanese realized they had missed the occupants of the hut they set the shelter on fire and walked back down the trail to Banaba. Rather than chancing a return by the patrol, Decker and Cracker spent the rest of the night hiding in the ravine.

The next day Decker moved the camp further into the jungle and left trail signs, a marked tree here and a bent limb there, to enable Mailheau to find him when he returned from headquarters. When Mailheau found Decker they had a long conversation about the near miss and the new camp.

They had found that organizing the Filipinos required more than contacting potential volunteers. There was ammunition to locate and store, and food, always in short supply, was constantly on the men's minds. Puli (tamarind) was a staple — similar to lima beans but sweeter, and puli beans had a nice pop when bitten into. Boiled to soften, they could be dried and stored for weeks and then boiled again for eating. The Negritos, who controlled the mountain crop, used mountain rice and puli-beans for bartering with lowland Filipinos to get needed implements, clothing, medicine, and even weapons. Mailheau particularly liked puli beans and avocados. During the dry season, fruits and vegetables were plentiful, but the rainy season was miserable and food was more difficult to procure and store without spoiling. The men stored rice and jerky for the rainy season, but food putrefied easily in the tropics and dysentery was a problem. Dried puli beans stored well.

Prior to Thanksgiving, Mrs. Hardin sent word through George that she was preparing a Thanksgiving meal and that she and her daughters Maling and Pading would bring it to the camp and celebrate with "the boys." This was a special time for the men of the 155th and their benefactors of Banaba. They spent the day enjoying the feast of rice, chicken, and camotes with lots of fruit. It felt like family to everyone that day and was reminiscent of the first Thanksgiving celebrated in the New World.[4]

In the latter part of January 1944, Bert Pettitt moved all the equipment from the camp on the Cabanabanan River to a new location north of Infanta. Pettitt then rejoined Bernard Anderson at his request and proceeded with him to another camp four kilometers south of Laganbyan. When they arrived, a letter was waiting from a Captain Montalban, liaison officer from the Tenth Military District of Mindinao.

Anderson proceeded to Mainit, Tayabas, to meet Captain Montalban, while Pettitt remained to see that the new headquarters was completed. When Anderson returned he brought good news that a fairly reliable contact had been made with forces operating in the Southwest Pacific. He also had American cigarettes and candy as additional proof. Captain Montalban wanted Anderson to go to Mindanao with Mauro Prieto to act as a contact agent and interpreter.[5]

The mission of Pettitt, John Schafer, and Mauro Prieto from Anderson's camp was to report to Colonel W. Fertig on all possible landing points for submarines from Dingalon Bay to Capalong, Comarines Norte, and to accompany a submarine to one of the possible landing points. Further, in the event that they could not accompany a submarine, they were to return to Luzon with what supplies could be obtained from the Tenth Military District, using any transportation available.

The party was taken to Mindanao by Mauro Rama, a member of "Quezon's Own Guerrillas." Arrangements for transportation were made by Captain Montalban. The group left Luzon at Mulanay, Bondoc Peninsula, on April 7, 1944, and arrived in Tobigon, Bohol, on April 13. Because of the delay by the commanding officer of the Bohol forces in supplying the group with arms which had been issued to Mauro Rama, the party did not leave Bohol until May 6. They then left with Major Zapanta and arrived at Cabadbaran, Agusan Province, the next day. From here they traveled to Loreto, Agusan Province, and arrived at the Headquarters of the Tenth Military District on May 25.

A written report of possible landing points on Luzon was turned in to the commanding officer. There was no reply until June 25 when the group left with medicine, clothing, 5,000 pesos in Japanese War Notes and 24,000 pesos in Mindanao Emergency Currency for the liaison officer of the Tenth Military District on Bohol. The group proceeded to Bohol and picked up other supplies.

Then it was on to Balinguan, Occidental Misamis, on July 18 to purchase a sailing boat with the expense money given to them by the Tenth Military District commanding officer. The boat was supposed to be able to hold 4,000 kilograms — 8,800 pounds. John Schafer remained in Balinguan to get the boat in order and procure supplies and crew. Pettitt and Mauro Prieto proceeded to Balingasag, and sent a radio message to the commanding officer of the Tenth Military District for authority to use the 24,000 pesos intended for Bohol, as it had been learned that Bohol had been invaded by the Japanese and the money would not be delivered in time. Authority to keep the money arrived on July 25.

John Schafer arrived in Balingasag on August 12 and he left on August 14 for destinations in the Occidental Misamis, as directed by the Tenth Military District, to pick up supplies for Luzon. Mauro Prieto accompanied Schafer.

Pettitt proceeded to contract for another sailing boat, but because of enemy actions in the vicinity and difficulty in getting a crew he was unable to secure a banca (boat) until September 7. The date set for departure was September 19, but increased enemy action caused the boat to be captured and burned on September 17.

With the radio out of commission, Pettitt proceeded to Sumilao, Bukidnon, and made radio contact with the Tenth Military District. Hearing that Schafer was in Dipolog, Occidental, Misamis, Pettitt proceeded to the coast at Alibijed, learning that Schafer had passed there on his way to Cameguin Island. Pettitt then found a boat and rejoined Schafer on November 3 at Kinoguitan, and they proceeded to Mombajao, arriving November 5.

A radio message to the Tenth Military District was sent requesting authority to proceed to Luzon via Leyte. Authority was not granted but arrangements were made to pick up the men by plane, a PBY, on December 7. On this day they flew to Tacloban, Leyte, and reported to the G-3 Philippine Sub-Division.[6]

After the surrender of Bill and Martin Fassoth, Catalina Fassoth continued to help those men at liberty on Luzon with food. With Louis Bell's death, Vernon and Bill Jr. were now under the command of John Boone. Vernon was the more active of the two brothers, in charge of procuring supplies as a captain of the Headquarters Service Company for Boone's unit, in addition to commanding the messenger center.

Bill Jr. was the provost marshal for Boone's unit and thus was in charge of the military police. His unit would investigate those people with alleged ties to the Japanese and would arrest them if enough evidence was found.

Not having any training, Vernon Fassoth learned the job by using his ingenuity to obtain rice and other staples from the local populace who supported the guerrillas. He relied on four barrios to get most of the supplies and used a bull cart to collect the rice. The barrios were expected to supply ten percent of their rice crop to the guerrillas. In some situations the guerrillas were able to gain support by promising to protect the barrios from bandits and thieves.

In 1943 there was a lot of food. The Japanese went from house to house, confiscating whatever they could find. They took from the granaries, and whereever they could get food. This was a blunder by the Japanese. Feeling that any food produced would be taken from them, the populace did not plant in 1943. As a result, in 1944 there was little food, and everybody nearly starved. No rice, because no one planted. The populace was reduced to eating banana stalks, or anything they could get from the land that grew wild or volunteered. This complicated Vernon Fassoth's efforts.[7]

In early March 1944, Earl Oatman was sent to Cabanatuan Prison Camp. The prison camp was built on land that had been used for rice paddies. It originally served as a training base for an infantry division of the Philippine Army before the Japanese attacked the Philippines. At Cabanatuan, Oatman's name was added to a list of nine other POW's. Oatman was told that if any one on the list escaped, the others would be executed by the Japanese.

Oatman soon found Hank Winslow at Cabanatuan, as Winslow had been transferred there several months before Oatman's arrival.[8]

Millard Hileman, Paul Vacher, Bill Main and several other American prisoners had been transferred from Bilibid to Cabanatuan Prison Camp. All prisoners who had escaped from the Japanese either directly or from the Death March, were designated special prisoners and required to wear a red tag.

At Cabanatuan the prisoners had formed small groups, usually two to four men, who honored an unspoken promise of mutual survival. The core of the understanding was sharing any extra food obtained by anyone in the group, an activity known as "quanning." The word was created from the Filipino word "quan" (or "kuwan") which referred to a small kitchen.

Vacher, Main and Hileman trusted one another and instinctively became quan partners. A fourth man, Henry Patton, who had been at the Fassoths' camp, and also had met the others at Bilibid, joined the quan. Patton's strong character had clashed with Vacher's at different times, but Hileman was friends with both of them, so the quan came together.

Tom Rayburn had also made the trip to Cabanatuan and he and Hileman resumed their bridge game with the other men in the camp.[9]

In the summer of 1944, sailboats began to arrive along the east coast of Luzon with materials for the guerrillas, the most valuable being radios. These new radios could be packed by one man, rather than the old sets that had to be moved in pieces by several men. The new radios could be run by a bicycle-type transformer, again allowing the rapid movement of the set to avoid detection. After several weeks of trial and error, Volckmann, Lapham, and Anderson were routinely communicating with each other and were linked to SWPA (South West Pacific Area) as well.

To raise their morale and taunt the Japanese, General MacArthur would radio his orders, addressing them "to my commanders in the Philippines."

With the arrival of the radios there also came some arms, ammunition, chocolate, toothpaste, razors, needles, cigarettes, and American magazines. In August 1944 they came in a trickle, but with the landing of the first submarine in Dibut Bay about September 1 they began to arrive in floods.[10]

Some of the radio messages were garbled in their transmission as per the following: "THE FOLLOWING AMERICANS DESIRE FAMILIES BE NOTIFIED: 2nd LIEU HC CONNORS (Henry Clay Conner, Jr.) STAFF SGT JOSE PHWOONAHCY (Joseph W. Donahey) PRIVATE FRANK SOVOEY (Frank Gyovai) PRIVATE ROBERT F. MILEHIEE (Robert T. Mailheau) PRIVATE EOTLEY DECKER (Doyle V. Decker) PRIVATE ROBERTELLPT CAMBELL (Robert A. Campbell) THE ABOVE NAMES WERE NOT REPEATED AND THEIR ACCURACY IS DOUBTFUL. THIS MESSAGE IS BEING SERVICED."[11]

No individual was able to unify the guerrilla movement on Luzon. Doyle Decker, who spent most of the war in Clay Conner's 155th Provisional Guer-

S E C R E T

20 NOVEMBER 1944

TO   :   GENERAL MACARTHUR

FROM   :   LAPHAM

DR HOME   22 NOVEMBER

THE FOLLOWING AMERICANS DESIRE FAMILIES BE NOTIFIED:

2ND LIEUT HC (HG) CONNORS *

STAFF SGT JOSE PHWOONAHCY *

PRIVATE FRANK SOVOEY *

PRIVATE ROBERT F MILEHIEE *

PRIVATE EOTLEY DECKER *

PRIVATE ROBERTELLPT CAMBELL *

* THE ABOVE NAMES WERE NOT REPEATED AND THEIR ACCURACY IS DOUBTFUL. THIS MESSAGE IS BEING SERVICED.

TOR: 230106/Z
TYPED: 230735/Z
SG

S E C R E T

Copy of communication from Bob Lapham to General MacArthur, concerning names of men at liberty (National Archives).

rilla Battalion, felt the answer was obvious: all the guerrilla leaders were ego-
ists striving to be little kings in the areas they controlled — a view shared by
others who had been enlisted in the prewar U.S. Army.[12] Bernard Anderson
largely agreed, notably in the case of his rival Ed Ramsey, but he added that
he did not think the ambition to command was itself reprehensible.[13]

The lack of a central command on Luzon would prove to be a strength
rather than an impediment. The Japanese could not penetrate the guerrilla
movement by toppling any one unit. Because of the lack of a central command no unit depended on another. They were however very careful not to
let the names of their Filipino supporters fall into enemy hands, because on
those few occasions when it happened the results were devastating to the families.

When the American troops returned to Luzon, all the guerrilla units
were instrumental in routing the Japanese troops. Because the guerrillas had
largely committed themselves to intelligence, the Japanese were at a disad-
vantage trying to protect their troops and supplies.

Chapter 10

Preparations

Until the middle of 1944, most guerrilla organizations had been more about survival and organization than causing the Japanese any damage. The fact that these groups existed was a concern of the Japanese hierarchy, but that hierarchy didn't know how devastating the guerrillas were to become when the American troops returned to Luzon.

After Major Russell Volkmann took over command of USAFIP, NL (United Stated Armed Forces in Philippines, North Luzon), it was evident that changes would be necessary to carry out the mission assigned by SWPA. With Captain Donald Blackburn's help, Volckmann began to outline new strategies concerning the unit's organization, acquisition of supplies, and ability to communicate with other guerrilla units and make contact with MacArthur's headquarters. This was no small task and took over one and a half years to accomplish, under difficult circumstances. As the reorganization of Volckmann's group was taking place, a general directive was issued from MacArthur's headquarters, restating the general mission, with strong emphasis on intelligence and avoidance of enemy contact. This became known as the "Lay Low Order."[1]

The Japanese began organizing spies and secret agents to gain intelligence throughout North Luzon. They would either convince or bribe a mayor or some other major administrator within a district with a large sum of war currency. He was expected to employ several people and was pledged a sizable windfall for particularly good intelligence. This scheme was so successful in some districts that civilians could not collaborate with the guerrillas for fear of Japanese reprisal against them and their families.

General Headquarters, USAFIP, NL had placed emphasis on counterespionage and the eradication of all spies and secret agents in a district. This
strategy was given wide promotion and was pursued persistently. Those found
guilty of spying for the Japanese were eradicated. Every attempt was made to
expose the key players in every spy organization. After six months of inten-
sive counterintelligence efforts, most of the informants had left and were hiding within districts with large Japanese garrisons. Despite their attempts to
hide, the guerrillas' agents ultimately found many of these people. During
the counterespionage campaign, some Filipino agents spying for the Japanese
took shelter in the town of Cervantes in Ilocos Sur. One night, guerrillas of
the First District searched the town. The Japanese retreated to their foxholes,
and the guerrillas burned the structure in which the informants had hidden.

The elimination of Japan's secret agents had sweeping results. The loyal
and sympathetic civilians were convinced that they could safely support
USAFIP, and those who had been hesitant began helping the guerrillas.

The counterespionage was not without risk. Those sympathetic to the
Japanese used this opportunity to turn in neighbors for revenge and economic
gain. Many have maintained that Volckmann's group killed several innocent
victims.

In May 1944, American officers in the guerrilla movement in North
Luzon presented Volckmann a resolution, signed by the commanders in their
area of operation, giving Volckmann the unofficial rank of colonel. This was
fitting, as many American commanders on Luzon had given themselves the
field rank of colonel.

Don Blackburn had been unable to communicate with Ralph Praeger
and Tom Jones in the northernmost provinces of Luzon. Blackburn's guerrilla force, in a foray into the capital of Apayao, recovered records of the sub-
province's puppet governor, and from these the location of Major Praeger and
his assistant, Captain Thomas Jones, was learned. The puppet governor had
been bribed by the governor of the mountain province to cooperate with
Japanese forces in capturing Praeger and Jones.

The Eleventh Infantry swiftly located the collaborators, and when reports
of the retaliation reached the populace, the people responded quickly, once
again supporting the Eleventh Infantry.[2]

In July 1944, Volckmann obtained a radio and was then able to communicate sporadically with the Southwest Pacific Command. In addition there
were occasional submarine contacts.

A dilemma arose for Volckmann's guerrillas. When General MacArthur
left Corregidor for Australia, President Quezon and Vice President Osmena
were taken first to Australia and then to the United States. When Quezon
died in 1944, Osmena became President of the Commonwealth of the Philip-

pines. Osmena's wife, who had remained in the Philippines, was meanwhile under close scrutiny by the Kempeitai. Mrs. Osmena sought freedom from this by moving her family from Manila to Baguio, but the Japanese continued surveillance there. As MacArthur's forces advanced toward the Philippine Islands, the Kempeitai increased its scrutiny of the family.

Mrs. Osmena who had many loyal contacts on Luzon, learned that the Japanese were contemplating the arrest of her and her family. She pleaded to Volckmann's agents in Baguio that her family be rescued and taken to the guerrillas' headquarters in the mountains. Such a mission was inherently dangerous. Volckmann radioed Mrs. Osmena's request to SWPA and asked for the new president's thoughts. President Osmena concluded that it would be safer for his family to remain in Baguio. When these views were reported to Mrs. Osmena, she objected to her husband's decision. On October 27, 1944, she sent a communication to Volckmann insisting that he help her family escape from Baguio on October 30.

A detailed plan, previously drawn up for this situation, was put into operation. Volckmann's agents prearranged with the Constabulary to document the Osmena family as having passed a checkpoint on the Kennon Road heading from Baguio to Manila. This was to direct the Kempeitai in the wrong direction long enough to give the family time to safely initiate travel to Volckmann's area.

The Osmena family, numbering seven, left Baguio by the Naguilian road on the morning of October 30. Units of the Sixty-sixth Infantry met the party four kilometers outside of Baguio, and there pushed off a cliff the station wagon in which they had escaped. Then the guerrillas guided the family to Volckmann's headquarters. Because of Mrs. Osmena's age and her daughter-in-law's pregnancy, they were carried on makeshift chairs. The plan worked to perfection and Mrs. Osmena and her four children were situated in a small camp near Volckmann's headquarters. Mrs. Osmena's daughter-in-law was taken to the First Field Hospital in the area of the 121st Infantry, where a month later a healthy son was born. The affable Osmenas lived near Volckmann's guerrillas until late January 1945 when they traveled to General MacArthur's center of operations at Dagupan and were reunited with the president.[3]

On June 25, 1944, Earl Oatman learned that he was on a list of 400 POW's scheduled to leave Cabanatuan on a work detail. The rumored destination was Japan. Oatman talked with Hank Winslow and found that neither Wnslow nor any of the special prisoners, those wearing red tags because they had been recaptured, were on the list.

On June 28, the 400 prisoners traveled in boxcars to Manila, arriving in the afternoon, and then walked from the train station to Bilibid Prison

Hospital. Here they discovered that an additional 500 prisoners from Mindanao and 60 from Bilibid were also headed for Japan.

On July 2, the prisoners were loaded on the *Canadian Inventor III*, or *Mati Mati Maru*, where they were packed into the holds so tightly that the men had to alternate between sitting and lying, as there wasn't enough room for them to all lie down at once. The ship finally docked at Moji, Kyushu, Japan, on September 2, 1944. The men had been prisoners on the ship for sixty-two days in the most inhumane circumstances imaginable.[4]

On July 13, 1944, more men were shipped from Cabanatuan to Manila and loaded on a ship for Japan. Included were Millard Hileman, Paul Vacher, Bill Main, Mike Slish, Henry Patton, Harold Irving, and Ray Schletterer. They were crammed into the *Nissyo Maru*, an old transport ship tied to the pier. Its crewmen pointed and laughed at the prisoners.[5] After a harrowing time during an attack by an American submarine wolfpack, the *Nissyo Maru* arrived undamaged in Moji on August 3, 1944.[6]

After Nano Lucero had fully recovered his health, one of his wife's relatives, Julian, taught Nano how to survive in the jungle. Julian who didn't seem to have many friends, enjoyed teaching Lucero how to avoid the dangers of various poisonous plants and animals living in the tropical forest.

Julian had a talent for creating explosive devices, and with Lucero's help he killed a particularly unpopular Japanese overseer of the local cotton field. The overseer was a man of habit and could always be counted on to use the same road at the same time every day. This proved to be his downfall, as Julian and Nano planted some explosives in the road one day and waited for the overseer. Just as he came along, Julian detonated the explosive. The overseer never knew what happened. The execution took place away from any barrio, to lower the risk that the local Japanese garrison might take reprisal.[7]

Ideally, a suspected spy would have been turned over to a civilian court for a formal trial under American or Philippine law. But Ray Hunt did not have the convenience of such a court or of any regularly constituted court-martial system. In the summer of 1944, Hunt did the best he could: he organized a company of military police whose duty it was to capture anyone suspected of spying, or of committing murder, rape, robbery, or any other serious crime against a civilian. When a case was presented against someone, the suspect was arrested, brought before the officers of his military unit, and tried. It wasn't a trial that would have passed muster with the American Bar Association, because those who voted for judgment were typically simple men untaught in the law, but it was a rung above a kangaroo court.[8]

Claire Phillips with her dark hair and eyes, decided to become an Italian since that would make her an ally of the Japanese. She contacted a young Spaniard who had been a friend of her husband, John Phillips, before the outbreak of war. He was an accomplished linguist and worked as a translator at the Italian consulate in Manila. In spite of his chance of being found out by the Japanese, the Spaniard obtained counterfeit Italian credentials for Phillips.[9]

With papers in hand, Claire Phillips started the Club Tsubaki, featuring a floor show every night. Patrons would be greeted at the door by the club's owner, a glamorous, thirty-three-year-old woman dressed in a white evening gown with a plunging neckline and a slit halfway up her thigh. Phillips would set up each party with a suggestively dressed hostess who was theirs for the night. The hostess would pour the Japanese clients' drinks, stroke their hair, light their cigarettes, and keep up constant flattery in an ambiguous mix of English, Japanese, Spanish, and Tagalog.[10]

After several drinks, Japanese officers became more prone to divulge things that would make them seem more important in the eyes of their attentive companions. Intelligence gained in this way was of no value unless it could be broadcast to General MacArthur's headquarters. So Phillips made contact with Corporal John Boone, who had served in the Thirty-first Infantry with her husband. Boone was in the hills north of Bataan, and had organized a guerrilla force that now totalled fifty Americans and nearly a thousand Filipinos.

In keeping with his responsibility as commander of such a large force, Boone had been promoted by Ed Ramsey to the rank of colonel. His code name was Compadre. Each week, at enormous risk, Phillip's couriers evaded Japanese military police in Manila and relayed her information to Boone in the hills. She signed the documents with her code name High Pockets, a nom de guerre that came about because of an inclination for safeguarding valuables in her bra.

At first Boone had no way of transmitting this information to an American headquarters. Through her sources, however, High Pockets managed to acquire a radio transmitter and receiver from a Filipino in Manila, and piece by piece the set was lugged to Boone's camp by a succession of Filipino couriers. Boone then transmitted High Pocket's information to an American guerrilla station on Mindanao, six hundred miles to the south, from where it was communicated to MacArthur.[11]

Doyle Decker was receiving intelligence from High Pockets through John Boone and sending it on to Clay Conner, who in turned sent it on to Colonel Gyles Merrill. In addition they received the *Manila Tribune*. The Americans could read the *Tribune* because it was written primarily in English, the second language of the Philippines. A few articles were in Japanese, but these used the Roman alphabet rather than kanji to aid in translation.

Because Japanese armies were constantly "winning" great battles over the Americans on islands ever closer to the Philippines, the GI's construed that American troops were advancing toward Luzon. From these battles allegedly won by the Japanese, the Americans gained hope for the day MacArthur would return in triumph. Not only did High Pockets supply the 155th with valuable intelligence, but they now had news of how the American troops were progressing. This, in turn, gave renewed hope to the Negritos and Filipino members of the unit.[12]

Continued contact with the lowland allies was important, as at times the Filipino spirit boosted the morale of the American guerrillas. Bob Mailheau and Doyle Decker were successful in recruiting some of the younger men into the "Barrio Defense System," intended to protect the barrios when American troops returned to Luzon. The Japanese forces were expected to attempt to burn all villages at the end of their occupation. The approach to organizing the barrios in the USAFFE sphere of control of the 155th (Pampanga, Eastern Zambales, and Tarlac) was to keep it simple and emphasize espionage and intelligence gathering. Ever mindful of previous Japanese reprisals against barrios whose patriots attacked patrols, resulting in injury, death, and destruction of their barrios and neighboring villages, the 155th insisted that barrios leave the combat to the fighting troops in the foothills and mountains.

The *teniente del barrio,* or village leader, was also the leader of the Barrio Defense System. Most of the *tenientes* accepted the responsibility, but a few older ones appointed trusted compadres to fulfill the mission. There were nearly fifty barrios under the authority of the 155th. Each *teniente* or compadre designated two groups, a "watch" group and a "defense" group. The watch group consisted of four to six men, while the defense group had six to twelve. The watch groups did just that — watch, day and night. Each man pulled his shift according to the direction of the *teniente* and reported anything of an unusual or suspicious nature in a timely manner.

The defense groups carried reportable information to the next barrio closest to the 155th sub-headquarters near Banaba. The barrio next to the information source relayed the information to *their* closest barrio, and so on until Mailheau or Decker received it. The information was reviewed and evaluated, then forwarded to the 155th headquarters via scout or Negrito runner.

Japanese activity in the townships, barrios, and surrounding areas was closely monitored through the system. Especially important was the system's ability to detect patrols and their probable destinations. If by reason of numbers and weaponry the patrol appeared severe and threatening, the combat guerillas could be forewarned to prepare for a potential encounter.

On occasion some of the young members of the Barrio Watch and

Defense Groups volunteered for combat guerrilla training and duty. The Philippine Scout contingent of the 155th was responsible for training these youngsters. Hand-to-hand combat came naturally to the Filipino troops, as many were schooled as youngsters in Asian arts of self-defense. Handling weapons was demonstrated and practiced without the benefit of live firing. Ammunition was in short supply, but more importantly, the Japanese would hear the noise and determine the training location.[13]

In July 1944, Ray Hunt received a transmitter, in a set built in the Dutch East Indies. This was one of over 100 transmitters smuggled into Luzon by submarine. In addition to this valuable tool to communicate with MacArthur's headquarters, there were some magazines, cigarettes, matches, newspapers, gum, candy bars, toothpaste, and propaganda with the words "I Shall Return" emblazoned on it, intended to raise the moral of the men and women in guerrilla warfare.

The radio got its power from being pedaled like a bicycle. One had to pump vigorously to receive a message on it, and build up muscles to perform for long periods in order to transmit. The contraption had other drawbacks, as well. Unlike the new English models, this one was too heavy for a man to carry. It had to be hauled over rough roads and trails and across open fields either in a cart or on the back of a carabao. In this way was continuously shaken, and sometimes it fell off its conveyance. Hunt felt that his unit spent half of their time repairing the radio, frequently without spare parts. When the gadget did work, the guerrillas risked nuisances of a different sort: they had to change their location after each transmission for fear that the Japanese might locate them by triangulation. More important, Hunt's unit was now able to establish rendezvous points with U.S. submarines and get consignments of all sorts of sorely needed arms and supplies on a somewhat regular basis.

By the time of the Leyte landing in October 1944, a network of 134 underground radio stations and 23 weather observation positions had been established all over the Philippines. They supplied MacArthur's headquarters with detailed intelligence about everything down to which barbershop cut the hair of which Japanese lieutenant.[14]

Bernard Anderson had a firm foothold in north central Luzon. He had developed a strong relationship with Marking's guerrillas lead by Marcos Augustin. Marking's mistress, a half–American journalist named Yay Panlilio, particularly admired Anderson. She found that he was not moody or given to fits of uncivilized conduct like so many guerrillas, but was a quiet, considerate man who did not disparage other outfits, and who stayed away from towns so that Japanese would not punish civilians who might have seen him but failed to turn him in.

Bob Lapham had a similarly good opinion of Anderson. He found Andy to be an especially generous man, extraordinarily so for one in such harsh conditions. When a submarine from Australia brought him forty-seven tons of supplies in mid–1944, Andy promptly apportioned forty tons among his Filipino aides and supporters. In December of that year a detachment from the Hunters, another guerrilla band operating near Manila, came to Anderson's camp to ask for arms and supplies. Andy gave the guerrillas seventy tommy guns, twenty-five new carbines, five .45-caliber pistols, some medicine, and many cigarettes — all followed by what was, for them, a sumptuous Christmas party.[15]

Ed Ramsey's guerrillas engaged in sabotage only occasionally and with great care. Joe Barker and Ramsey had agreed that such disruption was to be performed only when it created little risk to the civilian population. MacArthur had communicated this position in messages to the guerrillas in the Philippines. He didn't want the American forces at liberty to alienate the population through needless acts of aggression. The Japanese had already accomplished this in their occupational tactics. The Americans were to avoid any action that might provoke Japanese reprisals. Instead, individual units were instructed to employ sabotage only when clear, low-risk enemy objectives existed. Aiming generally at Japanese military targets, operatives poured sugar into the gas tanks of planes and vehicles, set fire to depots, or attacked military convoys in the countryside.

Sabotage provided an important confidence-building function, but it remained secondary to the goals of MacArthur's directive: organization and intelligence gathering.[16]

By the early spring of 1944, the 155th had completed its organization and training, and was engaged in espionage, intelligence gathering, and guerrilla warfare sorties. The four Americans had recruited several hundred Negrito soldiers and two dozen Philippine Scouts.

The 155th continued to maintain its headquarters on Mt. Pinatubo in the Zambales mountain range, where Clay Conner and Frank Gyovai performed the duties of operations, intelligence, logistics, and supply. Conner, wanting a camp closer to intelligence-gathering sources, had Bob Mailheau and Doyle Decker maintain a sub-headquarters near the barrio of Banaba. This camp was moved from time to time to avoid detection by Japanese patrol, while remaining located in the foothills south of Fort Stotsenburg and Clark Field.

Although operations of the 155th were successful and morale was good, after eleven months of operation an inspirational ingredient seemed to be lacking.

One evening Mailheau and Decker were sitting around the campfire talking. A recently recruited staff member and Philippine Scout, Sergeant Agapito Macasual (Max), joined in the discussion and brought them up to date on his latest adventure.

Max told them that after his capture on Bataan, he was forced into the ranks of the Japanese-commanded Philippine Constabulary. He had been collaborating with the guerrilla movement for several months, so it was time to arrange his liberation from the Constabulary as he had been giving the guerrillas information about the location of certain supplies, especially ammunition and fuel depots, and was afraid the Kempeitai was getting wise to his activities. A trap was set whereby he would lead a guerrilla-hunting Japanese patrol into an ambush. The patrol was guided to a predetermined location where he made certain that he was far enough ahead so that when the shooting started he could run for the guerrillas' position and terminate his tenure with the Japanese. As far as the Japanese were concerned, he was killed with the rest of the patrol.

Decker and Mailheau listened with interest, asking questions about other activities in which Max had participated. Mailheau asserted that the unit needed something to unite them, something to increase morale.

"You know, an American flag would really give us something to rally around," he stated, "a symbol to inspire and give us a motivational push, to make all our tears and fears and pain worthwhile."

As Decker and Max nodded in agreement, Max told them that he knew where such a flag might exist.

Mailheau and Decker were mesmerized as Max told another story.

A sergeant, Gaetano Bato, the designated regimental flag bearer, was entrusted with the safekeeping of the Twenty-sixth Cavalry flag. The previous flag bearer had been shot in battle, but on falling from his horse he stuck the flag in the earth so it wouldn't touch the ground. Sergeant Bato retrieved the flag and was the standard bearer at the last stand by the Twenty-sixth Regiment and the American and Filipino armies as they were falling back from their defensive position against the advancing Japanese army on Bataan.

Prior to the surrender of the troops on Bataan, Bato was ordered by his commanding officer to not surrender but to evade capture and keep the flag safe from the Japanese. He and a few companions made their way through Japanese lines to their home barrio, a short distance from Fort Stotsenburg. Sergeant Bato had his wife tuck the flag into a pillowcase and hide this in one of their chests of drawers. Despite the capture of Bato and his compatriots by the Japanese a short time later, the flag remained hidden in the Bato home. After a period of internship and Japanese indoctrination efforts, Bato and several of his comrades had been released but forced to work for the Japanese Army at Fort Stotsenburg.

Since Max was a Twenty-sixth trooper, he concluded that it shouldn't be difficult for him to make contact with some of the others and determine if Sergeant Bato was still alive and had the flag.

"How soon can you do this, Max?" asked Mailheau.

"At first light."

Three days later, Max returned with a big smile. Not only was Sergeant Bato alive, he would be honored to turn the flag over to the 155th. Max had made arrangements for Sergeant Bato and some of his fellow troopers to meet with Mailheau and Decker at a place that only he and Max knew about. They would meet at night to avoid detection.

The next evening Mailheau, Decker, and Max walked down the trail to rendezvous with Sergeant Bato and several of his companions. All were alert to Japanese patrols and possible ambush. There was a nervous anticipation and an air of excitement. After introductions of Bato's group by Max, and a delicious meal prepared from stolen Japanese commissary supplies, Bato presented the flag to Mailheau.

With tears of pride, Bato made the presentation. "It is with great honor that we return this flag to an American unit. Take good care of it and remember that it was never surrendered nor has it ever touched the ground."

Bato paused for a moment and then asked, "Is it possible for us to become a part of your unit?"

Mailheau and Decker nodded in agreement, and then everyone shook hands and hugged. Mailheau told the group that he would clear everything with Major Conner and get word back to them through Sergeant Macasual as soon as possible.

The next day, Mailheau, Decker, and Max returned to their camp near Banaba. Mailheau sent a runner with word to Conner and Gyovai of their joyous acquisition. Conner was delighted and instructed Mailheau to welcome Bato and his friends to "our guerrilla family." He also asked Mailheau and Decker to notify all the unit commanders with the 155th in the lowlands to attend a special ceremony to be convened as soon as possible.

Four days later, all the leaders of various units under the 155th assembled near Mailheau's and Decker's camp. When everyone had gathered, Bato and Max unfurled the Twenty-sixth Cavalry's flag and made it fast to a bamboo staff that Gyovai had hastily cut.

Everyone was transfixed. The Americans were lost in their thoughts as they looked at the symbol of their country. Here was America, and with their hearts pounding, the men stood taller, their chests pushed out farther. They were standing on holy ground.

The Negritos and Filipinos saw what was happening among the Americans. The pride evident in the Americans' posture was contagious, and each man felt himself part of something larger. There was a renewed commitment to country and a strengthening of mind and body. The guerrillas would overcome all odds and keep the enemy off balance for the remainder of the war.

"By God, even if it takes ten years for them to return," Conner asserted, "we will be here to welcome back MacArthur and the American troops."

Then, spontaneously, the words came forth: "I pledge allegiance to the flag, of the United States of America, and to the Republic for which it stands, one nation, indivisible, with liberty and justice for all."

Tears streamed down the Americans' faces. And though the Negritos were not accustomed to seeing men cry, it didn't matter. For each had tears in his eyes. They saw men who loved their country, as the Negritos loved the mountains. All the unit commanders were impressed. Not a shred of doubt remained that the Americans could be trusted.

With the proximity of the sub-headquarters to the lowlands, Conner and Gyovai decided to take the flag with them to headquarters. "I don't want those Jap bastards capturing this flag," said Conner.

In the following weeks word of the flag spread and the Japanese made numerous attempts to locate and destroy the symbol of the 155th. While the dense jungle prevented sighting from the air, Negrito guerrillas kept all approaches protected and secure. At headquarters the flag was raised each morning and lowered each evening, as it would be in a regular army unit.

The presentation of the flag improved morale and led to additional strength for the 155th. With the addition of Bato came a commitment from another Scout leader, Lieutenant Felipe Maningo, who had combat honors in the battles of Bataan and a strong following in the area.[17]

On Luzon, in mid–1944, with the American troops advancing toward the Philippines, all the guerrilla units stepped up their recruiting efforts in an attempt to boost their command. Majors Bernard Anderson, Edwin Ramsey, and Robert Lapham began a frantic contest to expand and organize their relative areas of responsibility, sometimes at each other's expense. Intelligence messages forwarded to MacArthur's headquarters were chaotic with information about who was in control of what areas and who was under their commands. Firefights broke out between members of rival guerrilla organizations as they tried to take control of what they deemed their area of command. One message to MacArthur stated, "These happenings seem to suit the Japanese and have become a source of their mirth."

John Boone considered his unit a part of Major Ramsey's East Central Luzon Guerrilla Army, although Bernard Anderson also claimed Boone's group and included Boone's men in the troop counts he sent to MacArthur. Anderson listed Robert Lapham under his control, and stretched his area to include Ramsey's organization. Ramsey, meanwhile, refused Anderson's overtures. At one point Robert Lapham sent a message to MacArthur's headquarters asking for illumination of everyone's position. Ramsey went so far as to send a message asking MacArthur to send a general to take over. MacArthur, with more significant problems to consider, did not reply to any of the requests.

Lieutenant Cabangbang, who had been sent via submarine by MacArthur to solidify the guerrilla command, broke the news: none of them were in charge. General MacArthur had sent specific orders that the various guerrilla commanders were to each operate independently and report directly to the commanding general. Unified leadership behind Japanese lines, throughout the vastness of the Philippine Islands or even on Luzon itself, was impractical.[18] This also helped the guerrillas avoid a devastating blow had the Japanese been able to capture the leader of a central command.

As the American troops neared the Philippines, Lieutenant Felipe Maningo, a Philippine Scout, brought 150 former Scouts with him to join Clay Conner's 155th. Conner set up an observation post in Banaba, a town in the foothills close to Fort Stotsenburg and Clark Field, and Lieutenant Maningo recruited a network of Filipino agents who worked at the two Japanese military bases. Doyle Decker, manning the observation post at Banaba, had made contact with Claire Phillips in Manila. They had established a courier arrangement to pass information the workers collected on the Japanese bases "though channels" to General MacArthur.[19]

Humbo and Mario had been sent by Clay Conner to Mailheau and Decker's camp to report rumors that the Japanese would soon reinforce Clark Field with a large group of airplanes. This could mean that action was finally coming to Luzon. Discussing the probabilities, Mailheau and Decker decided that they should move closer to the Banaba area, to reconnoiter Japanese movements and activities. They would also procure medicine to treat Decker's dysentery. Mailheau sent a message by Humbo and Mario to Conner requesting permission to relocate the camp near Banaba.

The fog was heavy on the morning of September 21, 1944, and while Mailheau and Decker were eating breakfast they heard a large flight of airplanes heading for Clark Field. Unable to see anything, they assumed it was Japanese planes such as they often heard flying south from Taiwan. A short time later there was a loud roar as more planes approached Clark Field. The sound was different this time, so Mailheau and Decker walked to a lookout point on a nearby ridge. The fog lifted and the sky was full of U.S. Navy aircraft. Yank planes had followed the Japanese aircraft and were bombing and strafing the planes as they taxied to the hangar line. The U.S. planes with new American decals were a beautiful sight for Mailheau and Decker.

"Looks like Uncle Sam has come up with some new designs," observed Mailheau. "And, God, can they fly."

A few Japanese planes took off from Clark Field, but Navy fighters were on them like wolves on lambs. Spent shells and casing from the air battles were falling from the air, but the casings didn't bother Mailheau and Decker.

"Those are our planes, Decker. We are going to make it. After all this time, the Americans are back and we're going to make it. Jesus, thank you. What a beautiful sight."

The raid lasted almost an hour. Leaning on each other for support Mailheau and Decker cried like babies. This was too good to be true. There wasn't any better medicine than seeing American planes attacking the Japanese air force and Clark Field. Later in the afternoon the American planes returned and another battle filled the sky.

The two Americans knew the troops couldn't be far behind; it would just be a matter of time. They had a lot of work to do before then.

Several Japanese planes were shot out of the sky in the two air raids. Frank Gyovai came down from headquarters to report that they had seen the planes, adding, "The Negritos have killed some of the Jap pilots who parachuted to the ground before their planes crashed."

Decker pitied the pilots. The Negritos had their own law. They had suffered at the hands of the Japanese and had vowed revenge. God help any pilot caught in the mountains. He would never see the "Land of the Rising Sun" again.

In response to Mailheau and Decker's request to move back to Banaba, Conner sent word through Gyovai for them to return as quickly as possible and gather as much intelligence as they could on Japanese activity, numbers, locations of facilities in and around Clark Field, and anything else of military importance.

Because of Mailheau's recent bout with tonsillitis and Decker's dysentery, it took longer than normal to trudge down the trail to Banaba.

Several days after they reached their deserted hut near Banaba, Conner sent them a small amount of medicine, cigarettes, and matchbooks with the "I Shall Return" pledge on the covers. The supplies were delivered through Colonel Merrill from a submarine rendezvous. Humbo was pleased with the package he delivered to camp. In a few days, Mailheau and Decker were back on their feet.[20]

On September 21, 1944, Ray Hunt was standing outdoors when he heard a long, low rumble. He strained his eyes southward and saw columns of smoke climbing into the sky from the direction of Clark Field. Hunt concluded that American planes had bombed an air field. The men with Hunt burst out with cries of joy and pounded each other on the back without regard. Yay Panlilio wrote that even Marking's dog succumbed to the hysteria, whining, barking, and quivering with excitement as the guerrillas whooped and hollered and cried.[21]

Vernon Fassoth and his guerrillas also saw the planes attack Clark Field. They were ecstatic and knew it wouldn't be long before MacArthur and the American troops would return to the Philippines, and to Luzon in particular.[22]

Both sides shot down several aircraft. The guerrillas tried to reach downed American pilots and crewmen before the Japanese captured them. Rescued pilots were guided to rendezvous points by Negrito and Filipino guerrillas where they were protected until they could be sent through Japanese lines to returning American forces.

Mailheau and Conner were in Lieutenant Maningo's barrio, helping him organize his unit and recruit additional Philippine Scouts, when an American fighter shot down a Japanese plane. The pilot parachuted down right into the middle of the barrio. Due to its close proximity to Fort Stotsenburg, a Japanese patrol would soon be on its way to rescue the pilot.

Since nearby barrio had been destroyed and all its inhabitants killed a few days prior when the residents had tried to capture a downed Japanese pilot, the decision was made for the Filipinos to turn the Japanese pilot over to the patrol rather than take a chance of exposing Maningo and his scouts as guerrillas. It was a tough call, but the Japanese patrol was pleased to have their pilot returned by the barrio. Mailheau and Conner hid in a hut and watched with satisfaction as Maningo and his men ingratiated themselves to their former captors, enhancing the undercover work of their unit.[23]

On October 11, 1944, the *Arisan Maru* left Manila with about 1,800 POW's in the cargo holds. That ship turned south to Palawan Island and anchored off Palawan until October 20 when it returned to Manila to join Convoy MATA-30 which sailed on the next day. On October 23 when the convoy was about 200 miles northwest of Luzon, two packs of U.S. submarines (a total of nine) began attacking this convoy. At about 5:30 P.M. on October 24, 1944, the USS *Shark* (some believe USS *Snook*) sent three torpedoes into the *Arisan Maru*. The ship broke in two pieces which floated for a while. The result was death for all except nine of the POW's. This was the largest loss of American lives in a single disaster at sea. Among those killed were three former residents of the Fassoths' camp, Benjamin Baruch, John A. Breder, and Lieutenant Arnold Warshell, the camp doctor.[24]

Lieutenant John M. Kerrey, uncle of former Nebraska senator J. Robert Kerrey, died a tragic death. He had left the Fassoths' camp and gone north to be near Colonel Volckmann and Captain Blackburn. When a submarine came in to deliver supplies in October 1944, Al Hendrickson told him to follow a difficult foot trail down the coastline to meet the submarine. Rather than hike through the mountains and jungle, Lieutenant Kerry was anxious and went out to the submarine in a rubber boat. Capsizing in a rough sea, Lieutenant Kerry drowned on October 17, 1944.[25]

Captain Wilber Lage's health had deteriorated to such a state that he was put on a submarine the *Narwhal*, and sent with two other Americans to Australia.[26]

Chapter 11

MacArthur Returns

O beautiful for heroes proved
In liberating strife,
Who more than self their country loved,
And mercy more than life.
—("America the Beautiful," third stanza)
Katharine Lee Bates & Samuel A Ward

November 29 began a series of miscalculations by many of John Boone's guerrilla units. Inspired by the invasion of Leyte by the American troops and ignoring Boone's directive to not engage the enemy, Captain Magtanggol and his men, wearing Japanese army uniforms, marched into Orani, attacked the city hall and shot the Japanese guards. They subsequently ambushed a Japanese patrol, killing nineteen enemy soldiers. Then a group from the Third (Seaside) Regiment on the west coast invaded the Wain logging camp north of Mariveles, owned by the Japanese, and killed eight Japanese civilians.

Five days later the Japanese retaliated. A Japanese unit lead by Lieutenant Kanesero attacked Bagac, the home municipality of Boone's Third Regiment. As retribution for the eight dead Japanese, eight men from the village were selected from a group of twenty and bayoneted to death. Then the Japanese soldiers attacked and destroyed the Third Regimental headquarters. The Third Regiment struck back and ambushed a Japanese convoy on the Pilar-Bagac road, killing eight Japanese soldiers and capturing a truckload of supplies.

Lieutenant Kanesero appealed for help from Manila to squelch the energized guerrillas. Reinforcements were sent and four hundred Japanese soldiers surrounded Morong and then burned the village. To prevent further retaliation, the remainder of the Third Regiment evacuated all the surviving citizens into the mountains.

Keeping pressure on Boone's guerrillas, Captain Tamura invaded Boone's headquarters on Mount Malasimbo. on December 7. The Japanese soldiers killed two men and confiscated a letter and a large amount of Japanese currency that had just arrived from Ed Ramsey.

The next day, Boone's Fourth Regiment headquarters, just outside the little village of Tuyo, Balanga, was attacked by Kanesero and his troops. Tuyo was defeated and all 150 male residents of the town were arrested. Then the men were lined up and passed in front of a hooded "scorpion" who identified twenty men as guerrillas. At midnight the twenty victims were taken to the mango grove behind the Balanga elementary school and beheaded. In continued retaliation, Kanesero arrested two sisters of one of the executed men and held them prisoner forcing them to work for the Japanese soldiers. After three days of captivity, the girls were raped every day until December 20, when a detail of soldiers took them behind the elementary school and put them to death — one by bayonet and one by saber.

The Japanese attacked Barrio Montilla on December 9 and Sibacan the next day, where more than fifty men were executed and the village was burned to the ground. Twenty-six more men were killed in the zonification of Santa Rosa. To escape the Japanese onslaught, the Fourth Regiment evacuated civilians from the barrios around Balanga.

Either in retaliation or plain stupidity, someone seized a drunken Japanese soldier in the street in Dinalupihan late at night and choked him to death. Captain Tamura immediately invaded Dinalupihan and killed twenty suspected guerrillas. Reprisals escalated when Filipino guerrillas shot Captain Tamura's wife, Besing.

Lieutenant Kanesero had barrio Kamachile surrounded, arrested all 186 male residents of the village, and then Japanese soldiers took eighty of the males behind the Balanga elementary school and executed all of them, including two boys ages five and seven. Then the barrio was burned.[1]

When American planes began bombing fuel dumps and ammunition storage areas, Doyle Decker saw the results of the intelligence information he had gathered and forwarded to headquarters by Negrito runners. Not wanting their supplies to fall into the hands of the American forces, the Japanese prepared for the inevitable invasion and began to destroy their fuel and ammo dumps.

With the daily bombing by American aircraft, Filipinos, eager to join in the fighting, affiliated with the 155th in droves. For several months Clay Conner had the Negritos prepare traps and other jungle apparatus along the Iba trail, which crossed the Zambales mountain range from Clark Field to Subic Bay. The trail was the probable escape route Japanese troops would use when

American troops laid siege to Clark Field and Fort Stotsenburg. Pig traps were particularly gruesome. Negritos would normally set the spear traps along an animal trail to kill an unsuspecting pig. To block the Iba trail, Negritos raised the angle of the traps so that they would throw lances at the height of a human mid-section. A man receiving a bamboo spear in his abdomen died a slow, painful death. Excruciating screams unnerved the other men in a patrol, adding panic to their retreat.

When the Japanese began to search for escape routes, they didn't venture far into the mountains because they were reluctant to confront the Negritos. Each time a Japanese patrol ventured further into the mountains along the Iba trail, the booby traps took their toll. Negritos on the slopes also bagged their share of victims with bows and arrows, bolstered by rifles and shotguns scrounged from battle sites on Bataan. The search for escape avenues resulted in large troop losses for the Japanese.

Beside hit-and-run tactics against the Japanese along the Iba trail, Negritos worked feverishly carrying messages between American guerrilla bands, keeping the units informed of the latest operations and delivering orders from Colonel Merrill.

Meanwhile, Lieutenant Maningo and his men made several raids on Fort Stotsenburg, seizing Japanese uniforms and supplies. His unit used the uniforms to disguise themselves as Japanese soldiers and then to gain intelligence and steal supplies from nearby installations.

The increasing numbers joining the 155th made it difficult to find enough provisions for the unit. Conner gave Gyovai this responsibility, and with assistance from Mailheau and Decker they located abandoned groves of papaya, avocados, and mangos, supplemented by beef from a heard of wild cattle. The support of the local populace helped the men to find enough to subsist. Japanese troops confiscated food in the lowlands, giving the 155th additional recruiting leverage with their supplies. Filipinos in the lowlands were becoming more dependent on the guerrilla units for food and therefore were eager to remain in their favor.

In early December, Mailheau returned to the camp near Banaba to assist Decker with intelligence gathering from the lowlands.[2]

The *Oryoku Maru* left Pier 7, Manila, late on December 13, 1944, with 1,619 POW's crammed into the three cargo holds. Japanese civilians occupied the passenger cabins.

Aircraft from the USS *Hornet* sighted the *Oryoku Maru* on December 14, as it sailed north along the west coast of Bataan Peninsula, and they attacked it many times that day. On the morning of December 15, aircraft from the *Hornet* again attacked the *Oryoku Maru* as it steamed across Subic

Bay toward Olongapo Point. One American bomb made a direct hit on the hatch of the aft cargo hold, killing about 250 POW's. Former Fassoth camp resident Shelby Newman was among the dead.[3]

The surviving POW's from the *Oryoku Maru* were held for six days on a single tennis court at the former Olongapo Naval Base and then taken by truck to San Fernando, Pampanga. Next they were taken by rail to San Fernando, La Union, on Lingayan Gulf, where they arrived about 2:00 on Christmas morning.

On December 27, the POW's who had survived the attacks on the *Oryoku Maru* were loaded into the cargo holds of two ships — the *Enoura Maru* and the *Brazil Maru*—for the voyage to Takao, Formosa, where they arrived on December 31. On January 6, 1945, the Japanese consolidated all surviving POW's into the holds of the *Enoura Maru*. On January 9, the *Enoura Maru* was still in the harbor at Takao (and moored to the same buoy with a Japanese tanker, making them a prime target) when aircraft from the USS *Hornet* attacked. One of the bombs hit the forward hold, killing about 350 POW's.

On January 13, all surviving POW's were moved to the *Brazil Maru* and that ship departed for Japan on January 14. On the *Brazil Maru* POW's died at a rate of up to fifty a day. When the *Brazil Maru* arrived at Moji, Japan, and unloaded its cargo of POW's, only about 425 were alive — out of 1,619 who began the trip on the *Oryoku Maru* on December 13, 1944. Former Fassoth camp resident Louis N. Dosh was recorded as having died on the *Brazil Maru* on January 20, 1945.[4]

By January 3, 1945, Doyle Decker and Bob Mailheau, manning the observation post at Banaba, had collected some interesting intelligence and forwarded their reports to Conner for review. Tunnels and concealed concrete bunkers were being constructed in the east face of the Zambales Mountains, above Fort Stotsenburg. The work started several weeks previous and was still in progress. Several of the tunnels were enormous — large enough to accommodate heavy artillery pieces. The construction extended across a broad canyon called Guligado's Pass, overlooking Luzon's central plain.

Japanese convoys loaded with men and equipment were streaming north up the highways from Manila into the mountains of North Luzon. The truck convoys included motorcycles, tanks, and staff cars, followed by busloads of Japanese civilians. Trains were also filled with Japanese troops headed north, and foot soldiers marched northward using both highways and pushing wooden carts filled with materials. It was rumored that the Japanese commanding general, Yamashita, had moved his headquarters to the Philippine summer palace at Baguio and had taken the Philippines administration of President Jose Laurel with him.[5]

On December 27, 1945, Colonel Russell Volckmann and his men recovered documents from a crashed Japanese plane telling of the plans of General Yamashita to pull back his troops and shore batteries to avoid heavy bombardments. He wanted to position his large force on Luzon in the mountains to the east of Lingayen Gulf.

Volckmann radioed MacArthur's headquarters: "There will be no, repeat no, opposition on the (Lingayen) beaches." But, apparently, the urgent message had been pigeonholed somewhere in the headquarters maze.[6]

By early January 1945, MacArthur felt his forces had secured Leyte and Mindoro and he was ready to commence the ultimate stage of his Philippine campaign, the offensive on Luzon. He had assembled a flotilla of 164 ships, accompanied by 3,000 landing craft and includeding 280,000 troops. General Yamashita's force of 275,000 men, who had three and a half years to prepare, was ready for the confrontation. On Luzon, however, were the guerrillas, estimated by several sources at over 40,000, armed with every manner of weapon from machine guns to swords, and ready to engage the Japanese. The battle for Luzon became the climactic struggle of the war in the southwest Pacific.

On January 8, Ramsey's guerrillas were at his temporary headquarters near Tala and their transmitter was back in operation. That afternoon he received a message from MacArthur. "MacArthur to Ramsey," it began. "Starting immediately, destroy trucks, planes concealed in dispersal areas, ammunition, oil and supply dumps.... Unleash maximum possible violence against the enemy."[7]

By January 8, 1945, units of USAFIP, NL had engaged the Japanese on several fronts and were releasing their pent-up anger. Although they had been relentless in their pursuit of the guerrillas, the Japanese had underestimated the potency and ability of the organized populace. By the time they recognized the scope of the resistance they were facing, enormous damage had been inflicted on the Japanese lines of communication. Numerous small enemy garrisons were cut off and destroyed. Widespread demolitions, roadblocks, and destruction of vehicles significantly reduced their troop mobility and created additional supply problems.

On the morning of January 9, Russell Volckmann was called to a high observation post near his headquarters. From his vantage, Lingayen Gulf, some fifty miles to the southwest, materialized as a diminutive cove speckled with hundreds of model ships. This was the day he had prayed for during three long years. To those on Luzon, the promise, "I shall return," was now a reality.

During three long years the Americans in North Luzon emerged among a strange people as determined, self-reliant, and resourceful leaders. In their violent struggle they found satisfaction in molding an organization capable of releasing incredible hostility against a tyrannical enemy. To an extent, they were accountable only to themselves. They stood alone, with their failures measured by the loss of human lives and their achievements rewarded in hope for a once-vanquished nation.

In spite of the suffering and hardships, when offered the opportunity to return to the United States and their families many American guerrillas chose to remain and fight beside their Filipino families, whom they trusted and admired. Their success could be attributed to the skills they developed in three years of guerrilla warfare. When confronted with a difficulty, their response was to ask how to solve it, rather than to become entangled in reasons why the task was hopeless. Their ability to improvise and to put into practice the outwardly impractical was invaluable. Around this core was a Filipino fighting force of trustworthy, brave, resolute men supported by a courageous people. This force proved itself, in spite of inadequate arms and equipment, more than a match for the highly vaunted Japanese Army.

When the Sixth Army landed at Lingayen Gulf, the blueprint of the enemy's defense was apparent. During the month preceding the landing, Yamashita had withdrawn 120,000 to 150,000 troops into North Luzon. He positioned these forces on the topography of the mountains, craggy gorges, narrow valleys, slippery slopes, and trails that passed for roads. The ultimate defense required the American troops to dig the enemy out yard by yard. Yamashita's plan was to bog General MacArthur down so he would have to retain a large force over an extended period of time to conquer the mountain fortress.[8]

On January 11, 1945, Colonel Merrill sent runners with word that American troops had landed on Luzon. Clay Conner sent messengers to John Boone and the men in the lowlands, and obtained additional reports of the location of Japanese troops. He relayed these to Alfred Bruce, who in turn passed the information to other guerrilla units further north. Maps that Bob Mailheau and Doyle Decker had previously prepared became valuable in planning blocking positions for the different units as the Japanese attempted to escape.

Japanese troops did escape to the mountains, but the Negrito guerrillas, despite their limited weaponry, did a respectable job of bouncing them back into the lowlands where the Filipino guerrilla units were able to avenge many of the wrongs dealt them over the past three years. Japanese troops then forced their way to the Iba trail and suffered additional losses, as the Negritos slowed their advance with pig traps, bows and arrows, and firearms they had salvaged.

Overwhelming Japanese forces made it past the initial guerrilla defenses, but they suffered severe losses. The Negritos darted through the jungle beside and behind the Japanese, harassing them as they fled.

Kodairo, the leader of the Negrito guerrillas, informed Conner that his men had inflicted enough casualties to make the Japs think twice about occupying the Zambales Mountains.

One of the most important accomplishments through all the battles was the messenger service, which never faltered. Communications from the guerrillas got to American commanders, and soon Doyle Decker heard the sound of guns bombarding Fort Stotsenburg. Again positions were set to stem the expected rush of Japanese solders seeking other escape routes from Stotsenburg. Orders arrived from Colonel Cayler, Colonel Merrill's adjutant, to evacuate the position and move all civilian refugees from barrios in the region and guerrilla units to positions farther east. American forces were about to lay down a terrific barrage, with the air force and the artillery combining their powers to force a quick surrender of Fort Stotsenburg. Conner sent Colonel Merrill the maps that Mailheau and Decker had obtained from Tony, a commercial artist who helped with intelligence in the area, and from his associates, maps showing Japanese caves and tunnels constructed in the hills west of the fort. A decision was made to try a bombardment rather than risk heavy casualties in a direct assault.

Conner gave orders for evacuation and told the guerrillas that once they had moved the civilian refugees to safety they were to rendezvous north of Banaba. The rest of the day was spent going from barrio to barrio and encouraging the people to evacuate their homes.

Preparations of two years came to fruition. American troops had landed and the guerrillas were now able to fight the Japanese and defend their friends without fear of reprisals on innocent civilians.[9]

To aid the American troops, John Boone's First Regiment was given the mission to harass Japanese units using the Dinalupihan-Olongapo highway across the north end of Bataan. The Second and Third Regiments were to thwart Japanese attempts to utilize roads on either of the coasts. The Fourth Regiment blocked the Pilar-Bagac road across the middle of the peninsula. This was a problem, as the Fourth Regiment was too undersized to do much harm in the south. However, the guerrilla agents in the area monitored Japanese deployments and sent their reports to the north. The guerrilla regiments controlled the north and isolated the Japanese in southern Bataan.[10]

Bernard Anderson and Bob Lapham had long been concerned about the plight and potential for mass murder of the prisoners at the Cabanatuan prison camp. No one knew with any certainty how many men had passed through its gates. Rumors had circulated around the USAFFE headquarters in Australia since early 1944 that 250 American soldiers had been beaten to death by their captors on the first day of their imprisonment, that thousands had died since, that many hundred had been shipped to Japan on slave ships, that uncounted hundreds had been worked to death in the camp, that heaps of dead were routinely buried in common graves, that as many as 3,000 men were still alive there, though perhaps barely, since some of them were said to have lost as much as 100 pounds.

Lapham and Anderson had pondered the possibility of liberating the camp. Throughout 1944 they urged SWPA to let them try to rescue the POW's. They wanted to make an attempt in late October or early November 1944, but all they could ever get was assurance that when the landings began on Luzon, rescuing the prisoners would be given top priority. That never satisfied Anderson and Lapham, because they feared that once the Japanese thought such an invasion imminent, they would kill all the prisoners.[11]

Anderson had a personal score to settle with the Japanese: his young fiancée was imprisoned in the Santo Tomas civilian internment camp in Manila.[12]

Lapham rode his horse some forty miles from his hideout in Nueva Ecija province to alert G-2 about the situation he believed could develop at Cabanatuan. He told Horton White that 500 American soldiers were living in squalor in the camp after three years of starvation and slavery.[13]

While the Sixth Ranger Battalion was preparing to liberate Cabanatuan under the leadership of Lieutenant Colonel Henry Mucci and Captain Robert Prince, the guerrilla leaders of the 155th assembled at Banaba on the afternoon of January 28, 1945. They had spent the last several hours alerting Filipinos of approaching danger. The people were excited with the return of the American troops and anxious about their homes and possessions.

Clay Hogan and Frank MacGrath, the two pilots rescued by Conner's Negritos, had been sent with two of the 155th guerrilla guides to link up with American troops. Their mission: to coordinate the uniting of forces.

The U.S. Army had landed at Lingayen Gulf on the ninth and had driven south toward the Fort Stotsenburg area with the goal of liberating Manila. The Negritos had done an exceptional job of keeping the Japanese out of the mountains so they couldn't use the Iba tail as an escape route. General Krueger was commanding the Sixth Army and four divisions were sweeping the area as they approached Fort Stotsenburg. The 155th was to link with either the Thirty-seventh or Fortieth Divisions the next day near Angeles.

The guerrillas were moving about Banaba before daybreak. Some had slept, some had not, but all tossed and turned in anticipation of uniting with the American troops. They had one remaining assignment before linking up in Angeles. The remaining villagers needed to be evacuated to Hacienda Ramona, a barrio that was founded as living quarters for the workers of a large Spanish ranch established over one hundred years before. Positioned on the route between Banaba and Angeles, the area had been relatively untouched by war. Here, the evacuees would be safe from attacks by American bombers and artillery.

The guerrillas began their march to Hacienda Ramona at dawn with the remaining residents of Banaba and neighboring villages. Filipino and Negrito guerrillas of the 155th provided flank, point, and rear guard against potential Japanese snipers and patrols along the route. Anticipating heavy Japanese defenses in the mountains and sniper activity, Conner selected a lined path with trees camouflaging the way. After they arrived in Ramona, they traveled along a dry riverbed towards Angeles. The riverbed provided reasonable cover from Japanese artillery and snipers in the hills south of Fort Stotsenburg.

Kodairo was leading the column alongside Conner, with Gyovai carrying a flagstaff. Decker had tucked the Twenty-sixth flag under his arm and Mailheau followed in file with Campbell and Charles Stotts, a Welshman whom the Negritos had rescued when he swam ashore from a sinking prison ship.

Decker was impressed with the contingent and mentioned to Mailheau his worry about drawing too much attention. It took about two hours to get the locals to Hacienda Ramona and help them get settled. Conner and Kodairo left fifty Negrito guerrillas to guard the residents until more help could be arranged.

Then the 155th continued its journey to Angeles. Soon after entering the dry riverbed, an American reconnaissance plane was spotted overhead. No thought had been given to protecting the column from U.S. artillery, and because the group was traveling in the direction of the Japanese lines, they could have been mistaken for Japanese trying to outflank the U.S. Army front lines.

Mailheau yelled for Decker to unfurl the flag and grabbed a corner, with Gyovai and Conner following suit. They then held the flag above their heads and waved it horizontally up and down to let the spotter in the plane overhead know they were Americans.

The plane began to circle and lose altitude. When he recognized the flag he waggled his wings to let the men on the ground know he had seen the flag and recognized them as Americans. The rest of the men in the group jumped up and down, hooting and hollering. The plane then regained altitude and flew above the column as it continued its march.

Upon reaching the main road, they turned toward Angeles. Gyovai fixed the flag to the staff, and, as it flew at the head of the column the men broke out in song. With tears in their eyes, and each man singing as loudly as he could, they began: *California here I come, right back where I started from....*[14]

Excited in anticipation of meeting the American troops, they rounded a curve in the road and saw American tanks and trucks waiting for them. Soldiers tumbled out of their vehicles to shake hands with the guerrillas. After a short silence the men began to talk and ask questions as they were offered cigarettes and candy.

The soldiers were moved at the sight of the guerrillas and some had tears in their eyes. Trucks were waiting to transport the men to the 145th Infantry Headquarters, one of General Griswold's Fourteenth Corps units.

Mailheau asked one of the soldiers what unit had met them.

"Thirty-seventh Infantry and damn proud of it," was the answer.

The next day, in a special ceremony, Clay Conner presented General Griswold the Twenty-sixth flag and told him of its history. General Griswold was moved to tears as he accepted the flag.

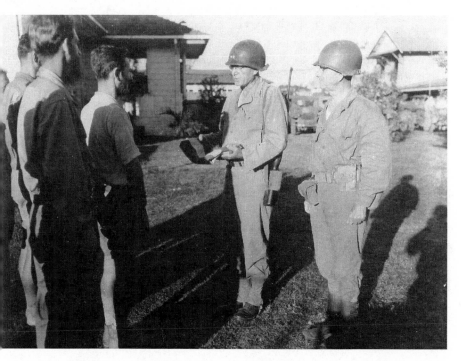

Clay Conner (third from left) presents the regimental colors of the Twenty-sixth Cavalry to General Oscar Griswold (center), about February 1, 1945 (National Archives).

"Men, you have proved your devotion to your country and your God many times in your actions and deeds. It is with the greatest humility that I accept this heroic symbol. God bless each and every one of you."[15]

With little time to prepare, the Sixth Ranger Battalion was given the mission to rescue five hundred prisoners at the Cabanatuan prison camp. Robert Lapham, in his report to Colonel Horton White, General Walter Kruger's intelligence chief, had laid out his fear that the prisoners would be killed by their Japanese guards as the liberating American troops approached the camp.

Lapham had nearly perfect intelligence regarding the Cabanatuan camp and the nearby village. He offered his guerrillas to help in the rescue. When Lieutenant Colonel Henry Mucci, a thirty-three-year-old West Point graduate and Bob Price, twenty-three-year-old ROTC graduate were assigned the mission, they immediately began to pore over the available intelligence and prepare to march their troops to the area.

Though originally planning to commence the rescue on the evening of January 29, the mission was setback to January 30 due to time constraints, and that was straining the mission to its limits.

Cabanatuan had as many as 3,000 men in its camp at any one time. Many died in the camp from disease, malnutrition and total lack of care by the Japanese. The deaths sometimes outpaced the ability to bury bodies, with putrefied corpses floating to the top of muddy mass graves during the rainy season. The remaining men in the camp were either civilians or soldiers too weak to be put on prison ships for Japan to work in the forced labor camps.

On the evening of January 30, with a Northrop P-31 flying over the camp using its twin, four-blade props powered by 2,000-horsepower Pratt-Whitney R-2800 engines to distract the Japanese guards, the Sixth Rangers crawled across the sparse fields toward the camp. Two guerrilla units from Bob Lapham's unit took positions across the river flowing near the camp, to block Japanese tanks and troops from reinforcing the camp during the raid.

At the appointed hour the raid began with such efficiency that the prison inmates were at first confused about their rescue. But in short order the prisoners were escorted to waiting Filipinos with carabaos and carts to move them to the safety of the American lines.

It was a joyous group of men who were transported to freedom after more than two years in sordid confinement and harsh treatment by the Japanese. Among those rescued were Bill and Martin Fassoth, along with Archie Bellair and Willard Smith who had been in the Fassoths' camp.[16]

One story that illustrates the love the Americans had for the Filipino people comes from John McCarty's book *Cabanatuan: Japanese Death Camp*.

Men of the 155th, about February 1, 1945. *Kneeling:* Clay Conner, Charles Stotts (British soldier), Bob Campbell, Bob Mailheau. *Standing:* Frank Gyovai, William Bressler, Doyle Decker, Alfred Bruce (Indiana Historical Society).

John was the medic for Battery H, 200th Coast Artillery, my father's unit. The story from McCarty's book as written by Vince Taylor:

> General Krueger had tents set up for us after our rescue. He had brought huge post and field stoves for the cooks to make us some good solid food in huge amounts. We had been starved for so long, but as we went through the chow line, we noticed the Filipino civilians roped out of the areas with guards to keep them back. We saw hundreds of young children, ribs showing, big stomachs caused by starvation during the years of occupation. The Filipinos had been so good to us. They had denied themselves food to try to get it to us.
>
> We took great big servings of everything and then walked over to the rope and scraped the food into whatever pots or containers these little children had. We had already been fed once that day. This might make us miss a meal and be a little hungry, but they were starving.
>
> American troops who had just recently landed had come over to see and visit with us. They were stunned by our actions. "Starved for three years and

Guerrilla leaders on Luzon after being awarded the Distinguished Service Cross on June 13, 1945. Front: Maj. Robert B. Lapham, Maj. Harry McKenzie, Maj. John P. Boone, Lt. Col. Bernard L Anderson. Back: Maj. Edwin P Ramsey, Capt. Alvin J. Feretta and Capt. Ray C Hunt (courtesy of Edwin P. Ramsey).

when they get food, they give it away!" They didn't know. Those Filipinos had kept us alive with bits of food and lots of love.

I was very proud to be an American that day, and very proud to be friends with the Filipinos.[17]

Friendly Filipinos and Negritos gave of themselves in many ways. American guerrillas who have written of their experiences have mentioned the times they were fed while the family went without food. But some islanders gave the ultimate price, their lives and the lives of their families.

Every American soldier who was in the Fassoths' camps, and who has written anything — be it a letter, article, or book — has expressed their undying gratitude for the valiant humanitarian efforts of Bill, Martin and Catalina Fassoth. To the last man, each has told how the camps saved their lives. I remember as a small boy my father telling stories of his time in the camp and the gratitude and admiration he had for the Fassoths. They were not authorized by the American government to put forth their efforts, at great risk to their property and lives, to save American soldiers. But truly God authorized these compassionate efforts and there is a special place in heaven for the Fassoths. Perhaps when their "boys" pass on through heaven's gates, the Fassoths will be there to meet them and hear from these men's lips, "Thank you for saving my life in that horrific time."

I have written this book to say my own thank you. Thank you for saving my father.

Appendix

The ceremonial surrender by Yamashita took place in Baguio on September 3, 1945. But isolated groups of Japanese soldiers, unaware that Hirohito had surrendered and the war was over, continued to resist, and various guerrilla forces continued to battle the Japanese and take prisoners for several more months. Nearly seventy thousand Japanese troops were taken out of the mountains of North Luzon and marched or trucked to San Fernando, La Union, where they were placed in prison and eventually shipped back to Japan.[1]

The guerrilla leaders on Luzon tackled the problem of record keeping by a variety of means. On one end of the spectrum was Captain Ray Hunt who kept no records at all, believing that if they were ever captured by the Japanese, those families listed would be executed. This was not an unfounded concern, as previous records had been seized and subsequently many guerrillas, those who aided them, and their families were killed. At the other end of the spectrum was Russell Volckmann who kept meticulous records and presented them to the American military authorities a few days after the troops landed in January 1945. While gallant, this effort risked the lives of brave men and women so that he could get his rightful share of credit for his unit's contribution to the war effort.[2]

The retaking of Luzon was different than any other campaign of World War II. It was achieved thanks to a largely loyal populace backing organized guerrilla forces to aid in the defeat of the Japanese army. This campaign for the Philippines was the most costly for the Japanese, as half their troops who died in the war did so in the Philippines.[3]

A TRUE COPY.

COMPTROLLER GENERAL OF THE UNITED STATES

WASHINGTON

B-69784   December 1, 1947

Mr. William J. Fassoth, Sr.,
    Santo Tomas, Lubao
        Pampanga
            Philippine Islands.

Dear Mr. Fassoth:

    There has been brought to my attention your letter of January
15, 1947, transmitted to this Office by the Office of the Judge Ad-
vocate General, War Department, relative to your claim in the amount
of 22,900 Pesos as reimbursement for personal funds and supplies alleged to have been furnished to American officers and enlisted men
at a rest camp operated by you in the Pampanga and Bataan Mountains,
Philippine Islands, during the period from April 1942 to April 1945.

    The said claim originally was referred to this Office by the
War Department under date of August 27, 1946, By settlement dated
October 30, 1946, this Office disallowed the claim for reasons sta-
ted in the said settlement as follows:

    "Your claim for 22,900 Pesos alleged to be due as reimbursement
of personal funds and supplies used in connection with a rest camp,
operated in the Pampanga and Bataan Mountains, Philippine Islands,
has been carefully examined and it is found that no part therefore may
be allowed for the reasons hereinafter stated.

    "The record of this office shows that from April 1942 until
April 5, 1943, you operated a rest camp in the Pampanga and Bataan
Mountains, where you sheltered, fed clothed and nursed back to
health numerous American officers and enlisted men, during which
period you used approximately 12,800 pesos of your own money to buy
food, clothing and supplies for use in the camp, 800 cavans of rice
at an estimated fair value of 2,8880 Pesos, and also issued receipts
in the approximate amount of 2,210 Pesos to various people to cover
food, supplies and labor furnished the camp.

    "The administrative office has reported that the money, food
and supplies were not réquisitioned by the United States Army or
any recognized guerrilla unit but were furnished voluntarily by you,
and therefore do not constitute procurements, nor was there created

Above and opposite: Letter of declination to Bill Fassoth from Comptroller General
(National Archives).

B-69784   - 2 -

any contractual liability either express or implied to pay for the same.

"You were not authorized to incur the expenses for which you seek reimbursement. It was a voluntary act on your part which does not create any obligation, legal or implied on the part of the United States to reimburse you. When services are rendered without expectation on the part of the one rendering the service, and are accepted without intention of incurring an obligation to pay on the part of the one receiving the benefit, no contract or agreement to pay is implied.

"I therefore certify that no balance is found due you from the United States."

In view of the facts of this matter as shown in the record, the said disallowance must be sustained, there being no legal basis for payment of the claim. Furthermore, the claim is not one containing such elements of legal liability or equity as would justify this Office in reporting it to the Congress under the act of April 10, 1928, 45 Stat. 413, with the recommendation that it be paid. The said act provides:

"That when there is filed in the General Accounting Office a claim or demand against the United States that may not lawfully be adjusted by the use of an appropriation therefore made, but which claim or demand in the judgement of the Comptroller General of the United States contains such elements of legal liability or equity as to be deserving of the consideration of the Congress, he shall submit the same to the Congress by a special report containing the material facts and his recommendation thereon."

There is no element of equity in your claim within the meaning of the said act of April 10, 1928, in-asmuch as the expenditures involved were made voluntarily by you with notice, actual or implied, that you were not entitled to reimbursement therefor, 17 Comp. Gen. 720, and decisions therein cited, also, the record indicates that reimbursement was in no manner contemplated by you at the time the expenditures were made.

What is said here is not to be understood as precluding the Department of the Army from taking such action as it may deem proper to bring your claim before the Congress for its consideration.

                          Respectfully,

                          (Sgd.) Not legible
                          Acting Comptroller General
                             of the United States

Many of the guerrilla leaders and Americans in their units gave Filipino families IOUs for the aid they rendered. The IOUs were later honored by the American government. These families put their lives at risk by keeping the debt receipts. If they had been found by the Japanese, and some were, the families were summarily executed.

Why none of the leading officers who received treatment in the Fassoths' camps ever came forward and offered testimony about the efforts by the Fassoths is probably a result of Bill Fassoth refusing to let them turn the sanctuaries into military camps. He also destroyed all records for the same reason as Ray Hunt did, to keep the material from being compromised.

It is from the stories of the men who were rescued by the Fassoths that this book has been written, to finally give the Fassoths the recognition and compensation they richly deserve.

Bill, Catalina and Martin Fassoth, Medal of Freedom honorees (Fassoth family collection).

Vernon Fassoth, his children and grandchildren at the Fassoth home, Labor Day weekend, 2005.

Bill, Martin, and Catalina, along with others who helped the American escapees on Luzon, were awarded the Presidential Medal of Freedom at Clark Field by General George F. Moore on behalf of President Harry Truman.

Because there was trouble with the Huks in the area, Bill and Martin Fassoth gave up on the idea of returning to the sugarcane business at their plantation, and instead went to work at Clark Air Base as civil service employees.

Bill died in 1957 of a heart attack at age 67, Martin died of kidney failure in 1959, and Catalina died of brain cancer in Lubao in 1962.

Bill Jr. went to work at Clark Air Base and retired early with a bad heart in 1977. He died in a car accident in Lubao in 1982.[4]

Vernon Fassoth and his wife Aurora moved their family to Griffith, Indiana, in 1954. Vernon still lives in Griffith and has 12 children. Aurora died in 2001. The author and his wife were privileged to attend their family reunion on Labor Day weekend in 2005.

Hipolita San Jose, the nurse at the Fassoths' camps, was found by Frank Bernacki after the war and died after a mental breakdown several weeks later.[5]

Men Who Rested at the Fassoths' Camps

Two affidavits were submitted by Bill Fassoth at the end of the war. One, dated April 30, 1947, was submitted to the U.S. Army. The other, dated November 1947, was submitted to the Philippine government. Many of the names were either misspelled or had typographical errors. I have tried to get the correct spelling and determine each man's identity.

EXECUTED, DIED, OR WENT MISSING

Hugh Gene Strickland, died 4-29-1942 after resting in Fassoth's camp
Owen Keiper, died at the Fassoths' camp about 7-1-1942
Bob Reeves, died at the Fassoths' camp early July 1942
Larsen,[6] died at the Fassoths' camp, July 1942 (no first name given by any source)
Jack Spies, killed by unfriendly Filipinos 10-21-1942
Jim Raulston, died 12-8-1942
John P. Taylor, died 12-14-1942
Jack Bart, died 1-10-1943
William Fought, died 1-31-1943
Louis Bell, died 1-31-1943
Cecil G. (Duke) Jarvis, died 5-31-1943
Manuel Montoya, died 7-4-1943
Hayden Lawrence, executed 9-23-1943
Coleman Banks, executed 9-30-1943
Joseph R. Barker, executed 9-30-1943
Martin Moses, executed 9-30-1943
Arthur Noble, executed 9-30-1943
Jack Renn, executed 9-30-1943
Roy Thomas, executed 9-30-1943
Donald G. (Jerry) Sourbrier, executed 9-30-1943
Eugene Zingheim, killed at Capas, Tarlac 9-30-1943
Johnny L. Storey, died February 1944
Fred Stamper, executed 6-23-1944
Fred "Tibuc Tibuc" Alvidrez, killed 9-2-1944
John M. Kerrey, drowned 10-24-1944
Benjamin Baruch, died on *Arisan Maru* 10-24-1944
John A. Breder, died on *Arisan Maru* 10-24-1944
Arnold Warshell, died on *Arisan Maru* 10-24-1944
Shelby Newman, died on *Oryoku Maru* 12-14-1944
Louis N. Dosh, died on *Brazil Maru* 1-20-1945
Harry Magnuson, died at Fukuoka #4
George Mogyorosi, died of pneumonia at one of the camps in Fukuoka
Raymond Schletterer, died of pneumonia at Fukuoka #3 January 1945
Margarito Agridano, believed killed, listed as missing
Forrest Henderson, bayoneted by Japanese at Barrio Pio, Pampanga
Raymond Herbert, killed by Huks per John N. Johns, letter to Wayne Sanford
Ernest Kelly, listed as missing
Rudolph Wurzbach, killed by Japanese per Vernon Fassoth

PRISONERS AT WAR'S END

Archie D. Bellair, Cabanatuan
Louis F. Barella, Fukuoka #3, Kyushu Island 34-130
Richard Beck, Cabanatuan
David Capps, Osaka Main Camp Chikko 34-135
Daniel Cahill, last seen at Bilibid
Walter Chatham, Fukuoka #1, Kahii (Pine Tree Camp) Kyushu Island 33-130
    (This camp was less than 50 miles from ground zero when the atom bomb
    hit Nagasaki)
Gerald W. Coward, Fukuoka #1, Kashii 33-130
Gerald D. Foley, Fukuoka #1, Kashii 33-130
Sill Herring, Fukuoka, per Hileman
Alvin Inghram, Osaka Main Camp Chikko Osaka 34-135
Harold Irving, Fukuoka #1, Kashii 33-130
Luther H. MacKenzie, Fukuoka #1, Kashii 33-130
Howard Mann, Fukuoka #1, Kashii 33-130
Homer Martin, Billibid, per Byers AG-384 A-5
Hugh B. McCoy, Fukuoka, per American roster, page 7
Earl Oatman, Osaka Main Camp Chikko Osaka 34-125
Raymond D. O'Conner, Tokyo POW Camp (Shinjuku) Tokyo Bay Area 35-
    140
Henry R. Patton, Fukuoka #1, Kashii 33-130
Thomas D. Rayburn, Fukuoka #1, Kashii 33-130
Hugh W. Rives, last seen at Bilibid
Andrew L. Roskopf, Billibid 14-121
Ralph Schibley, Billibid 14-121
Michael Slish, Fukuoka #1, Kashii 33-130
Willard Smith, Cabanatuan 15-121
Pierce Wade, Fukuoka #1, Kashii 33-130
Earl Walk, Billibid
Henry Winslow, Fukuoka
Jack N. Woods, Osaka Main Camp Chikko Osaka 34-135
Elmer D. Young?, Billibid * Elmer B. Young died. (I could not determine which
    Elmer Young)

GUERRILLAS AT LIBERTY AT WAR'S END

Bernard L. Anderson, commanded own unit
Leon Beck, Thirty-first Infantry, with Gyles Merrill
Frank Bernacki, 808th MP, with Gyles Merrill
Donald Blackburn, with Russell Volckmann

John P. Boone, Thirty-first Infantry, commanded own unit
James P. Boyd, Seventeenth Ordnance, with John Boone
Willard A. Bresler, at liberty
Al Bruce, Twelfth MP, commanded own unit under Bob Lapham
Robert A. Campbell, 200th Coastal Artillery, with Clay Conner
Bob Chapin, Forty-fifth Infantry, with Edgar Wright under Gyles Merrill
Henry Clay Conner, Twenty-seventh Bomb, commanded 155th Guerrillas
Doyle Decker, 200th Coastal Artillery, with Clay Conner
Bernice R. Fletcher, Quartermaster Corps, with John Boone
William Gardner, Thirty-First Infantry, with Gyles Merrill
Frank Gyovai, Seventeenth Ordnance, with Clay Conner
Eddie Higginbottom, Air Corps 48th Material Squadron, with John Boone
Arthur Hagins, Quartermaster Corp, with John Boone
Ray C. Hunt, with Bob Lapham
John N. Johns, at liberty
Cletus W. Johnson, Thirty-first Infantry, with John Boone
Winston Jones, 88th Field Artillery, with Gyles Merrill
Edward C. Keith, airlifted out of Luzon 12-29-1944
Wilber Lage, with Bob Lapham, escaped by submarine December 1944
Nano Lucero, 200th Coastal Artillery, at liberty
Bert E. Pettitt, with Bernard Anderson
Edwin P. Ramsey, Twenty-sixth Cavalry, commanded own unit
Joseph Schoebert, at liberty
Russell Volckmann, commanded own unit
Gerald Wade, Nineteenth Bomb Group, with John Boone
Clinton V. Wolfe, 200th Coastal Artillery, with Gyles Merrill

Unable to Determine

Ted Miller
Lieutenant Moore, (Howard? Roger?) unable to determine first name
Charles B. Nicely, Sergeant, Sixteenth Bomb Group
Earl Ogle
William Sudimack (or Sudimak)
MacKenzie, unable to determine first name

Of the guerrilla units on Luzon, all but one American lead unit was commanded by a former member of Fassoth's camps. Without the help of the Fassoths not only would many additional lives have been lost but guerrilla warfare on the island may not have so dramatically led to the Japanese defeat.

Chapter Notes

Chapter 1

1. Wade, Pierce, "War Reports," *World War II Chronicle*, November/December 1991, 14.
2. *Ibid.*
3. *Ibid.*
4. *Ibid.*
5. *Ibid.*
6. Oatman, Earl R., *Bataan: Only the Beginning* (E. R. Oatman, 1991), 6.
7. *Ibid.*, 10.
8. *Ibid.*
9. *Ibid.*, 11.
10. Sanford, Wayne, "Anderson's Guerrillas," *World War II Chronicle*, March/April 1990, 5.
11. Volckmann, R. W., *We Remained: Three Years Behind Enemy Lines in the Philippines* (New York: W. W. Norton, 1954), 11.
12. Morton, Louis, *The Fall of the Philippines* (Washington, DC: Office of the Chief of Military History, Department of the Army, 1953). War Plan Orange (WPO-3) was put into effect. The plan called for the defense forces in the Philippines to withdraw to the Bataan Peninsula of Luzon and to Corregidor, an island fortress in Manila Bay two miles from the southern tip of Bataan, where they would fight a delaying action. Japanese ships would not be able to use Manila's harbor because of the big guns on Corregidor. This was to give the United States time to relieve the garrison by means of a powerful fleet steaming from Pearl Harbor. Only, now there was no fleet to stream to the rescue.

Chapter 2

1. Morton, Louis, *The Fall of the Philippines* (Dept. of the Army, 1953), 145–148. Unknown to all but the highest command in the Philippines, the Pensacola Convoy, on its way to Manila with supplies, was ordered by the Joint Army-Navy Board to change course and sail to Brisbane, Australia. The convoy, led by the heavy navy cruiser *Pensacola*, was steaming to Manila, bringing fifty-two A-24 bombers, eighteen P-40 fighter planes, 340 trucks and jeeps, forty-eight 75mm guns, 600 tons of bombs, 3.5 million rounds of machine-gun ammunition, 9,000 drums of aviation fuel and 4,600 men. With the losses in Honolulu and the doubtful situation in the Philippines, the Army-Navy Board felt these supplies were needed in Australia.
2. Ramsey, Edwin Price, and Stephen J. Rivele, *Lieutenant Ramsey's War* (New York: Knightsbridge, 1990), 64–66. Ramsey's charge at Morong, January 16, 1942, was the last mounted cavalry charge in Unites States military history.
3. Morton, 184.
4. Oatman, 18, 19.
5. Fassoth affidavit, 6.
6. Hunt, Ray C., and Bernard Norling,

Behind Japanese Lines (Lexington: University Press of Kentucky, 1986), 11, 12.

7. Decker, Malcolm, *On a Mountainside* (Las Cruces, N.M.: Yucca Tree Press, 2004), 13–15.

8. Dizon affidavit. According to Robert Lapham in *Lapham's Raiders* (14–17), Ralph McGuire was a civil engineer who became a captain in the Philippine army. Some of the enlisted men were Sergeants Bruce, Fred Sladky, and Everett Brooks; and Corporals Daniel Cahill and George McCarty. Also in the group was Thorp's secretary, Herminia Dizon.

Chapter 3

1. Whitman, John W., *Bataan: Our Last Ditch* (New York: Hippocrene Books, 1990).

2. The "Big" and "Little" Pockets were much like the trench warfare of World War I, but lasting several days rather than two years.

3. Morton, 369.

4. Filipino term for unmilled rice.

5. The seventeen-year-old boy was Fred Kelly, the girl his sister Padring (*Time*, December 24, 1945). Catalina had asked their mother Romana Romero to help with the cooking.

6. Fassoth affidavit, 8.

7. A species of bamboo growing in the forest.

8. Fassoth affidavit, 8, 9.

9. Sanford, Wayne, "His Friends Called Him 'Chief,'" *World War II Chronicle*, September/October 1989, 3, 5.

10. Morton, 426.

11. Ashton, Paul, *Bataan Diary* (P. Ashton, 1984), 132.

12. Conner, *The Wartime Recollections of Henry Clay Conner, Jr.*, 118.

13. Whitman, 540.

14. Hunt and Norling, 20.

15. *Ibid.*, 22.

16. Toland, John, *But Not in Shame: The Six Months After Pearl Harbor* (New York: Random House, 1961), 296.

17. *Ibid.*, 297.

18. Sanford, "His Friends," 7.

19. M. Decker, 22, 23. Unknown to D. Decker, Lucero, and Wolfe at this time, the sergeant and captain had deserted from their battery a week or so before, taken food from the scanty stores of their starving comrades, and fled. After the war, a meeting of the officers of the unit decided that rather than court-martial the men, they would never mention their names, in order to protect their families from shame. For this reason, I will refer to them only as the sergeant and captain.

20. Ramsey and Rivele, 83.

21. *Ibid.*, 84. Finding a boat and escaping to one of the southern islands and eventually to Australia was a common theme among those men who escaped from Bataan.

22. Conner, *Wartime Recollections*, 122, 123.

23. Whitman, 597.

Chapter 4

1. Letter from Frank Bernacki to Doyle Decker, August 1, 1985.

2. Browne, Gordon, *Behind Japanese Lines with the Oklahoma Kid: The Leon Beck Story* (unpublished).

3. Toland, 324.

4. M. Decker, 25–31.

5. Hunt and Norling, 34.

6. John M. Kerrey, uncle of former Nebraska senator J. Robert Kerrey. He meets a tragic death described in chapter 9. Hunt and Norling, 173, also misspelled the name "Kiery."

7. Hunt and Norling, 32–37.

8. Oatman, 36.

9. *Ibid.* 48.

10. Ashton, 140.

11. Conner, *Wartime Recollections*, 125.

12. Sanford, "Anderson's Guerrillas," *World War II Chronicle*, March/April 1990, 5. One of the lieutenants was Bert Pettitt. The two enlisted men were Private Ernest Kelly and Howard Mann.

13. Conner, *Wartime Recollections*, 130.

14. Ramsey and Rivele, 87.

15. *Ibid.*, 87, 88. This passage was so intense and goes to the core of what the men experienced that I have taken it nearly ver-

batim from Ramsey's book, though without directly quoting.

16. Conner, *Wartime Recollections*, 159.

17. Schaefer, Chris, *Bataan Diary* (Houston, TX: Riverview Pub., 2004), 83–86.

18. Ibid, 93.

19. Conner, Henry Clay. "We Fought Fear on Luzon," *True*, August 1946, 72.

20. Volckmann, 43.

21. Confirmed by a report submitted to Bernard Anderson by Bert Pettitt dated January 26, 1946.

22. Refers to non–Christian peoples of northern Luzon, especially the Bontok.

23. Several sources say the amount was 15 pesos.

24. Morton, 344. Unknown to the group, they were in the midst of one of the major battles fought on Bataan, called the "Pockets." The Japanese had tried to penetrate the American lines and each paid a terrible price, with the Japanese 65 Brigade losing over 4,000 of 6,500 men and the Americans 2,231 of 2,881 men.

25. The spelling of Roskopf varies according to different sources, as does that of Raulston. Several sources have misspelled Lou Dosh's name "Dosch." Bernard Norling incorrectly identified Louis Dosh as Samuel Dosch in *Behind Japanese Lines*.

26. I have not been able to identify Sergeant Phillips. He was not on Fassoth's roster, nor on anyone else's list I can find. It is possible that my father misidentified him.

27. This long passage describes the trials and difficulties facing all the escapees working their way out of Bataan.

28. Conner, *Wartime Recollections*, 196.

29. Oatman, 127.

30. M. Decker, 56.

31. Interview of Vernon Fassoth by Chris Schaefer, April 22–July 28, 2005.

32. Norling, Bernard, *The Intrepid Guerrillas of Northern Luzon* (Lexington: University Press of Kentucky, 1999), 92.

Chapter 5

1. From various family materials supplied by Monica Fassoth, daughter of Vernon Fassoth.

2. Wurzbach's name is spelled various ways, but I think this is the correct spelling.

3. Fassoth's affidavit, 10.

4. Ramsey and Rivele, 95.

5. Oatman, 51.

6. Ramsey and Rivele, 97.

7. *Ibid.*, 99.

8. Earl Oatman wrote that the tall grass was cogon grass. Vernon Fassoth in an interview said it was elib grass, or *Aegilops cylindria*; though tall, at four to five feet, this is a shorter grass than the cogon grasses that grow eight to nine feet tall.

9. Fassoth affidavit, 13.

10. Oatman, 53, 54.

11. Fassoth affidavit, 14.

12. Interview by Chris Schaefer with Vernon Fassoth. Lebrado Tubo was the girl's father; Maming and Coching were Catalina's nieces by her sister who had died a few years before the war, often referred to as "the girls" in several sources.

13. Fassoth affidavit, 12.

14. Oatman, 63.

15. Fassoth affidavit, 13, 14.

16. Oatman, 60.

17. There are several references to Larsen, but none gives a first name.

18. Fassoth's affidavit, 15. Also, an illustration by Doyle Decker shows the three graves. The deaths occurred after June 1942 as Don Blackburn in a letter to Doug Clanin dated October 4, 1985, described Russell Volckmann performing the burial ceremony for Lieutenant Reeves. Reeves was described in the letter as being from Colorado Springs, Colorado, and having graduated from Dartmouth or Cornell.

19. Fassoth affidavit, 15.

20. One must experience the rainy season, or monsoons themselves to understand how much and for how long it can rain. I have experienced downpours interrupted by heavy drizzle for as long as three weeks.

21. Harkins, Philip, *Blackburn's Headhunters* (New York: W. W. Norton, 1955), 58.

22. *Ibid.*, 59. This story seems embellished. In a letter to Doug Clanin, dated October 4, 1985, Blackburn had used the name Red Boyd in Harkins' book, but acknowledged that it was Red Wolfe. Black-

burn gives himself too much credit for turning the attitude of the camp around; most records from the enlisted men who survived the camp would discount this recollection. In the letter Blackburn did not take the conversation as one of hostility towards officers, just the rules of the camp. Red Wolfe didn't seem like a troublemaker, and in fact was seeking Russell Volckmann's advice on some matters that disturbed him a few days later.

23. Interview by author with Nano Lucero, February 28, 2006.

24. Interview by Chris Schaefer with Vernon Fassoth.

25. This edict by Bill Fassoth would prove to save him, Martin, and several Americans who where later captured or surrendered. Because the camp was not a military compound the Japanese did not treat those captured at the camp or who later surrendered without weapons as guerrillas. All those captured as guerrillas were executed. However, this is probably the one reason that no higher-ranking officer would validate the Fassoths' request after the war for compensation of the money they spent supplying the camp.

26. Hukbo ng Bayan Laban sa Hapon (People's Anti-Japanese Army), or Huks. Originally organized by the Communist Party as a guerrilla movement against Japanese centering in Pangasinan, the organization in response to peasant grievances also attacked wealthy landowners and collaborators. Because of their political activities, under the leadership of Luis Taruc, the Americans refused to recognize the Huks as official guerrilla units. Luis Taruc had been the head of the socialist movement before the war. The Communists had infiltrated the group and inducted its members into the Huk organization, as they all wanted the defeat of the Japanese.

27. Pettitt report.

28. *Ibid.*, 62.

29. Oatman, 62.

30. M. Decker, 62, 63.

31. A term used to refer to non–Christian peoples of northern Luzon, especially the Bontok (from which the term "boondocks" originated). The term does not usually refer to a specific ethnolinguistic group,

and its connotation of "'hillbilly'" makes it unacceptable to most tribal peoples to which it refers.

32. M. Decker, 63, 64.

33. The Decker family still has the Bible. It is a prized possession.

34. See copy of document Bob Lapham radioed out to MacArthur's headquarters.

35. M. Decker, 63–65.

36. Bob Reeves, Owen Keiper, and Larsen. Hunt recounted three others and noted the death of Bob Reeves. All other references, Conner, Volckmann, Blackburn, Boone and Fassoth, say that three died in camp: Reeves, Keiper and Larsen.

37. M. Decker, 65.

38. See note 36.

39. Pettitt report.

40. Fassoth affidavit, 16, 17.

41. Affidavit of Herminia Dizon dated July 24, 1946.

42. Fassoth affidavit, 18.

43. Fassoth affidavit, 19.

44. Letter from Frank Bernacki to Doyle Decker, dated August 1, 1985.

45. Knox, Donald, *Death March: The Survivors of Bataan* (New York: Harcourt Brace Jovanovich, 1981), 314.

46. *Ibid.*, 69, 70.

47. Conner, *Wartime Recollections*, 199–203.

48. M. Decker, 65, 66.

Chapter 6

1. Hunt and Norling, 56.

2. Lapham and Norling, 36.

3. Interview with Vernon Fassoth, May 24, 2007.

4. Fassoth affidavit, 19.

5. M. Decker, 65.

6. Oatman, 71, 72.

7. All my sources refer to one or more of these men. All agree that six were captured, but to date my research has not found who the other three were.

8. Fassoth affidavit, 19, 20.

9. Hunt and Norling, 45, 46.

10. Ramsey and Rivele, 139.

11. Email from Fred Kelly, Romana Romero's son, to author, March 24, 2002.

12. Oatman, 76, 77.
13. Fassoth affidavit, 21–24.
14. Interview with Vernon Fassoth by Chris Schaefer.
15. Hunt and Norling, 56.
16. From Visayan Island.
17. Oatman, 81, 82.
18. M. Decker, 67–75.
19. Affidavit by Herminia Dizon, July 24, 1946.
20. Vernon Fassoth interview by Chris Schaefer.
21. Letter from Ramsey to Vernon Fassoth, February 12, 1998.
22. Interview with Vernon Fassoth by author, May 24, 2007.
23. Interview with Vernon Fassoth by Chris Schaefer and author, May 25, 2007.
24. Conner, "We Fought Fear on Luzon," 75.
25. Conner, *Wartime Recollections*, 208.
26. *Ibid.*, 258.
27. *Ibid.*, 251.
28. M. Decker, 80–89.
29. Hileman, Millard E., and Paul Fridlund, 1051: An American POW's Remarkable Journey through World War II (Walla Walla, WA: Words Worth Press, 1992), 170–174.
30. Ramsey and Rivele, 142.
31. *Ibid.*, 143. Ramsey and Barker had come into possession of a book of writings by Chairman Mao and had studied it intently. Boone's children still have the written document signed by Ed Ramsey authorizing the marriage of their parents.

Chapter 7

1. Schaefer, 148.
2. *Ibid.*, 146, 147.
3. Conner interview with Doug Clanin, Indiana Historical Society.
4. Vernon Fassoth interview with Chris Schaefer.
5. Conner interview with Doug Clanin, Indiana Historical Society.
6. Volckmann, 120, 121.
7. Huks, according to Bill Fassoth.
8. Bill Fassoth did not identify Johns in

his affidavit, but Ray Hunt does in the next section of the story.
9. Fassoth affidavit, 25.
10. Hunt and Norling, 56.
11. Ibid.
12. Pettitt report.
13. Lapham and Norling, 111.
14. Sanford, Wayne, "*Organization of Guerrilla Warfare*," 9–10.
15. Fassoth affidavit, 27.
16. Had Bill Fassoth turned his camp into a military or guerrilla base it is likely that Merrill or one of the other colonels would have authorized his expenditures at the end of the war. As it was, no one of authority came forward to help him.
17. Oatman, 86–96.
18. Hileman and Fridlund, 180, 181.
19. *Ibid.*, 182.
20. Oatman, 104, 112.
21. In an e-mail to the author on January 6, 2007, Ed Ramsey said he had heard that Bell was ambushed by the Japanese on his way to southern Luzon. Conner thought Bell had died from typhoid, but no one is certain of the cause of his death. The National Archives list Bell's last known status as missing.
22. Gyovai was right about Kelly, but not about Mann. The latter was captured and eventually liberated from Fukuoka POW Camp #1.
23. Conner, *Wartime Recollections*, 307–366.
24. M. Decker, 118, 119.
25. Pettitt report.
26. Hunt and Norling, 57–60.
27. Schaefer, 191; interview of Vernon Fassoth by Chris Schaefer.
28. Letter dated August 1, 1985, from Frank Bernacki to Doyle Decker.
29. Frank Bernacki did not realize that Bill Jr. had been dispatched by his father to arrange the surrender and still held hard feelings toward Bill Jr. expressed in a letter to Doyle Decker dated August 1, 1985.
30. Fassoth affidavit, 27–31.
31. E-mail to author from Fred Kelly, Roman's Romero's son.
32. This is the same cure that almost killed Clay Conner. Obviously Mr. Barron

knew how to brew the tea, though ineffectively.

33. Oatman, 114–130

34. Browne, 24. Actually Stamper fell ill, and, fearing he would die without proper medical attention, he turned himself in to the Japanese, hoping they would put him in a hospital. On June 23, 1944, Stamper was taken to the city square of San Fernando and beheaded.

Chapter 8

1. Volckmann, 119.
2. Lapham and Norling, 113.
3. This is one form of the water treatment described by Oatman. There are others.
4. Oatman, 133–155.
5. Hileman and Fridlund, 207.
6. *Ibid.*, 208.
7. *Ibid.*, 210.
8. On October 4, 1943, Colonel Thorp, Colonel Straughn, Colonel Nakar and others were executed at I La Loma, according to the affidavit by Herminia Dizon, July 24, 1942. Other sources show the date as September 30, 1943 (see story later in this chapter). Chris Schaefer in *Bataan Diary*, quoting Ignacio Santos and Lieutenant Richard W. Sakakida, uses the date of October 8, 1943. (Both Santos and Sakakida witnessed the men's executions.)
9. Hileman and Fridlund, 221, 222.
10. *Ibid.*, 222, 223.
11. Philippine Jurisprudence G.R. No. L-880, December 17, 1947: People of the Philippines vs. Fortunato Munoz.
12. Another form of the water treatment. Conner, *Wartime Recollections*, 468.
13. Conner, *Wartime Recollections*, 468, 469. Ray Herbert's death was confirmed by Johnny Johns in a letter to Wayne Sanford dated February 4, 1984.
14. Conner, "We Fought Fear," 89, 90.
15. Schaefer, 208, 209. Chris Schaefer did exhaustive research on this event. Several stories have emerged from this day. (Some contend this event occurred over two days.)
16. *Ibid.*, page 209.
17. Lapham and Norling, 54.

Chapter 9

1. Lebrado was married to Catalina Fassoth's sister. Her nieces, called "the Lebrado girls" (Maming and Coching) were from this marriage. Interview with Vernon Fassoth by Chris Schaefer.
2. Interview with Vernon Fassoth by Chris Schaefer.
3. M. Decker, 91–126
4. *Ibid.*, 128–130.
5. Pettitt report.
6. Pettitt report.
7. Interview with Vernon Fassoth by Chris Schaefer.
8. Oatman, 169–176.
9. Hileman and Fridlund, 240–243.
10. Lapham & Norling, 148. Not every guerrilla unit received many supplies, due to terrain and command.
11. Archived copy of message radioed and received from Robert Lapham.
12. Letter to Wayne Sanford from Doyle Decker, March 24, 1985.
13. Lapham and Norling, 113.

Chapter 10

1. Volckmann, 122.
2. *Ibid.*, 125–152.
3. *Ibid.*, 160–161.
4. Oatman, 186–193.
5. Hileman and Fridlund, 261.
6. Jorgensen, Ruth E., "The Hell Ships of World War Two," http://www.west-point.org/family/adbc/hellship.htm.
7. Lucero interview with author, February 28, 2006.
8. Hunt and Norling, 129.
9. Breuer, William B., "The Great Raid on Cabanatuan (New York: J. Wiley and Sons, 1994)," 103. Sergeant John Phillips later died at Cabanatuan.
10. Sides, Hampton, "*Ghost Soldiers* (New York: Doubleday, 2001)," 184, 185.
11. Breuer, 103–105.
12. M. Decker, 135–137.
13. *Ibid.*, 140, 141.
14. Hunt and Norling, 161, 162.

15. Lapham and Norling, 70.
16. Ramsey and Rivele, 254, 255.
17. M. Decker, 152–155.
18. Schaefer, 253, 254.
19. *Ibid.*, 255, 256.
20. M. Decker, 162–164.
21. Hunt and Norling, 178.
22. Vernon Fassoth interview with author, May 24, 2007.
23. M. Decker, 168.
24. Michno, Gregory F., *Death on the Hellships: Prisoners at Sea in the Pacific War* (Annapolis, MD: Naval Institute Press, 2001)," 258. Also: Jorgensen, Ruth E., "The Hell Ships of World War Two," http://www.west-point.org/family/adbc/hellship.htm.
25. Lapham and Norling, 157; Hunt and Norling, 36; interview with Vernon Fassoth by Chris Schaefer.
26. Hunt and Norling, 173.

Chapter 11

1. Schaefer, 291–293.
2. M. Decker, 175, 176.
3. Jorgensen, Ruth E., "The Hell Ships of World War Two," http://www.west-point.org/family/adbc/hellship.htm.
4. *Ibid.*
5. Schaefer, 304, 305.

6. Breuer, 154.
7. Ramsey and Revile, 301.
8. Volckmann, 182–193.
9. M. Decker, 180–182.
10. Schafer, 297, 298.
11. Lapham and Norling, 177.
12. Breuer, 128.
13. Sides, 20.
14. M. Decker, 193.
15. *Ibid.*, 197.
16. Byers, list of prisoners at Cabanatuan and Bilibid, National Archives. I use this list as it was complied by WO E. G. Byers, USN, an American POW who worked for the Japanese in Bilibid Prison Records section.
17. Taylor Vince, *Cabanatuan* (Waco, TX: Texian Press, 1985), 143, 144.

Appendix

1. Volckmann, page 218.
2. Norling, 216.
3. Lapham and Norling, page 184.
4. Letter from Vernon Fassoth to Doyle Decker, April 5, 1984.
5. Letter from Frank Bernacki to Doyle Decker, May 22, 1985.
6. Vernon Fassoth believes Larsen's first name was Jim.

Bibliography

Much of the research for this book comes from the collection of audio tapes and transcriptions, correspondence, diaries, histories, newspaper clippings, and photocopies from the National Archives of documents, orders, maps and replies of inquires that Wayne Sanford and Doug Clanin compiled in their research of guerrilla warfare on Luzon, Philippine Islands.

Ashton, Paul. *"And Somebody Gives a Damn!"* P. Ashton, 1990.

_____. *Bataan Diary.* P. Ashton, 1984.

Bernacki, Frank. Letters to Doyle Decker on the Fassoths' camp and experiences on Luzon, with comments about other men he was in contact with during and after the war. 1985–1986.

Boone, Phil. Letter to Doug Clanin, dated February 17, 1988.

Breuer, William B. *The Great Raid on Cabanatuan.* New York: John Wiley & Sons, 1994.

Browne, Gordon. *Behind Japanese Lines with the Oklahoma Kid: The Leon Beck Story.* Unpub.

Cave, Dorothy. *Beyond Courage.* Las Cruces, N.M.: Yucca Tree Press, 1992.

Conner, Henry Clay. Documents, memos and orders from the National Archives; 1956 "This is Your Life" videotape.

_____. *The Wartime Recollections of Henry Clay Conner, Jr.* Unpublished manuscript.

_____. "We Fought Fear on Luzon." *True,* August 1946, 69–87.

Decker, Doyle. Diary of events on Luzon; letters to Dorothy Cave, Wayne Sanford, and Doug Clanin pertaining to activity in guerrilla warfare and experiences on Luzon; miscellaneous writings; audiotape of interview with Vernon Fassoth and Leon Beck discussing the Fassoths' Camp. Indianapolis: Indiana Historical Society.

Decker, Malcolm. *On a Mountainside: The 155th Provisional Guerrilla Battalion Against the Japanese on Luzon.* Las Cruces, N.M.: Yucca Tree Press, 2004.

Dizon, Herminia S. Affidavit covering the guerrilla activities of Colonel Claude A. Thorp, July 29, 1947.

Falk, Stanley L. *Bataan: The March of Death.* New York: PBJ Books, 1982.

"Fassoth Affadavit." RG 407: Records of the Adjutant General's Office, Philippine Archives Collection, Box 258. National Archives.

Fassoth, Vernon. Documents from the National Archives.

_____. Interviews with author, May 22–May 31, 2007.

_____. Interviews with Chris Schaefer, April 22–23, May 4, and July 4, 2004; July 28, 2005.

_____. Letters to Doyle Decker, 1984–1987.

Fassoth, William J. Sr. *The Story of Fassoth's Camp.* Item 136 in Box 258, National Archives.

Griess, Thomas E. *Atlas of the Second World War: Asia and the Pacific.* Wayne, N.J.: Avery Publishing Group, 1985.

Griswold, Oscar W. Letter dated September 28, 1945, to Major H. C. Conner; letter dated March 12, 1949, to Bob Mailheau.

Gyovai, Frank. Interviews and correspondence with Wayne Sanford.

_____. Letters to Doyle Decker 1982–1985.

Harkins, Philip. *Blackburn's Headhunters.* New York: W. W. Norton, 1955.

Hileman, Millard E., and Paul Fridlund. *1051: An American POW's Remarkable Journey Through World War II.* Walla Walla, WA: Words Worth Press, 1992.

Hunt, Ray C., and Bernard Norling. *Behind Japanese Lines.* Lexington: University Press of Kentucky, 1986.

Knox, Donald. *Death March: The Survivors of Bataan.* New York: Harcourt Brace Jovanovich, 1981.

Lapham, Robert, and Bernard Norling. *Lapham's Raiders: Guerrillas in the Philippines 1942–1945.* Lexington: University Press of Kentucky, 1996.

Lee, Henry G. *Nothing but Praise.* Culver City, CA: Murray & Gee, 1948.

Mailheau, Bob. Miscellaneous writings. Indianapolis: Indiana Historical Society.

Maring, Ester G., and Joel M. Maring. *Historical and Cultural Dictionary of the Philippines.* Metuchen, N.J.: Scarecrow Press, 1973.

Morton, Louis. *The Fall of the Philippines.* Washington, DC: Office of the Chief of Military History, Department of the Army, 1953.

Norling, Bernard. *The Intrepid Guerrillas of North Luzon.* Lexington: University Press of Kentucky, 1999.

Norman, Elizabeth M. *We Band of Angels.* New York: Random House, 1999.

Oatman, Earl R. *Bataan: Only the Beginning.* E. R. Oatman, 1991.

Olson, John E. *O'Donnell: Andersonville of the Pacific.* J. E. Olson, 1985.

_____, with Frank O. Anders. *Anywhere, Anytime: The History of the 57th Infantry.* J. E. Olson, 1991.

Ramsey, Edwin Price, and Stephen J. Rivele. *Lieutenant Ramsey's War.* New York: Knightsbridge, 1990.

"Report of Activities of Bert E. Pettitt from 9 April 1942 to 7 December 1944 in the Philippine Islands." National Archives. January 26, 1946.

Reynolds, Russell B. *The Officer's Guide.* Harrisburg, PA: Stackpole Books, 1968; originally published 1930.

Sanford, Wayne. "Anderson's Guerrillas." *World War II Chronicle,* March/April 1990.

_____. "His Friends Called Him 'Chief.'" *World War II Chronicle,* September/October 1989.

_____. "Organization of Guerrilla Warfare." *World War II Chronicle,* 1989.

Schaefer, Chris. *Bataan Diary: An American Family in World War II, 1941–1945.* Houston, TX: Riverview Publishing, 2004.

Schultz, Duane P. *Hero of Bataan: The Story of General Jonathan M. Wainwright.* New York: St. Martin's Press, 1981.

Sides, Hampton. *Ghost Soldiers.* New York: Doubleday, 2001.

Taylor, Vince. *Cabanatuan: Japanese Death Camp.* Waco, TX: Texian Press, 1985.

Thorp, Claude. Documents and orders from the National Archives.

Toland, John. *But Not in Shame: The Six Months After Pearl Harbor.* New York: Random House, 1961.

Volckmann, R. W. *We Remained: Three Years Behind Enemy Lines in the Philippines.* New York: W. W. Norton, 1954.

Wade, Pierce. "War Reports." *World War II Chronicle,* November/December 1991.

Whitman, John W. *Bataan: Our Last Ditch.* New York: Hippocrene Books, 1990.

Winslow, Hank, and Earl Oatman. Interview by author, September 1996.

Index

215

Mac — State Farm
camdenton